CW00926547

Inclusion, Equality & Diversity in Working with Children

Sue Griffin

www.heinemann.co.uk

✓ Free online support
✓ Useful weblinks
✓ 24 hour online ordering

01865 888118

Heinemann

Heinemann is an imprint of Pearson Education Limited, a company incorporated in England and Wales, having its registered office at Edinburgh Gate, Harlow, Essex, CM20 2JE. Registered company number: 872828

www.heinemann.co.uk

Heinemann is a registered trademark of Pearson Education Limited

Text © Sue Griffin 2008

First published 2008

12 11 10
10 9 8 7 6 5 4 3

British Library Cataloguing in Publication Data
A catalogue record for this book is available from the British Library

ISBN 978 0 435402 40 2

Edited by TAG Publishing and Caroline Lowe
Typeset by Saxon Graphics
Original illustrations © Pearson Education Limited 2008
Picture research by Liz Savery
Cover photo/illustration © iStockPhoto.com / Stefanie Timmermann
Printed in Malaysia (CTP-VP)

Acknowledgements

The author and publisher would like to thank the following individuals and organisations for permission to reproduce photographs on the following pages:

Alamy / Bubbles Photolibrary: 85; Alamy / Photofusion Picture Library: 22; Alamy / PhotoAlto: 81; Alamy / WoodyStock: 122; Alamy / Amoret Tanner: 168; Corbis / Bettmann: 183; Corbis / Bloomimage: 81; Corbis / Comstock Select: 70; Corbis / Don Hammond / Design Pics: 146; Corbis / Jennie Woodcock: 24; Corbis / JLP / Jose L. Pelaez: 79; Corbis / Helen King: 216; Digital Vision: 9; Fotolia / Anita Patterson-Peppers: 144; Fotolia / Miroslav: 11; Getty Images: 133, 135; Getty Images / AFP: 46; Sally & Richard Greenhill: 188; Sue Griffin: 114; The Illustrated London News Picture Library: 181; PA Photos / Stefan Rousseau / PA Archive: 175; Pearson Education Ltd / Gareth Boden: 221; Pearson Education Ltd / Gerald Sunderland: 73; Pearson Education Ltd / Jules Selmes: 87, 137, 147, 215; Pearson Education Ltd / Lord & Leverett: 225; Pearson Education Ltd / Tudor Photography: 29, 89, 125; Persona Doll Training: 104; Shutterstock: 197

Every effort has been made to contact copyright holders of material reproduced in this book. Any omissions will be rectified in subsequent printings if notice is given to the publishers.

Websites
The websites used in this book were correct and up-to-date at the time of publication. It is essential for tutors to preview each website before using it in class so as to ensure that the URL is still accurate, relevant and appropriate. We suggest that tutors bookmark useful websites and consider enabling students to access them through the school/college intranet.

Contents

Dedication

This book is dedicated to Miranda and Rosalind, from whom I have learned so much, and to Beatrice and Florence, from whom I am still learning.

About the author

Sue Griffin

Sue Griffin has been involved in the early years and childcare field for 30 years. She worked for 18 years for the National Childminding Association and played a key role in developing the first national qualification and quality assurance schemes for childminders. She was a member of the Under Sevens Project team in 1989–90 which developed the first NVQs. She was involved in the playgroup movement in the 1980s and was national chair of the Pre-school Playgroups Association.

She is now semi-retired, working as a writer and freelance consultant. Her book *Getting Started in Home-based Childcare* for new childminders and nannies was published in 2006.

Sue is a magistrate and sits on the family panel in Cambridgeshire. She enjoys being a granny.

Other titles in the Professional Development series

Planning for the Foundation Stage 0 435 40167 X

Research Methods in Health, Care and Early Years 0 435 401168 8

Baby and Child Health 0 435 40151 3

Supporting Special Needs 0 435 40162 9

Managing Children's Behaviour 0 435 45532 X

Protecting Children 0 435 45679 2

How to Observe Children 0 435 40186 6

Planning Play and the Early Years, 2nd edition 0 435 40119 X

Working with Babies and Children under Three 0 435 9873 1

Understanding Early Years Theory in Practice 0 435 40213 7

Foreword

Terms like equality, inclusion and diversity are used a lot when working with children, but sadly they are sometimes used without much thought. You should expect to see them in policies, standards and curricula, and might comment if they are not made explicit, but there is no point having them on the page if they cannot be seen in practice – in the way you relate to colleagues, to children and to families. Many people still do not understand or think about the ways in which prejudice and discrimination function in society. Furthermore, many early years practitioners fail to realise the vital role they can have in effecting change through their work with children, whose ideas about the world are not yet fixed. Change can only happen, however, if practitioners are open to change in their own lives, and are willing to examine their everyday practice with children and families through observation and reflection.

Observation and reflection are at the heart of the Early Years Foundation Stage and of the various quality improvement processes which all settings are now putting into practice. This book therefore comes at just the right time to link in with such developments. The author, Sue Griffin, makes it clear from the start that this is a practical guide, which explains definitions and concepts but then expects the reader to go back to work and make changes.

Beginning with the central concept of fairness, which is familiar to most children, the author introduces key concepts and definitions which are then mapped very clearly to practical experiences and exercises that arise in the reader's own setting and with the young children which he or she knows. In this, readers are challenged to think hard and ask serious questions of themselves and others. This is not just an intellectual exercise – it is about embedding a particular way of thinking in our daily practice with children and families. Thus, while there is enough repetition of key ideas and definitions to make it possible to skip to chapters as needed, I would recommend a full read through to begin with.

When considering how to implement equality, inclusion and diversity in practice, you may be aware that some sections of the media (and, perhaps, some of your colleagues) deride these efforts as 'politically correct' or even 'crazy'. The author tackles this ignorance head-on, stating clearly why there is nothing misguided about such an approach. Rather, it is about the early years worker doing his or her best for all children and, importantly, about self-respect and the ability to think creatively and get better at what we do.

Pioneering work has been done over the past 30 years in the fields described in this book, particularly race, disability and gender. Building on this work, the author has produced an excellent guide to equalities for those who work with young children. In many ways, it is a guide to dealing with 'difference'. As the author says, this should help early years workers to "consider differences in a positive way, as something to enjoy and be interested in." This book is certainly something to enjoy and be interested in.

Sue Owen
Director, Early Childhood Unit, National Children's Bureau

Introduction

'It's not fair' is a frequent children's complaint. The English language is full of phrases like 'fair play' and 'a fair crack of the whip', even 'fair trade'. We value being 'fair minded', and most people think that all children should have a 'fair chance' to get a good start in life.

When we talk about fairness we often mean that no one should have an advantage over other people in any aspect of their life solely because they were born into a certain group in society or grew up in a particular location. If we're being 'fair', we do our best to make sure that everyone has the same chances to benefit from the good things of life, to enjoy well-being, and to have opportunities to progress and achieve success.

Unfairness is widespread in society. Some children and adults have advantages and opportunities not available to others. Most people accept that some individuals will have a larger share of the material goods of the world, and also accept that people will have varied experiences depending on how effectively they use their talents and skills – that seems 'fair enough'. But it feels unfair if benefits are derived only from, for example, the social position a person is born into. When a person is denied such benefits because of the social position they are born into, that is seen as unfair because they are denied equality of opportunity.

The principles of inclusion, equality and diversity should underpin all work with children and, as this book will show, it can be useful to keep this idea of 'fairness' at the centre of your thinking about these concepts. Thinking about how to promote these principles becomes more complex as we unpick the full meaning of the principles, and we can get lost in discussing whether or not we should use certain language or specific resources. If we can bring our reflections back to whether something is 'fair' to everyone concerned, then we may be more able to make good decisions and maintain good practice in working with children and families, and in turn ensure that they are included fully in settings and can benefit from equality of opportunity.

In Chapter 2 each aspect of difference is considered and explored separately. However, in the rest of the book these various aspects are interwoven as we examine themes of provision and practice. This is in order to address the issues of inclusion, equality and diversity in a holistic way. For example, Chapter 4 considers how to create an inclusive environment across the range of gender, ethnicity and culture, disability and other aspects of difference.

Creating an environment which will include a disabled girl of Chinese origins from a single-parent family requires practitioners to look at all aspects of her identity. A child is not just defined by one aspect of difference.

Terminology

It can become confusing when people use the same terms but not with the same meanings. For example, it has become clear that discussions in recent times about 'multiculturalism' have been very muddled due to different people attributing different meanings to the term. The area of practice which this book focuses on is full of terminology which needs to be properly defined. It is therefore worthwhile to clarify constantly what is actually meant by some of the terms that are widely used.

My first encounters with some of the ideas explored in this book were as part of what was called 'anti-racist' training in the 1980s. By the 1990s, I was reading about and discussing with others in the field of working with children ideas of 'equal opportunities' or 'anti-discrimination' or 'multiculturalism'. By the end of the 20th century I found myself attending 'diversity' training, and in the 21st century exploring with colleagues in the sector the concepts of 'inclusion'. Although this training, writing and discussion was approached in different ways, many of the messages remained similar across the decades.

In this book the term *practitioner* is used to mean anyone who works with children, such as childminders and nannies, pre-school and nursery workers, teachers and learning support staff, playworkers and other workers in after-school clubs or playschemes, and sports coaches. The term *setting* is used for places and situations where practitioners work with children, such as home-based settings, pre-schools, nurseries, schools, play settings, sports pitches/fields/courts/tracks and so on.

Values of the sector

The values concerning inclusion, equality and diversity embedded in working with children are expressed in many ways by different organisations.

◆ Article 2 of the United Nations Convention on the Rights of the Child (UNCRC) requires that children are 'protected against all forms of discrimination'.

◆ The Common Core of Skills and Knowledge for everyone who works with children, young people and families in England aims to reflect a set of common values for practitioners that:

  – promote equality

- respect diversity
- challenge stereotypes

'Helping to improve the life chances of all children and young people':

◆ The National Occupational Standards in Children's Care, Learning and Development (CCLD) are underpinned by a number of values which set out the ethical or moral basis for professional work with children and families across the UK. Two of these values are:

- individuality, difference and diversity are valued and celebrated
- equality of opportunity and anti-discriminatory practice are actively promoted.

◆ The standards for Qualified Teacher status in the UK ask teachers to 'respect pupils' social, cultural, linguistic, religious and ethnic backgrounds'.

◆ The National Occupational Standards for Playwork in the UK include 'promote a diverse and inclusive environment' as one of the standards and state that to achieve this one must:

- make sure the environment reflects and promotes diversity and inclusion
- make sure there are resources which are accessible to all children
- promote the environment to children and young people who may experience barriers to participation and provide them with appropriate forms of support
- provide a positive role model for issues to do with diversity and inclusion
- provide opportunities for children and young people to understand and value diversity and inclusion
- promote diversity and inclusion to colleagues and other relevant adults and, where necessary, provide them with relevant support
- deal with words and behaviour that challenge diversity and inclusion in a way that is appropriate to the people involved.

◆ The Early Years Foundation Stage (EYFS), which must be complied with in all registered and maintained early years settings in England, says: 'Providers have a responsibility to ensure positive attitudes to diversity and difference – not only so that every child is included and not disadvantaged, but also so that they learn from the earliest age to value diversity in others and grow up making a positive contribution to society.'
It also says: 'All children, irrespective of ethnicity, culture or religion, home language, family background, learning difficulties or disabilities, gender or ability should have the opportunity to experience a challenging and enjoyable programme of learning and development.'
Although the EYFS relates to early years provision, it contains much

which will be useful to practitioners, whatever your work setting and whatever the age group of the children we work with.

◆ The National Childminding Association's Quality Standards (due for revision 2008) expect their childminder and nanny members to:

- treat each child as an individual and with equal concern
- give every child equal chances to learn and develop
- take into account each child's age and stage of development, gender, ethnicity, home language and any disability
- encourage children to develop a sense of their own identity and culture
- help children to learn about cultures different from their own, and to develop positive attitudes towards people who are different from themselves.

Give every child equal chances

◆ The Code of Practice for Sports Coaches developed by sports coach UK says, 'Coaches must respect the rights, dignity and worth of every human being … [and] must treat everyone equitably and sensitively, within the context of their activity and ability, regardless of gender, ethnic origin, cultural background, sexual orientation, religion or political affiliation.'

Whatever your role in working with children, it is likely that there are explicit expectations that the underlying values for your work will be related to inclusion, equality and diversity. In this book we will explore these values and consider how they can be put into practice in the reality of everyday work, no matter what setting you work in.

A journey of learning

The aspects of inclusion, equality and diversity practice are challenging. It is therefore essential that anyone who works with children spends time sorting out their thoughts, ideas and opinions about:

- why the principles of inclusion, equality and diversity matter so much in our society
- why they are especially important in planning and delivering services for children and families
- how such principles can be put into practice.

Many practitioners find that some of the ideas and issues about inclusion, equality and diversity are difficult to explore and think about. Some feel tentative about approaching this area of practice, worrying that they will lay themselves open to criticism if they don't get things 'right'. However, we are all on a journey of learning about these central aspects of practice in working with children. None of us has all the answers or has yet thought about all the sensitive issues involved. What matters is that practitioners maintain an open mind and are ready to seek new knowledge and develop new skills. If we give careful thought to how we can develop your own practice, we can ensure that we play our part in promoting and protecting all children's rights to opportunities in life.

Chapter 1

Why does it matter?

In this chapter, we look at why promoting inclusion, equality and diversity is so important in work with children, whichever part of the UK you work in. We explore what is meant by some key terms such as:

- equality of opportunity
- discrimination
- prejudice
- anti-discriminatory practice
- inclusion
- stereotypes
- diversity.

We identify some of the barriers to inclusion and equality of opportunity that children and families may encounter, which make it difficult for them to participate in settings and benefit from what the settings offer.

It is every child's right to experience equality of opportunity

Ensuring inclusion, promoting equality, valuing diversity: making a difference

Elements of the British media sometimes attack efforts to tackle the issues surrounding inclusion, equality and diversity in the context of working with children. Headlines about 'Racism in the nursery' and invented tales about 'Baa, baa, green sheep' pour scorn on or poke fun at attempts by early years practitioners and settings to discuss the agenda of inclusion, equality and diversity. Carefully thought-out policies and practices in a range of settings are often dismissed as mere 'political correctness'. The serious and socially desirable aims of offering all children good chances in life, and helping them learn how to respect one another and live in harmony, are derided as trivial and unimportant.

Such negativism can undermine the confidence and the determination of all practitioners to make a difference to the lives and the future of children and young people. It can help you to resist such pressures if you are clear about why this aspect of your work is so important, and why it is worth making the effort to maintain high standards in ensuring inclusion, promoting equality and valuing diversity.

Equality of opportunity

When you think about your intentions in working with children, you probably feel strongly that you want to:

◆ offer each child the very best chances to develop and learn

◆ help them feel good about themselves and be happy

◆ help them experience success and achievement

◆ enable them to move on to the next stage of their life with confidence and the skills they will need to progress.

To be able to do this, you need to offer each child **equality of opportunity**.

WHAT DOES THIS MEAN?

Equality of opportunity *means that each individual in society experiences opportunities to achieve and flourish which are as good as the opportunities experienced by other people.*

Equality of opportunity is not the same as everyone 'being equal'. Promoting equality of opportunity is sometimes mistakenly seen as trying to level everything out and make everyone the same, but that is not the aim at all. We all know that various individuals achieve at different levels and develop in different ways. It would be fruitless and pointless to try to make everyone equal. What matters for children is that they have *opportunities* which are equal – that they experience a 'level playing field' which gives each of them a fair chance to make the most of their lives, and that they are not held back by unfair barriers. It is each child's right to experience equality of opportunity.

Barriers to equality of opportunity

It is important that we are able to acknowledge that equality of opportunity does not exist in our society today, despite many efforts to improve the situation. Social inequalities are deeply embedded; it is an indisputable fact that some people have fewer, or more restricted, opportunities to achieve and flourish than other people do. Some children, from their earliest days and weeks, have the odds stacked against them when it comes to their chances of leading a successful and satisfying life; various influences get in the way of this happening, or hold them back.

Even very young children can have doors of opportunity closed to them. As someone who works with children, your role is to:

◆ identify why this is happening

◆ find ways of keeping those doors as wide open as possible.

Opportunities for both children and adults are often restricted in our society because of:

◆ discrimination and prejudice

◆ stereotyping and failure to treat them as individuals.

Keep the doors of opportunity open as wide as possible

Discrimination and prejudice

The most evident barrier to equality of opportunity arises through **discrimination**.

> ## WHAT DOES THIS MEAN?
>
> **Discrimination** *means treating someone less or more favourably than other people because they or their family are seen as belonging to a particular group in society. Discrimination obviously has a positive side for some – the people who are not discriminated against benefit from an unfair advantage. However, it is the negative side of discrimination that needs our attention because it limits the opportunities that some people have in life.*

Even very young children experience discrimination as the result of:

◆ the colour of their skin or other aspects of their ethnicity

◆ the traditions and way of life of their family, arising from culture and religion

◆ any impairments they may have

◆ their gender

◆ their social background – the class or socio-economic group of their family

◆ the structure or composition of their family

◆ family medical conditions such as HIV / AIDS.

For many, this restricts the opportunities open to them in their lives.

Sometimes discrimination occurs in multiple ways. For example, a black child who is also disabled may experience discrimination on both grounds.

> ## REFLECTING
>
> Think about some of the situations where you have observed or heard of discrimination based on these or any other factors, or discrimination you have experienced for yourself. What form did the less or more favourable treatment take? How do you think the person being discriminated against felt? What effects did it have on the person's life, both short-term and long-term?

Discrimination is harmful. When children are discriminated against (and so experience inequality of opportunity), they are harmed because:

◆ they are denied advantages that others have, so they don't have the chance to fulfil their potential

◆ they don't progress and experience success in their lives, and the negative effect this has on their self-esteem may dampen their motivation to learn

◆ they are excluded from certain roles.

All of this means that their potential is lost to society.

Discrimination is usually based on **prejudice**.

Prejudice can lead to assumptions such as:

◆ black / female / disabled / homosexual people are of less value, or are inferior to, or of less worth or significance than white / male / non-disabled / heterosexual people

◆ black / female / disabled people are less capable than white / male / non-disabled people

◆ one culture or religion or social group is superior to another, embodying the 'right' way to live

◆ if a family is not a two-parent nuclear family with parents of different genders and the same ethnicity, it is not 'normal'.

Many people in Britain, such as black people, Muslims and members of other cultural / religious groups, disabled people, women, people from certain social backgrounds, people with HIV / AIDS and homosexual people, endure prejudice, discrimination and lack of respect as a daily part of life. This can affect even small children. Prejudice and discrimination can be expressed in many ways including:

◆ racism in all its forms ranging from petty insults to violence, with examples including:

  – ignoring someone from an ethnic minority

  – white people avoiding touch with a black person; for example, a white shop worker putting change on the counter rather than directly into the hand of a black person

  – making fun of the way that someone with English as an additional language speaks or Anglicising their name

  – white patients rejecting the attentions and touch of black nurses, doctors and other medical practitioners

  – unchallenged assumptions that any thieving in a rural area is inevitably perpetrated by the local traveller community

  – racist name-calling in the street or playground

  – physical attacks on someone because of their skin colour or their cultural form of dress

- derogatory remarks about people who live in a specific area, or excluding behaviour even to the extent of someone being denied employment opportunities because of their postcode
- male dismissal of the significance of female roles and qualities, and undervaluing the contribution made to society by women, which leads to disparity in pay and fewer opportunities for women to reach the top in work roles (the 'glass ceiling')
- buildings and public transport which disabled people find difficult to get in to or to move around in
- avoiding all physical contact with people with HIV/AIDS
- homophobic abuse.

At the extremes, racial and homophobic prejudice turns to hatred and leads to acts of violence.

Prejudice is harmful. When children have prejudice expressed against them, they are harmed because, at the very least, they are hurt and offended. But prejudiced attitudes and remarks can also damage their **self-image**, **self-esteem** and **self-confidence**.

WHAT DOES THIS MEAN?

Self-image *is the picture we have of ourselves – who we are and what we are like, and how we fit into the world.*

Self-esteem *is valuing ourselves, and seeing ourselves as having value in other people's eyes.*

Self-confidence *is feeling able to do things and capable of achieving.*

People with a clear self-image and high self-esteem are confident enough to tackle new activities and experiences, to take responsibility for themselves, to care for others and to make choices and decisions.

In Chapter 3 we will look at how prejudice and discrimination can have destructive effects on children's self-esteem, blighting their future development. This is a major reason for being determined to tackle prejudice and discrimination. Discrimination is contrary to the values of practice in working with children and a denial of children's rights. This is why it is so important that you base your work on **anti-discriminatory** or **anti-bias** practice.

> ## WHAT DOES THIS MEAN?
>
> **Anti-discriminatory** (*or* **anti-bias**) *practice means:*
> ◆ *taking positive action to counter discrimination*
> ◆ *identifying and challenging prejudice*
> ◆ *being positive about the differences and similarities between people.*

You can take this positive action through many aspects of your practice. You can also help children to learn less prejudiced attitudes and to not behave in discriminatory ways. We will look at these in Chapters 4 and 6.

Inclusion

Because of the harm they do, it is clear that discrimination and prejudice have no place in settings where children are cared for, educated or have opportunities to play. We will see in Chapter 5 what the law has to say about how settings must behave towards children and families in order not to discriminate. But good practice goes far beyond what the law commands. Settings should always aim for the opposite of discrimination – **inclusion**.

> ## WHAT DOES THIS MEAN?
>
> **Inclusion** *is a process of identifying, understanding and breaking down barriers to participation and belonging. (Definition developed by the Early Childhood Forum.)*

It is important to look for the barriers to children and families becoming part of a setting and being included on an equal footing with other children and families. When you understand the origins of such barriers and how they exclude children and families, you will be able to start to remove them and make sure that all children and families can be (and feel themselves to be) part of your setting.

All settings for children and families like to think that they reject discrimination and that they reach out and are inclusive, but barriers to the inclusion of children and families may not be immediately obvious. The barriers to participating and feeling that they belong may link to a family's ethnic or cultural group, the disability of a family member, the composition or social background of the family, or some other reason. We will look at improving inclusion by breaking down such barriers in Chapters 4 and 6.

WHAT IT LOOKS LIKE IN PRACTICE

As part of his course, Dalvinder decided to study some settings which provide for children and families in his area, to see what barriers to inclusion he could identify. He found settings that were unintentionally pushing some children and families away by making them feel uncomfortable or that they did not belong. This was because of the following reasons:

◆ There was no visual representation of the full range of the languages spoken in the area in the setting, and no one in the setting could speak those languages.

◆ All the staff were from an ethnic background that was different from that of most of the families in the area.

◆ Resources (like the cooking utensils in the role-play area and dressing-up clothes), the food provided and the festivals celebrated reflected the home culture of a narrow range of cultures, not the broad range found in the area.

◆ Staff were not familiar with naming systems in particular cultures and did not address parents in ways seen as courteous in those cultures.

◆ Vacancies were not advertised in the full range of languages familiar to families in the area, or in places where they would see the information (such as places of worship or community meeting places).

◆ Open days to 'come and have a look at what we do' were sometime held on dates that clashed with festivals celebrated by cultures represented in the local community.

◆ Practitioners in the setting projected nervousness about their knowledge and skills in working with disabled children, so parents of disabled children got the impression that their child could not be included.

◆ Disabled family members encountered physical barriers such as steps and stairs.

◆ Some families from the surrounding rural areas could not get there because of lack of transport.

◆ Some parents with restricted literacy skills found the formal and complex English used in the information the setting distributed in the locality difficult to understand.

◆ Some families could not afford the charges made by the setting.

◆ Admission forms asked for a child's 'Christian name', and families from other religions or who were not religious felt this meant they were not welcome in the setting.

◆ Families and even staff displayed a lack of acceptance of the local traveller community.

◆ When children or adults spoke or behaved in discriminatory ways, they were not challenged.

Stereotypes

A way of denying children equality of opportunity which is more subtle than discrimination, but is nonetheless powerful, is falling into the trap of **stereotypes**.

WHAT DOES THIS MEAN?

Stereotypes *are generalisations about a person, assumptions (usually inaccurate) that because he or she is part of a particular group, that individual will:*

◆ *have certain characteristics*

◆ *have the same needs as all other members of that group*

◆ *will or should behave in a particular way.*

When we first meet someone we tend to make assumptions about them, based largely on their appearance and the way they speak and behave. If we identify a group of people they belong to, we may also generalise from what we know in broad terms about that group. This can cause us to assume that this individual will share the characteristics and needs that are sometimes or often true for the whole group.

Over the years, my husband has bewildered several boyfriends of our daughters by not conforming to the stereotype of being a man and wanting to watch football on television. While it is true that the majority of men do seem to be at least interested in (if not fanatical about) sport, there are many individual men who are not. It is best to be wary of leaping from knowing that something is often true about members of a group to assuming that it is true of a specific member of the group.

Up to a point, stereotypes are useful. They can help us to make probable predictions about a person. The assumptions we may make about a person based on their apparent membership of a group, provide us with a starting point for our interaction with them before we have had the chance to gather information about them as an individual. If we meet a person wearing garments which indicate that they are Jewish or Muslim, for example, we would hold back from offering them certain foods until we had asked whether they adhere strictly to the dietary laws of their religion.

The danger in making assumptions and generalisations arises if we assume that because a child is deaf or blind, or a family is Christian/Muslim/Jewish, or a person is homosexual, they will be like all other deaf or blind children, Christian/Muslim/Jewish families or homosexual people. We have to remember that there are as many differences within such groups as there are between them.

◆ Not all deaf people use sign language and not all blind people use guide dogs.

◆ Not all members of a religion adhere strictly to its dietary laws or rules about dress.

◆ Not all gay men are 'camp' and not all lesbian women are 'butch'.

WHAT IT LOOKS LIKE IN PRACTICE

Chloe kept a record of some of the stereotypical assumptions and comments she heard from other practitioners, to remind her to be wary of falling into the same trap herself. She listed the following:

◆ 'African Caribbean boys are very physical and run around a lot.'

◆ 'Asian mothers don't speak much English.'

◆ 'Children with Down's syndrome are affectionate.'

◆ 'Men can't hold two things in their head at the same time.'

◆ 'Girls like dressing up and imaginative play, but boys want to be rough or play with cars and trains.'

◆ 'The kids who live on the estate are badly behaved.'

Stereotyping can lead practitioners, without realising, into making assumptions about what an individual child can achieve based on one aspect of who they are. This will prevent us from nurturing the all-round development of the child. If we think about children in stereotyped ways, instead of seeing them as unique individuals, we may be limiting the expectations and aspirations which we – and they – have for:

◆ their abilities

◆ how it is appropriate for them to behave

◆ what their future achievements might be.

These limited expectations are likely to lead practitioners into failing to:

◆ offer challenging and stretching opportunities for learning

◆ encourage children to have ambitious aims for their future.

WHAT IT LOOKS LIKE IN PRACTICE

Also on Chloe's list were:

◆ 'Boys are interested in how things work, but they aren't keen on reading stories.'

◆ 'Girls are naturally inclined to be more interested in caring for others, and they're not going to become mechanics and engineers.'

◆ 'Disabled children can't join in with outdoor play on the slide and swings.'

◆ 'Black boys don't do well at school.'

Stereotyping can also give children messages that certain activities or ways of behaving are only suitable for certain children, and this may limit their access to learning opportunities.

REFLECTING

Think about the stereotypical assumptions you have observed other people making about a child or family, or which you have found yourself making (be very honest with yourself). What stereotypical expectations have you encountered about:

◆ what girls/boys can do or ought to do

◆ characteristics of children of various ethnic origins or cultural groups

◆ what disabled children are capable of

◆ the roles that men and women, or white people and black people, or disabled people and non-disabled people, can play in adult life

◆ the behaviour that might be expected of children from particular social groups or who live in specific areas or who speak with a particular accent?

How can these assumptions influence you to change your practice?

People more often apply stereotypes to a group of people they don't belong to themselves. For example, a woman is more likely than a man to say 'men make such a fuss when they're ill'; and middle-class people may regard working-class people who have a sense of grievance about the injustice of inequality as 'having a chip on their shoulder'. Often, people build up a stereotype from one or two experiences of a group they don't belong to – they generalise from a few examples to label the whole group. They may say, for example, 'We had trouble with a family of travellers in our village last year – but, of course, they're all a dishonest and dirty lot, aren't they?' Even when a person gets to know a member of a group who doesn't fit the stereotype, he or she may continue to hold on to a stereotypical viewpoint, seeing the individual they know as the exception: 'Well, I know my neighbour would never force his daughter into an arranged marriage, he's different, but it's the culture, isn't it?'

In Chapter 2, you will look in more detail at stereotypes, and in Chapter 4 at how you can reduce the influence of stereotypes in your work.

Treating children with equal concern

The key to steering away from stereotypes is to see each child as a unique individual. Each child is an individual, different from every other child; even twins or triplets who may look alike can have differing personalities, skills and abilities. Margaret Meade, the anthropologist, said, 'Remember you are unique – just like everyone else.' We will look at this more in Chapter 3.

Offering children equal opportunities to develop and learn doesn't mean treating them 'all the same'; practitioners have to treat children as individuals, **with equal concern**.

WHAT DOES THIS MEAN?

Treating children **with equal concern** *means taking as much care to promote the opportunities and progress of one child as you do for any other child. This may require you to adapt the way you work with a child to best meet their individual needs and characteristics. In this way you can make sure that each child has the opportunities which will help them to get the most out of life.*

The phrase 'treating children with equal concern' first appeared in the guidance to the Children Act 1989 and is a useful way of thinking about how we work with children.

Making sure that each child has opportunities that are as good as those which other children have may mean that sometimes you have to treat children differently from one another, according to their stage of development or some other aspect of their individuality. Disabled children, for example, sometimes require additional resources or adult support to be able to participate.

By viewing each child as an individual, you will be able to identify that child's particular requirements. By meeting those requirements, you can be sure you are offering the child opportunities equal to those experienced by other children. We will look at ways of doing this in Chapter 4.

Disabled children sometimes require additional resources to be able to participate

Diversity

An important part of anti-discriminatory practice is valuing and, indeed, celebrating **diversity**.

> ## WHAT DOES THIS MEAN?
>
> **Diversity** *refers to the differences between individuals and groups in society arising from gender, ethnic origins, social, cultural or religious background, family structure, disabilities, sexuality and appearance.*

The children you work with throughout your career will come from a variety of social and cultural backgrounds and live in families with a wide range of ways of life. It is important that you show by the way you communicate with children and their parents that you value and respect them and their family, however different they are from your own.

Differences between people can become a source of suspicion and antagonism, and are at the heart of divisions and unhappiness in society. You can play a part in preventing this. In your work with children, you can help them to see differences in a positive way – as interesting and enriching to all our lives. Children's learning from their earliest years can introduce them to the pleasure of exploring the immense variety of human life. Your role is to explain about the variety of humanity, so you can extend children's knowledge and understanding both of people who are like themselves and of people who are different from themselves. You can help children to develop positive and respectful attitudes towards:

- people from ethnic, cultural and social groups different from their own
- people who live in families different from their own
- disabled people
- people who look or sound different from themselves.

By doing this, you will reduce the likelihood of children developing prejudiced views. We will look at this in Chapter 3.

Enjoying the variety of humanity

It *does matter*

Because prejudice, discrimination and lack of equality of opportunity have destructive effects in our society, we cannot tolerate them. Lack of opportunity and discrimination exclude certain people from certain roles and activities, and so rob society of the potential skills and talents of part of the population. Prejudice damages the self-esteem of individuals and prevents them from developing their potential. It also leads to division and disharmony in society, which can be harmful to us all.

Because anti-discriminatory practice can help to overcome prejudice and discrimination, it must underpin all work with children and families. Settings should promote practice which offers equality of opportunity and is inclusive of all children.

A guiding principle for people who work with children should be that every child has the right to the best possible chances in life. The Early Years Foundation Stage (EYFS) says, 'All children are entitled to enjoy a full life in conditions which will help them take part in society and develop as an individual.' One of its commitments is, 'No child or family is discriminated against.' This should be a commitment for everyone who works with children and young people.

In England and Wales, the government's aim for all children from birth to 19 years, whatever their background or circumstances, is that they have the support they need to reach the Every Child Matters outcomes. These are:

◆ be healthy

◆ stay safe

◆ enjoy and achieve

◆ make a positive contribution

◆ achieve economic well-being.

Inclusion and equality are vital to these outcomes.

◆ *Be healthy*: Social inequalities are reflected in poorer health amongst socially excluded groups such as homeless people and families on low incomes. Experiencing prejudice and discrimination can have a negative effect on emotional well-being and mental health.

◆ *Stay safe*: Prejudice can lead to harassment and bullying and, at the extreme, to physical violence which threatens the safety of some citizens.

◆ *Enjoy and achieve*: Stereotyping, discrimination and lack of equality of opportunity can limit a person's enjoyment of life and undermine their chance of achieving success.

◆ *Make a positive contribution*: When an individual's educational opportunities are limited by stereotyping and discrimination, they face exclusion from aspects of social and economic life and are unable to contribute their potential talents.

◆ *Achieve economic well-being*: Limited educational opportunities arising from stereotyping and discrimination have long-lasting effects on a person's employment prospects, potential to earn and economic well-being.

Some children and families experience discrimination and prejudice, which lead to inequality of opportunity. For such people to reach the Every Child Matters outcomes, they will need considerable support.

People who work with children can have great influence on children's lives, especially the way in which impressionable young minds view the world. Through the way you treat each child as an individual, you can ensure they will get the best possible opportunities for development and progress, in ways that are fair to all. You can help children to grow up in a society in which differences amongst people are seen to enrich the lives of everyone, rather than being the source of intolerance, prejudice and discrimination, and in which people of differing backgrounds can live in greater harmony.

It matters wherever you work

There is still a tendency for some people to think that 'all of this anti-discrimination stuff' is not relevant to them because they live in an area which is predominantly white. They feel that the issues of diversity and equality are only relevant to inner-city areas where there are sizable minority ethnic populations. Such people might say 'we don't have that problem here'. This is not the case.

The issues of inclusion, equality and diversity matter to you as a person working with children wherever you work. The EYFS makes the point that: 'All practitioners will benefit from professional development in diversity, equality and anti-discriminatory practice whatever the ethnic, cultural or social make-up of the setting.'

As we will see in Chapter 2, inclusion and equality relate to other issues besides ethnic origins and cultural background, such as gender, disability, sexuality, social class and family patterns. But even if inclusion and equality only related to the issues of ethnicity and culture, they would still be significant for all UK citizens, wherever they live and work.

People who live in a largely white community may not have many first-hand opportunities of meeting and getting to know people of various ethnic origins or other cultures. They may not be aware of the intensity of discrimination against black people, because they don't observe it and don't have friends who experience it. But it is important to help children in such a community to learn about people who are different from themselves. They need to understand how to show respect for people who look, speak, dress, cook and eat food differently, and have a different way of life. All children, whatever the ethnic mix of the area they live in, are part of our diverse UK society, and when they grow up, they will live and work with people of various ethnic origins and cultural backgrounds. They should learn as early as possible to respect other people's ways of life and to value individuals equally.

In fact, of course, no community in Britain is 'all white'; even the most rural communities include people from ethnic minorities. These people may be very much in an ethnic or cultural minority (for example, only one per cent of the population in Cornwall is black), but they deserve to be free from discrimination and to be respected. Although, as we will see in Chapter 5, previous generations of immigrants who came from outside Europe and were easily identifiable by the colour of their skin settled in urban areas, many of the more recent immigrants from Eastern Europe are settling in rural areas. In addition, social and cultural groups who experience high levels of prejudice and discrimination, such as travellers, refugees and asylum seekers, live in all parts of the UK.

FOOD FOR FURTHER THOUGHT

What do you know about the variations in cultural, ethnic or social groups in the area where you work? What changes are you aware of in the ethnic and/or cultural mix in your locality in recent years? How are such changes affecting your community – what adaptations have been necessary? What have been the prevailing attitudes to the changes?

As someone who works with children, you have a responsibility to be well informed about a wide range of issues related to inclusion, equality and diversity, and to use your knowledge and understanding to develop your work practice in the best interests of children and families. You may find the consideration of some of these issues an uncomfortable or even challenging experience. However, it will be your commitment to promoting the best interests of the children you work with that will enable you to keep thinking about what is 'fair'.

Chapter 2

What makes us different and what makes us the same?

In this chapter, we explore differences between people based on:

◆ gender

◆ ethnicity

◆ cultural background (including religion and language)

◆ social background (including family grouping)

◆ disability

◆ sexuality

◆ appearance and accent.

We also consider some of the key issues for practice in working with children which arise from these differences.

Girls and boys enjoy movement and exploration in their play

Our shared humanity

All human beings have many important things in common. We each have similar basic needs for:

◆ food and shelter

◆ emotional stability and loving relationships

◆ an environment which protects our health and well-being

◆ opportunities to make the most of our lives.

This makes up our shared humanity.

However, as we have already seen in Chapter 1, there are many differences between people. These differences can be a source of great richness and variety in society. Unfortunately, these same differences are also often the source of prejudice and discrimination, disharmony and suspicion, as well as imposing restrictions on some children's life-chances – denying them equality of opportunity.

In your work with children, you need to:

◆ be aware of issues surrounding each of these aspects of diversity

◆ be vigilant to attitudes (your own and other people's) and situations which discriminate against certain children and deny them equality of opportunity

◆ influence policies and practices in your setting and adapt your own practice to ensure each child is:

  – truly included

  – treated with equal concern

  – offered equal opportunities to develop and learn.

It is essential to explore differences and highlight the ways they affect children, but it is also vital to remember the significance of our shared humanity.

Gender

One of the first pieces of information sought and given about a new baby (nowadays even before birth) is whether the child is a girl or a boy. This is one of the main factors identifying us as a human being, from the very beginning of our lives. As a practitioner who works with children and influences their future, you should think about the difference between a child's **sex** and his or her **gender identity**.

> ### (WHAT DOES THIS MEAN?)
>
> *A person's* **sex** *– male or female – is determined biologically; it derives from differences of the genitals and other physical characteristics such as adult body shape.*
>
> *A person's* **gender identity** *derives from their identity in society – what it means, psychologically and culturally, to be male or female, and what roles and behaviour are seen as appropriate or inappropriate for each gender.*

For almost all children, their sex is a given fact from conception, but their gender identity is influenced by:

◆ the society they live in

◆ the attitudes of adults and other children they encounter in life

◆ the opportunities they are offered for development.

The big question is whether a child's sex will inevitably and always shape their gender identity. If a child is born a boy or a girl, does that mean their future life is bound to follow a masculine or a feminine pathway? Can we predict how they will behave, what abilities they will have, what roles they will be capable of taking in society? And should the pattern of a person's life be entirely dependent on their sex?

Differences between the sexes

Much has been written and said about the differences between men and women, some sensible, some nonsense. There are biological differences between males and females, significantly in the hormones in the brain, and these differences cannot be denied. They do affect behaviour and abilities to some extent.

The average male brain has up to 20 times more of the hormone testosterone than the average female brain. Testosterone is associated with action-orientated and risk-taking behaviour, reduced levels of eye contact and restlessness. Conversely, the average female brain contains higher levels of serotonin and dopamine than the average male brain. It is thought that serotonin helps with processing and understanding emotions and regulates aggression, and dopamine helps concentration levels. Both these chemicals help information to be transmitted along the pathways in the brain. The comparative levels of these substances in males and females seem to link with the wider incidence in boys than in girls of dyslexia, autism and ADHD (attention deficit and hyperactivity disorder).

A picture of the differences in *average* patterns of behaviour and development in boys and girls has been built up from the accumulation of many reports and studies, together with practitioners' experiences and observations. These differences apply to *most* boys or *most* girls, not to all, but they point to some inherent differences between the sexes.

- Girls develop in some ways at a younger age than boys do, such as learning to speak, achieving bladder and bowel control, and acquiring independence and self-reliance.
- Girls gravitate towards adults and engage in conversation whereas boys prefer to engage in their own activities away from adults.
- Boys are more physically active than girls in the early years – they prefer movement, exploration and building.
- Boys enjoy activities that present them with challenges whereas girls prefer activities which rely on co-operation.
- Boys are more aggressive than girls.
- Boys have better spatial awareness than girls.

REFLECTING

How far does your own experience and observation reinforce these ideas about the differences between the sexes? Collect some evidence for yourself about how accurate you think these descriptions of gender differences in patterns of behaviour and development are. How might this understanding affect your interactions with children?

This information about gender differences is useful and interesting, but you must treat it with caution and recognise that the differences apply only *on average*. There are no differences, beyond the biological ones, between *all* boys and *all* girls. While it may be true to say that aggressiveness is more frequently found amongst boys than amongst girls, it is absolutely not true to say that all boys are 'naturally' aggressive. Thus, you cannot assume that a particular boy will be aggressive. It seems to be true that girls, on the whole, develop communication skills earlier then boys, but not all girls are better communicators than all boys, so you should not assume that a specific girl will naturally be a good communicator. No statement about boys or girls *in general* is true of *all* boys or girls. The key factor which should inform your practice is the understanding that, although a characteristic may be found in some or even most children of one sex, it will not necessarily be present in the particular child you are working with.

Nurture versus nature

It is always difficult to disentangle the threads of:

- *nature* (the biological characteristics a child is born with); and
- *nurture* (the different ways children are treated as they grow and develop).

It seems that there are differences in nature between the sexes, but it also seems that these differences are reinforced by nurture. We label boys and girls differently from infancy according to their sex. Even the youngest children are dressed differently. As the 20th century progressed, it became more common to dress girls in trousers and dungarees, and the practice of putting little boys in dresses died out. (I do have a delightful photograph of my father-in-law as a toddler in about 1918 in a frock adorned with frills.) But even today, clothes sold for boys are in strong and dark colours and it is not easy to find clothes for small girls that are not pink! Florists even ask whether pink or blue flowers should be sent to the mother of a newborn baby. Greetings cards to welcome a new baby are very definitely different for girl babies and boy babies, and most toys are still advertised and packaged as 'for boys' or 'for girls'.

If our assumptions about how boys and girls differ are too rigid, they can lead us into unhelpful ways of treating them differently. In this way, our assumptions become self-fulfilling prophecies: because of the way we treat them, children develop the very characteristics we assumed they already had. In one famous experiment reported by H. Frisch in 1977 ('Sex Stereotypes in Adult-Infant play', *Child Development*), adults were invited to play with 14-month-old children. They were told that some were boys and that others were girls. The adults responded differently to the children they thought were boys, offering them balls to play with, for example; with the children they thought were girls, the adults offered them dolls. In a similar experiment with six-month-old babies, the baby thought to be a girl was cuddled and the baby thought to be a boy was encouraged to crawl (C. Smith and B. Lloyd, 'Maternal Behaviour and Perceived Sex of Infants: Revisited', 1978). It seems that adults tend to treat boys and girls differently and have different expectations of them from infancy.

WHAT IT LOOKS LIKE IN PRACTICE

The childminding network that Meena belongs to had a discussion about gender roles and identity. They shared their observations of parents and other adults treating babies and very young children differently according to their sex, and described how they had noticed them handling and talking to children differently based on whether the child was male or female. Several of them had observed:

◆ boys being handled robustly and energetically, and encouraged to play with cars and trains

◆ girls being handled gently and talked to with eye contact, and encouraged to play with dolls and soft toys, and to look at books.

Children's gender identity is affected by the way adults treat them

If different sex children have different experiences from their earliest days, it would not be surprising if they developed gender-based preferences for toys or became more- or less-skilled communicators. The biological differences, the differences in nature, are often reinforced by the way children are treated, or nurtured.

REFLECTING

Over the next few weeks, look for examples of boys and girls being offered different play and learning opportunities (in your own setting and elsewhere). Are certain toys thought of as 'girl's toys' or 'boy's toys'? Are certain activities thought of as more suited or relevant to boys than girls, or vice versa? For example, are girls encouraged to do quiet and sedentary activities, and are boys encouraged to engage in energetic, physical and noisy play? Are boys and girls expected to take different responsibilities ('we need a big strong boy to carry this chair'; 'the girls can wash up the cooking bowls')?

What changes to your practice do you want to make as the result of your observations?

Twenty years ago it was largely assumed that there were no real differences between boys and girls, except those produced by nurture. It was therefore thought that, if boys and girls were treated the same, they would have equal opportunities. However, as more has been learned about biological and chemical differences, the view has developed that boys, on the whole, learn in ways that are different from the ways that girls, on average, learn. So, you do need to take differences of nature into account to be sure that you are appropriately and effectively supporting the learning of all children, whatever their sex. Practitioners may have to go about providing that support in different ways for girls and boys, and we will consider this in Chapter 4.

Learning gender identity

Children become aware of the sex they belong to at a very young age. They develop an understanding that there are two sexes, and even before their first birthday they may respond differently to males and females. We tell children from their earliest months that they are a girl or a boy, and they begin to acquire an understanding of their gender identity. Later, they develop knowledge of the different clothing, hairstyles, jobs, games and so on that are associated with each gender, and they begin to learn some of the **stereotypes** associated with gender identity.

WHAT DOES THIS MEAN?

Stereotypes *are generalisations about a person, assumptions (usually inaccurate) that because he or she is part of a particular group, that individual will:*
- *have certain characteristics*
- *have the same needs as all other members of that group*
- *will or should behave in a particular way.*

Before the age of two years, children may have expectations that girls play with dolls and boys play with cars. By the time children are three or four years, they regard certain tasks or activities as being either male or female. As discussed on pages 32 and 33, such information is gathered from the world around them and images from the media – it can even be suggested by the packaging on toys.

FOOD FOR FURTHER THOUGHT

How do you think you developed your image of yourself as a member of your gender? Think about influences like the role model of your parents and other family members, and the cultural and social influences in your life, including religion. In what ways do you now conform or not conform to the identity for your gender that you were brought up with?

If children receive messages that certain behaviour is expected or accepted from their own gender but not from the other, they are likely to start living up to the image they are formulating for their own gender. A boy may reason 'I know that

I'm a boy, and boys are supposed to behave like this, so I must behave like this.'
Even if he has a longing to push the doll around in the pram or use the ironing
board, he may not feel able to do so because 'that's not what boys do'.

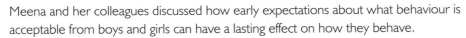

WHAT IT LOOKS LIKE IN PRACTICE

Meena and her colleagues discussed how early expectations about what behaviour is
acceptable from boys and girls can have a lasting effect on how they behave.

They thought about how:

◆ if boys are told 'big boys don't cry', they may learn to stifle their feelings (which they
have every right to express and communicate to others) and their frustration may
lead to aggression – towards others or towards themselves

◆ when girls are shown disapproval when they climb high or get dirty, they may
become fearful of taking physical risks or experiencing exploratory, messy play.

Sexism

All societies have built up traditional models of gender identity, which describe
what is seen as appropriate or 'proper' behaviour for males and females. These
models vary from society to society, and change over time, but a prevailing trend
is to see the male as superior to the female, and for men to have more choices,
autonomy and power. This is how **sexism** develops.

WHAT DOES THIS MEAN?

Sexism consists of attitudes, policies, institutional structures and actions that discriminate
against one sex (often, but not always, against women), limiting freedom and opportunities.

In Britain during the mid-20th century (when the grandparents of the children
you work with were growing up), there were clearly defined gender expectations.
It was thought that girls should be quiet, tidy and passive, and learn the skills
needed to become a wife and mother. It was thought that girls were not good at
maths and science, and that there was no need for them to move into higher
education, unless they were going to train as a teacher or nurse, jobs which would
fit in with being a housewife and rearing children. Female teachers and civil
servants were required to resign their jobs on marriage, and there was no
maternity leave, so pregnant women in employment could not continue to work.

It was thought that boys should be brave and strong, actively explore the world,
and learn skills to prepare them to be a family breadwinner. Jobs like firefighter or
plumber could only be done by men and there were still very few women in the
medical or legal professions. Additionally, men did not usually cook, do
housework or look after children – it was rare to see a man pushing a pram.

Of course, not all girls and boys and men and women experienced life in this way, but those were the prevailing expectations and views.

Society has changed a great deal in the last 50 years, but some of those attitudes still remain and practitioners need to consider them carefully to see if they continue to limit children's opportunities.

REFLECTING

How far do you think our society still assumes that girls and boys are different – that boys will behave and develop in different ways from girls? Think about how this links to the idea that all girls will behave and develop in ways similar to all other girls, and that all boys will behave and develop in ways similar to all other boys. Have you found that, even in the sector of working with children, some settings and practitioners still expect girls to learn to be quiet and gentle but tolerate more aggressive behaviour from boys?

Over the next few weeks, make a note of any examples or comments and assumptions you encounter (including your own – be honest!) about what is 'natural' or 'proper' as behaviour and development for boys or girls, or expectations about their personality. You might overhear a grandparent say 'he's a proper boy, he's never still for a moment and he's mad about cars' or 'she's a real little girl, so clean and tidy and loves pretty clothes'.

What do your findings tell you about how gender differences in children are perceived in our society today? Did you find any differences in the perceptions of men and women, or according to the age or culture of the speaker?

In the past, girls experienced **discrimination** in education

WHAT DOES THIS MEAN?

Discrimination *means treating someone less or more favourably than other people because they or their family are seen as belonging to a particular group in society. Discrimination obviously has a positive side for some – the people who are not discriminated against benefit from an unfair advantage. However, it is the negative side of discrimination that needs our attention because it limits the opportunities that some people have in life.*

During the 1950s and 1960s, children had to take an exam when they moved from primary to secondary school. The 'eleven plus' determined whether they went to a grammar school, which provided a traditional academic curriculum, or to a secondary modern, which provided more technical and vocational training. Secondary moderns tended to be significantly less well resourced than grammar schools and offered more limited opportunities to gain qualifications. The system was discriminatory because the numbers of places at grammar school for girls were the same (or sometimes smaller) than for boys, despite the fact that a higher proportion of girls than boys gained the top marks. This meant that many boys had the advantages of a grammar school education, even though they had not done as well as girls who were consigned to secondary moderns.

Until the 1980s, some UK universities restricted the proportion of women admitted. This practice continued until nearly the end of the 20th century in many medical schools, denying places to able girls and admitting less able boys. In previous generations, families often allowed boys to stay on for longer at school than their sisters, even if the girls were doing better than their brothers. The prevailing wisdom was that education would be wasted on a girl who would 'only' get married and have children. My father was regarded as foolish by his work colleagues in the building trade because, in the 1960s, he supported me in staying on at school and going on to higher education, rather than my leaving school to start earning and contributing to our family's low income.

Although our society has moved on from direct discrimination against the education of girls, practitioners still have to be vigilant that we do not allow more subtle discrimination to result from stereotyping girls' and boys' potential and abilities.

WHAT IT LOOKS LIKE IN PRACTICE

Meena's colleague, Ellie, pointed out that if they assumed that girls will not be good at maths and science, they might, even in the Early Years Foundation Stage, be having lower expectations of what girls can understand or offering them fewer opportunities to investigate mathematical or scientific concepts.

Sexism isn't only about disadvantaging girls. There are great concerns currently about the apparent under-achievement of boys in the school system. Girls out-perform boys at every subject in all stages of testing and examination throughout their school careers. Teachers widely report that working hard and studying are not seen as male or 'macho', and a central issue seems to be boys' greater reluctance to read. Concern is expressed by many early years professionals that part of the blame for this lies with the creeping formalisation of early years learning, especially in the area of literacy. The age at which young children are being expected to engage in learning in groups, largely passive and paying attention to the teacher, rather than learning through individual active exploration and play, is being steadily driven down. It is feared that the effect this is having on many boys is to alienate them from the whole process of learning and school, and this effect persists well beyond the early years.

It is also worrying that around 90 per cent of offenders who appear before the courts are male. Clearly society is not yet nurturing male children in ways that offer them and society a less disruptive lifestyle.

A 'gendered workforce'

One factor that needs to be considered is the imbalance of the sexes in the childcare workforce. More women than men work with children, and this is particularly marked in the early years. There are very few male nannies. Also, few male childminders work alone, tending to work in partnership with a female childminder. There are also few male pre-school and nursery workers, and the staff of primary schools have become much more 'feminised'.

This means that children see very little of men in the nurturing roles in the early years sector. They therefore do not benefit from the role model which male workers provide for them in terms of demonstrating how men can care for others. The idea that caring is 'women's work' is reinforced by the predominance of women in this kind of employment.

WHAT IT LOOKS LIKE IN PRACTICE

Meena said that a lot of progress has been made in recent years in getting across the message to girls that they can be assertive and active, and achieve in any area they find matches their talents and interests. But she felt that we seem to have taken our eye off the boys, who are often confused about expectations of them. They need a lot more help to embrace their caring, considerate characteristics and creative, artistic skills, and to understand the importance of taking a fair share of domestic roles.

Efforts have been made in recent years to recruit more men to the early years sector, but this has achieved only limited success. This seems to be partly linked to low pay and poor status, but also to the persistence of negative attitudes about men working with young children. Men who do choose this work report that they are often regarded with suspicion, as doing something which a 'real man' would not contemplate as a career. They find their motives are seen as questionable, and some parents are reluctant to see their children left in the care of male workers. There is much left to be done in breaking down these barriers to male participation in the children's workforce.

Your role

To be sure of providing all children with equality of opportunity in the context of gender, you need to identify ways in which children's opportunities – for both girls and boys – may be restricted by definitions of gender identity and expectations about abilities and roles. If children are offered opportunities for play and learning which are based on stereotyped expectations about what they are capable of and what they will be interested in, there is a risk that their development will be limited. Consider whether gender means that children must be confined to the behaviour, achievements and roles society has deemed appropriate for their sex, or whether their gender identity can be a more subtle mix of what is traditionally regarded as male and female.

You should be critical of assumptions about what boys and girls are, or do, or can become, and be open to a range of possibilities in guiding them towards their future. In Chapter 4, we will look at ways of offering all children opportunities to develop and learn in ways best suited to them, whatever their gender, by checking whether stereotypical expectations are limiting their opportunities for development and learning.

Ethnicity

When we look around us we see people who look different from ourselves. Probably the most striking difference is in the colour of skin, and this has led to the categorising of people as belonging to different '**races**'.

> ### WHAT DOES THIS MEAN?
>
> **Race** *has come to mean a group of human beings who are seen (by others or by themselves) as belonging to a separate group, different from other groups. The grouping is mainly based on skin tone, but may also relate to colour of eyes and hair, shape of features (such as the nose) or hair texture.*

There is no scientific basis for the concept of 'race'. All human beings are too closely related genetically to separate them out into groups. There are no genes or characteristics found in all members of a so-called 'race' which are not found in other groups. Furthermore, the variations in genetic make-up within so-called 'races' are as wide as the variations between the groups seen by some people as separate races.

Sometimes, the greater prevalence of the genetically inherited sickle cell disease and thalassaemia amongst people of black African descent is cited as proof that there is some sort of distinction between people of different races. However, sickle cell disease is the result of mutated genes, a circumstance which arises in parts of the world where malaria is common, and therefore affects people of various ethnic origins who trace their forebears back to the Indian sub-continent, south and central America, the middle east and the eastern Mediterranean.

The concept of 'race' sometimes gets muddled with the concept of **nation**, which means something a little different.

WHAT DOES THIS MEAN?

*A **nation** is a body of people who share a historical tradition and a language, and may also share a common descent from ancestors. They may all live within the same state or geographical area, or be spread over more than one territory.*

The idea of 'race' is therefore something constructed by society rather than a given fact. It makes no more sense to define someone as belonging to a specific 'race' because they have dark brown skin than if they have red hair. Nonetheless, the concept of 'race' is a powerful one and we cannot ignore the fact that it is how many people perceive their fellow human beings. Sometimes, this extends to seeing people of a different 'race' as a different species. Dislike, even revulsion, at the idea of people of different 'races' having children together was common in the past and still persists to some extent.

The notion of a 'pure race' was the basis of the worst actions of the Nazis under Hitler in Germany in the 1930s and 40s. This thinking had no grounding in scientific fact, although efforts were made to establish this. The current fascination with tracing family history is helping many people to understand that their ancestry is more complicated than they had assumed, as they find great-great grandparents from different 'races'. Everybody has a mixed inheritance of genes from their forebears, whether they were Celtic, African, Scandinavian or Arabic. People who look 'very white' have been shown through DNA samples to have black ancestors.

WHAT IT LOOKS LIKE IN PRACTICE

Meena and the other childminders in the network carried out a training exercise one of them had learned on a course. They imagined the room where they met as a map of the UK, and each of them stood in a place which represented the place where they had grown up. Meena stood part way up the room on the right hand side to represent Leicester, and Jaswinder stood on the left towards the end of the room to represent Glasgow. Ellie went out into the hallway to represent Ghana and Josh went outdoors to represent Argentina. Then they moved to different positions to represent where one or more of their grandparents had lived most of their lives. Meena stayed in Leicester, but Jaswinder moved out to the hallway to India. Ellie came in to Cardiff and Josh moved to Kent.

They all began to ask each other questions about where previous generations of their families had lived, and many of the childminders found they had ancestors who had lived in Ireland. They all agreed that there was no simple answer to the question 'where are you from?'

Racism

When the idea that there are separate human 'races' is muddled with nationhood, and this thinking is coupled with the idea that one 'race' or nation is superior to others, the result is **racism**.

WHAT DOES THIS MEAN?

Racism *consists of the attitudes and actions, often based on prejudice and deriving from stereotypes, that discriminate against certain people because they are seen as belonging to a particular 'race' which is seen as inferior to another.*

Racist attitudes include the view that people of some ethnic origins are less important or valuable than those of other ethnic origins, that they cannot be expected to benefit from education, or that they are not capable of achieving or of taking responsibility.

Extreme racism can lead to violence, but it also presents itself in attitudes that lead to discrimination in employment, housing and education. In 1993, Stephen Lawrence, a young black man, was attacked and killed on the streets of south London by a group of white youths simply because he was black. This brutal racist crime was made worse by the way the Metropolitan Police handled the investigation, demonstrating stereotypical and even prejudiced views about young black men. The Macpherson Report which followed the murder drew our attention to the concept of institutional racism, whereby the policies and practices of a corporate body (such as a police force) lead to the disadvantaging of black and other minority ethnic people.

When people think in stereotypical terms about people with skin of a particular tone, or features such as a nose of a particular shape, they fall into making assumptions about everyone with that skin tone or shape of nose. If those assumptions are that anyone with that skin tone or nose shape is inferior or suspect in some way, it is a short step to **prejudice** and so to the discrimination which engenders racism. Many white people still regard people with black or brown skin as less intelligent and capable than people with white skin, and widespread distrust of Jews and Arabs also continues.

WHAT DOES THIS MEAN?

Prejudice *is a judgment or opinion, often negative, of a person or group which is made without careful consideration of accurate relevant information. It normally leads to the view that some people are inferior to others, and of less worth and significance.*

Racism in Britain in the second half of the 20th century led to black and Asian adults experiencing the expression of open prejudice against them. These forms of racism included landladies' notices of the 1950s, such as 'No dogs, no Irish and no coloureds', the graffiti and insults of more recent years ('Pakis out'), as well as direct and indirect discrimination in getting jobs and housing. Asian families in some areas have experienced prolonged and persistent attacks on their homes and businesses, from graffiti to excrement through letter boxes to arson. In Stephen Lawrence's case, racism cost him his life.

Black and Asian children have also experienced prejudice and discrimination, most seriously in encountering low expectations about the capacity of black children to achieve academically and go on to train for professional jobs, coupled with expectations that black boys in particular will cause behavioural problems. These expectations are often self-fulfilling – if we see a child in stereotypical terms and expect little of them, they are likely to live down to our expectations.

It is also important to realise that racism isn't always about white people's attitudes to black people. I recall hearing an Asian woman talk about her childhood in a middle class, well-to-do family in East Africa, where they were used to having black servants. When her family was forced to leave Africa and came to live in Britain, she experienced racism directed against her for the first time. She came to realise that she and her family had made negative assumptions about black people and treated them with the same lack of respect she was now encountering towards herself from white British people. Similarly, the UK is currently experiencing increasing racism against groups of white people who have migrated to Britain from Eastern Europe. And, of course, some black people have stereotypical and prejudiced views of white people.

Even within ethnic groups, there can be a hierarchy of value attached to skin tone. For example, when an arranged marriage is sought in some Asian communities, it is not uncommon to see an emphasis on the 'fair skin' of a woman making her a more desirable wife. Some people of African ethnic background living in the UK hold negative views of black African Caribbean people; they stereotype them as lazy, poorly educated and part of the drug culture, with men seen to father children with different women and not support them financially.

REFLECTING

What experience have you had of racism? Look back at the stereotypes linked to ethnic origins you identified in the Reflecting activity on page 21.

Next, think about examples of discrimination you have encountered against adults or children because of their ethnic group. These might be examples from your own experience, of what you have observed, or what you have heard or read about.

Now, think of examples of prejudice expressed against adults or children because of their ethnic origins, again from your direct experience or observation, or that you have heard or read about.

How do the prejudice and discrimination that make up racism make you feel?

Not race but ethnicity

When talking about differences between people, it is more helpful to talk about **ethnicity**, which starts not from the flawed concept of 'race' but from the idea of shared genetic origins.

WHAT DOES THIS MEAN?

Ethnicity refers not only to people's genetic origins but also their shared heritage, traditions and language. It is a term which brings together understanding of everyone's mixed origins and inheritance of genes from many groups, rather than trying to separate people into different 'races'.

It is incorrect to talk about a group of people as 'the ethnic population'. We are all 'ethnic', including white British people. We all have ethnic origins. When the term 'ethnic population' is used, it usually applies to **minority ethnic groups**.

WHAT DOES THIS MEAN?

Minority ethnic groups are groups of people within a society who are similar to one another in ethnic origins, and different from and fewer in number than the majority ethnic group of that society.

It is patronising at best, derogatory at worst, and always inappropriate, to talk about members of minority ethnic groups as 'ethnics'. The use of 'ethnic' to describe, for example, designs on cloth or of jewellery, is often unhelpful in suggesting something exotic and foreign. Scottish tartan designs are as ethnic as the designs on cloth imported from India, and Cornish pasties are as much ethnic food as curry or spaghetti – they form part of a heritage and tradition.

The 2001 census recorded that the ethnicity of the UK population was:

◆ 92.1% white
◆ 4% Asian (including people of Indian, Pakistani and Bangladeshi origins)
◆ 2% black (including people of Caribbean and African origins)
◆ 0.4% Chinese
◆ 0.4% other ethnic groups
◆ 1.2% mixed ethnic origins.

However, these groups are not spread evenly throughout the country. In the London Borough of Tower Hamlets, 33.4% of the population was of Bangladeshi origin, whereas only 2% of the population in the south west and north east of England were from minority ethnic groups.

Minority ethnic groups are not static or given; the ethnic composition of local communities is changing all the time. An extraordinary example of this is the Brick Lane area of East London. Huguenot refugees (Protestant Christians escaping persecution in France) came to live there in the 17th century; Jews escaping Russia arrived in the late 19th century; immigrants from Bangladesh arrived in the late 20th century. A building that began as a church has subsequently been a synagogue and is now a mosque.

Immigrants, refugees, asylum seekers

There is sometimes a carelessness in the use of the word **immigrant** that suggests that all families in minority ethnic groups are new to this country.

WHAT DOES THIS MEAN?

An **immigrant** *is a person who has come to live in a country, emigrating from the country where they lived previously.*

Many members of ethnic minority groups in the UK are not immigrants. They are the second or third generation of their family to be born and live in the UK, and are British citizens. Some more recent arrivals (who are indeed immigrants) may be **asylum seekers** or **refugees**.

WHAT DOES THIS MEAN?

A **refugee** *is someone who is fleeing from their homeland because they can no longer live there, either because of famine, war or natural disaster like floods, or because they are facing persecution (perhaps because of their ethnic group or religion, or support for a political cause). When a refugee tries to find a safe place to live, away from these dangers, they become an* **asylum seeker***.*

Modern warfare disrupts the lives of civilians, displacing vast numbers of people. Almost 90 per cent of war casualties in modern warfare are civilians rather than military. In countries where the government is repressive, it can be dangerous to speak out against the ruling powers, and those who do so often flee their homes in fear of their own safety and that of their family. Asylum seekers and refugees have often had dreadful and terrifying experiences before they reach what they hope will be the safety of Britain.

Unfortunately, some media coverage of a few people who are trying to exploit the asylum system has diverted public attention away from the extreme plight of desperate people who are in sore need of help from their fellow human beings. Some newspaper stories imply that the UK receives more than our 'fair share' of refugees, yet seven other European countries grant asylum to more refugees per head of their existing population.

Congolese refugees cross into Uganda, fleeing from fighting

WHAT IT LOOKS LIKE IN PRACTICE

Cassie works in a project which supports families of asylum seekers and refugees. Some of the children have witnessed horrific violence and experienced great terror. Others have been caught up in bewildering and chaotic situations, resulting in their usual lives at home and in school being disrupted, and separation from members of their family.

Several of the children need considerable help in rebuilding their emotional well-being. They suffer from symptoms of trauma and their art work is full of their nightmares. Many of the children find it very difficult to trust any adult because of their experiences of violence and ill-treatment. Some of them react in extreme ways to, for example, loud noises or the sight of someone in a uniform. The lack of familiarity in everything, from the food which is unlike what they are accustomed to eating, to the absence of toys and books that they recognise, to the sounds of the language they hear being used around them, adds to their feelings of insecurity. They find it difficult to relax and to concentrate.

Immigrants, especially refugees and asylum seekers, often settle together in an area, in order to get support from one another and to join family and friends who have already settled. This can mean that a locality has a concentration of newly arrived families with intense needs, and this can present challenges for local health, housing and education services. Communities of people with an ethnicity and a culture new to an area can lead to suspicion and even fear from the existing population. This can provoke some unpleasant examples of racism, especially if the immigrants' skin colour or mode of dress mark them out as different.

Your role

For professionals working with children, racism is a serious issue to confront. It has huge implications for the coherence and harmony of our society, and it cannot be tolerated. As with sexism, racism can mean that the children you work with have unequal opportunities to progress and achieve, and you should be alert to when this is happening. You need to be well informed about all the ethnic groups in your area, whether or not the families in these groups use your setting. In particular, you need knowledge of the minority ethnic groups in your community.

WHAT IT LOOKS LIKE IN PRACTICE

Sarah decided to find out more about members of minority ethnic groups who lived in the area of the children's centre where she worked. When she mentioned this to her colleagues, some of them suggested that 'there aren't any' because they were in a small market town in a rural area and, walking round the streets, the area appeared to be 'white'.

But Sarah had already realised that, like nearly every town in Britain, they had a Chinese and an Indian take-away, and the families who ran these lived in the town. When one of the children was slightly injured in an accident in the centre, she took him to the local hospital and realised for the first time just how high a percentage of the staff were from minority ethnic groups. She read a report in the local paper about exploitation of workers from Eastern Europe in the local agricultural industry, and was amazed at the numbers quoted.

Sarah was able to share with her colleagues the fact that they worked in an area which was more multi-ethnic than they had recognised.

There was only one minority ethnic family who used the centre, children of a young Thai woman and her English husband. However, one of the members of staff was of South Asian descent and had come as a small child to live in the area with her family as refugees, when they were forced to leave East Africa.

Over your professional career, it is extremely unlikely that you will not work with children from minority ethnic groups. Your responsibility towards such children is to identify any stereotypes, discrimination and prejudice they encounter, and to implement strategies to prevent the effect this might have on denying them opportunities to learn and develop. We will look at this in Chapters 4 and 6.

Culture

Ethnicity and **culture** are closely linked, but 'race' and culture are not at all the same thing.

WHAT DOES THIS MEAN?

Culture *is about the attitudes and values underpinning patterns of tradition and custom which determine everyday aspects of life, such as:*

◆ *how we see the role of men and women in society*

◆ *the way we bring up our children*

◆ *the language we speak*

◆ *what, when and how we eat*

◆ *how we dress*

◆ *how we wash and care for ourselves*

◆ *the way we decorate and furnish our homes*

◆ *the religious practices we pursue regularly.*

Culture also includes things like:

◆ *drama, music, dance, literature and art*

◆ *how we celebrate special occasions such as weddings and festivals*

◆ *our attitudes to death and dying.*

Cultures are not static; they change over time as new generations reject or re-formulate some aspect of traditional ways of living.

Many of these patterns of everyday life have their origins in religious beliefs, or at least in the traditions which have grown up around a religion and its practices. For example, religious faith and traditions influence:

◆ the diet of many cultures – this may be avoiding certain meat such as pork, or being vegetarian

◆ the preparation of food – Kosher for practising Jews or Halal for practising Muslims

◆ dress – the Sikh turban, the Jewish yarmulke (or skullcap), and the Muslim hijab (head wear) and niqab (veil)

◆ decoration of the environment and creation of visual objects – Islam bars representation of living beings

◆ the role of women – Judaism, Islam and Christianity have all traditionally given women an inferior role in public life

◆ funeral arrangements and mourning.

Turban

Hijab

Yarmulke

Niqab

REFLECTING

Think about one or two cultures of which you have some knowledge. Use the list on the opposite page to identify the different ways each culture influences everyday life. What variations in following traditions and customs have you observed within each culture?

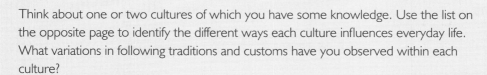

In the UK 2001 census, responses to the question about religion indicated that there were approximately:

- ◆ 41 million Christians (almost 72% of the population)
- ◆ 1.5 million Muslims (nearly 3%)
- ◆ 0.5 million Hindus (1%)
- ◆ 330,000 Sikhs (0.6%)
- ◆ 260,000 Jews (0.5%)
- ◆ 150,000 Buddhists (0.3%)
- ◆ 13 million with no religion or not indicating a religion (almost 23%).

One of the reasons people sometimes struggle with getting to grips with the concept of culture is that they find it difficult to identify and define their own culture. Because culture is about how we lead our everyday lives, it is concerned with matters which are deeply embedded in our psyches. We are so accustomed to our traditions and way of life that it is difficult to unpick them and see them as our 'culture' – they consist of things we take entirely for granted. This internalisation of our own culture can also lead us into false assumptions about our culture being the only 'proper' way of doing things, and other people's cultures being unsuitable or just plain wrong.

The relationship between ethnic origins and culture is complicated. It may be that a particular culture, especially when closely tied to a religion, is more often found in people of a particular ethnic background, but a culture is not 100 per cent exclusive to any particular ethnic group. There are white, European-origin Muslims as well as Muslims from Eastern and African ethnic origins. Equally, members of a given ethnic group may adhere to a range of cultures – again, religion often being instrumental. The small province of Northern Ireland is split culturally by membership of two denominations of the Christian religion. People of black African ethnic origins who live in the UK often follow very similar cultural traditions to their neighbours and work colleagues of European ethnic origin, especially if they have been born and educated here.

When cultures exist amicably alongside one another, they can bring new experiences and ideas to local communities. Sadly, cultural differences play almost as big a part as ethnicity in the development of prejudice and discrimination. In particular, **anti-Semitism** has been endemic in British society for centuries, and in recent years a distrust of Muslims has lead to **Islamaphobia**.

WHAT DOES THIS MEAN?

◆ **Anti-semitism** is prejudice and discrimination against Jewish people.
◆ **Islamophobia** is fear of Muslim people and the religion of Islam, which leads to prejudice and discrimination.

Travellers

One group of people for whom it is especially difficult to disentangle ethnicity and culture is travellers. There have been traveller communities throughout Europe for many centuries. Although true gypsies or Romanies can claim shared ethnic origins, there are other groups of different origins, such as 'new-age' travellers, who have assumed some of the Romany lifestyle. Early in the 21st century, the Commission for Racial Equality (CRE) estimated that there were about 300,000 travellers in the UK.

Travellers are by definition nomadic – they move from one place to another, stopping in one place for a few days or weeks or a season, before moving on to somewhere else. There are often regular patterns in their movements and they return to the same area frequently. Some groups of travellers move from one type of agricultural work to another, stopping for a while depending on the seasons of crops. Travellers who work in fairs or circuses have similar regular patterns of travel over a wide area.

What all travellers have in common is that, in almost all societies, they experience considerable prejudice and discrimination, hostility and exclusion from the settled population. There are widespread negative attitudes regarding the honesty, cleanliness, responsibility and reliability of travellers, much of it based on stereotypes and expressed in prejudiced terms. The settled community lacks knowledge and understanding of Romany culture and values. In Britain, there are long-running disputes between traveller communities and local authorities about the provision and use of designated sites with adequate facilities.

One possible piece of evidence of discrimination resulting in harm to travellers is the poor healthcare that they receive.

◆ The mortality rate amongst traveller children aged under 10 years is ten times as high as for the population as a whole.

◆ Only one per cent of the traveller population is aged over 65 years.

WHAT IT LOOKS LIKE IN PRACTICE

Naomi describes the work of her school with some of the traveller children who come and go.

'It can be frustrating that as soon as we get to know a child and begin a relationship, they move on. But we try very hard not to let this get in the way of our efforts to do our best for each child while we have contact with them.

We focus on the positive aspects of traveller children's learning, which grows out of their family's lifestyle. The children benefit emotionally from the close extended families of the traveller community, having many adults they relate to closely. We find that a lot of them have rich first-hand knowledge of the real world. They know much more about animals and plants and the weather than the other children. They have an understanding of travelling distances, and it's amazing what practical skills they develop, even at an early age. One boy explained to us about how the generator makes electricity and how often the petrol has to be topped up. We have all picked up some of the dialect words, like 'kushti' (good) and 'gorgios' (settled people).

From time to time, we have to introduce a traveller child to the mysteries of the flushing loo. Even stairs are unfamiliar to some of the little ones, and we need to be aware that being in the indoor space of the school for long periods each day is also a strange experience. It is important that we don't expect traveller children to spend too much time cooped up indoors, and this made us more aware of the needs of all the children for additional time to pursue learning activities out of doors.

Traveller families often have difficulty in getting access to health and educational services. We have met so many parents who had a disrupted education themselves and often they have limited literacy skills, so we're careful about not sending home a lot of written communications. However, we have found that some traveller parents are keen for their children to have opportunities to learn that they didn't have in their own childhood, and they do their best to support their children's 'book learning'.

We do have to tackle issues of discrimination and prejudice from the other children and, indeed, their parents. It is important to give the traveller children support to deal with the hostility they come up against.'

Language

Language is a key element of culture and a major issue for immigrant families. When someone emigrates from one country to another, most continue to speak the language they learned as children, even if they begin to learn the language of their new country. Immigrants to the UK will need to learn English if they are to seek worthwhile employment here and be able to make progress in their new home. They may become fluent enough in spoken English to get by in everyday life, but may never acquire enough for more complex communication such as debate or expression of emotions, or learn the idioms of the English language. They may not learn to write in English – in fact, some immigrants from poorer parts of the world such as Bangladesh, especially women, have never learned to write in their first language. Of course, this limits their employment opportunities in a society which communicates mainly in English.

Understandably, immigrants are likely to go on speaking their original language at home. Even if they become fluent in spoken and written English, they want to hold on to the language of their cultural background because it helps them to maintain links with their origins.

FOOD FOR FURTHER THOUGHT

Imagine you went to live permanently in another country where the main language spoken was different from the one you have grown up speaking. What language would you speak in your home and family? What language would you teach your children to speak first? What rhymes and songs would you sing and say to them? What fairy stories, myths and fables would you tell them?

Besides spoken language, there are cultural differences in body language. For example, in some cultures, looking someone directly in the eye when talking to them is seen as a sign of honesty and of listening with respect to the speaker. In other cultures, it has a directly opposite meaning: eye contact is seen as challenging and impolite. Thus, some African Caribbean children who politely keep their eyes cast down have sometimes been punished for lack of respect. Their demeanour has been interpreted as shifty and concealing the truth, but they were in fact avoiding the rudeness of looking an adult in the eye. Another gesture which is sometimes ambiguous is the sideways movement of the head, which is used by some people whose ethnic origins lie in the Indian sub-continent. This can denote 'yes, maybe' or 'no, probably', or something in between, and its subtlety is difficult for people from other cultures to understand.

Bilingualism

If you work in an area where immigrants or refugees come to settle, you may work with children who are still acquiring English as an additional language. It is often the children of a family who do this with greater ease than the adult family members do, being at the stage in their life when learning is easier and more rapid. These children then have the great advantage in life of becoming **bilingual** (or even multilingual), being able to speak English as well as their **home language**.

WHAT DOES THIS MEAN?

*Being **bilingual** means speaking and/or writing two languages. A child's **home language** is the first language they learn to speak, usually the language that is spoken by their first carers in the family's home.*

It is thought that 70 per cent of people in the world use more than one language in their everyday lives. The extent of bilingualism in the UK is often underestimated, but in fact many children in the UK are bilingual. You are therefore likely to work with bilingual children whose home language may be different from the language you usually speak. In some local authority areas, 20 to 30 (or even more) languages are in common use, reflecting diverse ethnic origins amongst the local community.

Bilingualism is an asset. Speaking more than one language can help children to become creative in the way they think, because of the way language and thought are intertwined. This can make it much easier to learn a third or even fourth language. A child who speaks Urdu at home, English at school and Arabic in the mosque is likely to have a rich appreciation of the potential to communicate in many different ways. Bilingual and multilingual children have a deep appreciation of symbols as the system on which language is built, and they become flexible thinkers.

PUTTING PRINCIPLES INTO PRACTICE

If you work with children who are acquiring English as an additional language, you should adopt the following practices:

◆ *Show respect for their home language – never give the impression that you consider one language better than another or to take precedence. It is vital that all children feel their home language is welcomed and valued in your setting.*

◆ *Never seek to suppress a child's first language, because they need the skills of speaking that language as the basis for acquiring a second (or third) language.*

◆ *Support children in retaining their home language so they continue to be able to communicate well in their family and community, especially if they are cared for by family members who themselves speak little English.*

◆ *Appreciate the significance of their home language in enabling them to sustain their sense of belonging to their cultural group, especially their religion.*

◆ *Be aware that, because they learn English first and fastest, other members of the family may become dependent on the children to translate and interpret for them, and this could put an unfair burden on children, involving them inappropriately in the lives of the adult members of their families. They may be, for example, expected to accompany parents to health and legal appointments. If this is happening, look for ways of supporting children to deal with such situations, and help the families find more appropriate interpretation services.*

If you speak more than one language, you will have a significant contribution to make to children's emergent bilingualism, but even if you are monolingual, you can do much to support this development. We will look at ways of supporting bilingual children in Chapter 4.

Negative attitudes to speaking a language other than English have been extensive in the past in Britain, and children in Wales, Scotland and Ireland used to be physically punished for speaking Welsh, Gallic or Gaelic in school. There are still some people whose attitude is that children should be discouraged from speaking their home language, arising from the mistaken belief that maintaining their home language will limit their ability to learn English. In fact, the brain has the capacity to expand linguistic skills and is not 'filled up' with learning one language.

You may encounter parents of monolingual children (who speak only English) who become suspicious upon hearing other languages spoken and encouraged in the setting. They may fear that the education of their own children will in some way be adversely affected by being exposed to 'foreign' languages. These same parents may go to some lengths to open up opportunities for their children to learn French or Italian, but object to their learning Gujarati songs or Turkish greetings. This reveals the potential racism implicit in the British tendency to see languages in a hierarchy of value. English is often put high on the scale of being desirable and important, followed by other European languages like Spanish and

German. Arabic and Chinese come way down this hierarchy, Asian languages like Urdu and Hindi are respected and valued much less, and African languages like Yoruba and Swahili positioned even lower on the scale. There may be occasions when practitioners need to challenge the racism of this attitude to language, and we will look at this in Chapter 6.

Your role

As with discrimination and prejudice related to 'race', your role is to ensure that children are able to have equality of opportunity in your setting, free from stereotypical assumptions about culture. We will look at this in Chapter 4. You should also become familiar with aspects of children's culture and demonstrate at all times that you respect the culture of their family. We will look at this in Chapter 3.

Social background

Overlying and interacting with a person's ethnic origins and cultural background is their social background – social class, economic stratum and family structure.

Social class

It is difficult to define social class even though it marks people off from one another in powerful ways. The advertising industry does so in terms of type of occupation or income level, when deciding how to pitch their message to particular social groups. But occupation and income are only part of what defines people as belonging to one class or another. Also playing a part are issues like:

- educational background (for example, being a university graduate)
- accent (for example, the upper class or 'cut-glass' accent)
- vocabulary (this is perhaps less important than a few decades ago, when saying 'serviette' or 'toilet' was regarded as more lower class than saying 'napkin' or 'lavatory')
- names given to children (which social class do you think the parents of a boy called Piers or St. John are likely to belong to?).

Income influences a person's ability to lead a particular lifestyle, but other influences of tradition are at work in determining the detail of day-to-day living, such as:

- meal times (dinner in the middle of the day or the evening) and the sort of food eaten (guacamole or mushy peas)
- following certain fashions in furnishing and decorating the home
- interaction with neighbours and friends (dinner parties or a pint in the pub)
- involvement in cultural and sporting activities (opera, theatre and cricket or tennis, or soaps on television, bingo and football)
- how money is spent (a holiday in a Tuscan villa or in a caravan in North Wales, certain kinds of car, private education).

Some of these factors reflect those of culture, and it could be argued that each social class has a culture of its own.

Many people in the UK have stereotyped attitudes and prejudices about those who lead their lives in a way that is different from their own because they belong to a different social class. And the whole point about social class is that it is hierarchical – each class is regarded as superior or inferior to others. People in higher classes may have a dismissive or condemning attitude to those in lower classes, and people in lower classes may feel resentment towards those in higher classes.

We may be tempted to dismiss much of this as 'snobbery' or even 'inverted snobbery', but we cannot ignore the fact that British society remains profoundly divided by social class.

WHAT IT LOOKS LIKE IN PRACTICE

Josie describes what happened when the private nursery she was working in negotiated funding arrangements with the local authority to become a SureStart children's centre.

'Several of the parents were very upset about the idea. We had comments like: "If you do that, all the kids from the estate by the by-pass will come here – and they're such a rough lot over there. There's druggies and jail birds and all sorts." "Those parents aren't the type I'd want to mix with." "There are so many single mums with their kids in that area. They'll all want to come and it will drag our children down to their level." "I moved to get away from the influence of those sort of families. I don't want my children getting into bad company." Some of them did take their children away and moved them to the new nursery down by the park. It made me so angry because of course only a minority of the families on the estate are involved in drugs and crime, and of course the parents of the children from the estate want the best for their kids and are doing their best. But they need a lot of help and support – which we can give here in the centre. There was one colleague on the staff team who seemed to think the estate children would have poor speech, be poorly behaved, not be used to books and not be able to play. It took her a while to see that they were all individuals with lots of potential.'

Some of the differences between social classes became less pronounced in Britain in the last decades of the 20th century, but they still exist. They affect children's life-chances when they lead to assumptions about children and families, which may limit expectations about the children's potential for learning and achievement.

Many people find it difficult to think and talk about social class without becoming subjective and even emotional. A person's class background influences the choices they make about how to conduct many of the details of their personal and family life. This is further complicated by some members of a class developing aspirations to move into another class. The social class you grew up in may be different from the social class you operate in as an adult.

Some people's educational opportunities and life experiences lead them to adopt a different way of life from that of their parents – they may become upwardly mobile, moving into a different class from the one they grew up in as a child. They may reject and even despise their old way of life or, at best, never feel totally at ease in either class situation. Some people, like me, have had sensitive and sometimes painful experiences of relationships with the family of origin becoming strained and uncomfortable when education has moved children away from the way of life of the family. Misunderstandings and resentments can arise when a young person begins to adopt ways of living which are at odds with that of his or her parents and extended family.

REFLECTING

What social class would you describe yourself as belonging to? Would you say you grew up in a different class than the one you are in now? Do you aspire to a class other than the one you belonged to as a child? Do you consider that you now belong to the same social class as the children you work with?

Do you think that the children and families you work with all belong to the same social class as one another? What aspects of their lives have led you to this conclusion – occupation, income level and educational attainments of the parents, where the families live, accent or some other factors?

Children growing up in families in different social strata have different prospects of standards of living when they become adults. This is especially linked to the benefits they are likely to derive from their education. Parents' attitudes to the significance and value of education play a great part in how well a child learns and achieves. We can think of the stereotype of the middle-class urban parent going to great lengths of moving house or attending church or paying fees to get their child into a 'good school', but much of the influence is more subtle. Class influence on children's educational achievements is attributed to many factors, such as:

◆ parents who devote time to reading and talking to their children, and taking them to see interesting places and things, explaining what they see

◆ books and other resources such as IT available in the home

◆ parents who feel at ease communicating with teachers.

In promoting equality for all children, you need to be aware of the influences of social class and to guard against assumptions about a child's potential based on his or her background. It is important that you do not condemn the way of life of families from a specific class, or assume that the parents are not interested in getting the best for their child. Never make assumptions about a family based on the area where they live.

Economic strata

Even though social class is about more than income levels, income does play a major role in determining social position. Even more importantly, the income level of parents is especially significant in determining children's prospects of good health and life-chances. It determines the area (inner-city/suburban/rural) and the quality of the housing the family can afford to live in, as well as the quality of food and access to leisure facilities, outings and holidays.

WHAT IT LOOKS LIKE IN PRACTICE

Compare the social and economic situation of these three children, all aged 10 years, and all with older siblings.

Georgia's mother is a consultant at a major teaching hospital and her father has a high-earning job in the City. Besides their spacious house in London, the family have a house in the country which they use at weekends and where Georgia keeps the pony she received for her last birthday. Both parents have large cars. The family take two or more foreign holidays a year, including long-haul flights. Georgia is learning to play the violin and goes to ballet lessons. She attends a private prep school where she gets good grades, and from which she will move on to the same well-known independent boarding school which her brother already attends. Her parents see the future for Georgia and her brother as involving one of the older universities and a choice of well-paid professional careers.

Jack's father is a manager of a local supermarket and his mother works in an administrative role for the probation service. They live in a modern three-bedroom semi-detached house in a pleasant village. The family spend some holidays visiting Jack's grandparents who live by the sea, but last year made their first trip to France. Jack's mother has a small, rather ancient car and his father drives the larger family car. Jack plays for the local under-twelves football team, and he and his friends practise on the village recreation ground. He attends the village primary school and has made good progress. Next term he will move on to the comprehensive in the nearby town, and he has been promised a bike for his next birthday so he can cycle to school with his older brother. His parents hope both boys will stay on at school for A-levels or go to college to get vocational qualifications.

Jordan's mother works part-time in the local corner shop and his father is a bus driver. The family lives in a fifth-floor two-bedroom flat on a 1980s housing estate. They have never been abroad but last summer spent a week in a B&B in Margate. They don't own a car. Jordan's last birthday present was some special trainers he had been wanting for some while. He spends a lot of time watching videos or playing computer games in the flat, as there is no play area near by. He attends the primary school on the estate where he lives. He gets good marks from time to time, when he makes an effort, but mostly he finds school quite boring. He will soon move to the same comprehensive as his older sister, a bus ride away. His parents assume that both children will leave school as soon as they can (as they did themselves) and get a job so they can earn their own keep.

All of these children have parents who care about them and want a good future for them, but each lives in different circumstances and has different expectations and prospects in life.

Growing up in different social and economic circumstances

A family is defined as living in poverty if its income is 60 per cent or less of the average household income. The numbers of children living in poverty rose rapidly during the 1980s. Although it has proved very difficult to reverse this, child poverty has fallen in the 21st century. The website www.poverty.org.uk gives the total number of children living in poverty in 2005/6 as 3.8 million, which represents a fall of over half a million since 1998/9.

Children are more likely to live in poverty if they live in workless households (a family where none of the adults is in employment), and half of children living in poverty are in such households. Poverty particularly affects single-parent families (half of whom are below the poverty line), children with teenage parents, and children with a disabled parent or a parent with mental health or addiction problems, all of whom may face difficulties in obtaining and sustaining employment. Child poverty is also more likely for families with a disabled child because of the extra costs involved in having a disabled child. Two-fifths of people in minority ethnic groups live in poverty, twice as many as in the white population.

There is a wide gap between the richest and the poorest families in the UK and these inequalities of life-chance affect many children. Infant mortality rates are more than twice as high in the lowest income group as in the highest, child accident rates are many times higher, and the chances of poor health later in life are greater. Statistically, children from lower income families are more likely than children from higher income groups to:

◆ have poorer health

◆ have lower achievement at school (and so have poorer employment prospects)

◆ get involved in crime.

This doesn't mean that all children from low income families are unhealthy, do badly at school and get into trouble with the law, but that poverty has a negative effect on children's well-being and life chances. Those who succeed do so against the pressures on them, just as some children from high income families do less well despite their advantages.

Economic inequality has a negative impact on children's ability to thrive and learn. A study by the London School of Economics and the University of Surrey published in December 2007 by the Sutton Trust (www.suttontrust.com) confirmed the effect of family income levels on children's progress and achievements in education. They found that children from homes in the lowest income stratum who show themselves to be able and achieving well before the age of 3 years are overtaken in test scores by children of lower ability but higher income background by the age of 7 years. Children from wealthy homes do better at school than children who are initially brighter than them but who come from poorer families.

REFLECTING

Find out about the level of benefits for families – how much would an unemployed single mother of two school-age children normally get to live on each week?

How much do you think she will be able to spend on food after paying rent, bills for gas, electricity and water, children's clothes and other essentials?

Take a look at the prices and quality of food in local shops compared with supermarkets which require shoppers to travel. What 'healthy choices' do you think this mother would be able to afford for her children?

Family structure

Another aspect of social background is family grouping.

REFLECTING

What images come to mind when you hear the word 'family'? Does your mental picture of a family include:

- children and parents
- two parents or a single parent
- half-siblings and step-parents
- people of another generation besides the children and parents – grandparents, aunts and uncles
- parents of the same gender
- parents of different ethnic groups
- an age range from youngest to oldest child of less than five years, or more than ten years
- parents under 20 years or over 50 years?

Even though the image persists of the 'normal' family with two parents of different gender and the same ethnicity, married to one another with two children (maybe of different genders), there are great variations within families in modern Britain.

- Step-families are much more numerous than they used to be.
- There are more families in which the parents belong to different ethnic groups.

- Large or extended families are more common in some cultures which place emphasis on interdependence and mutual support. You may work with children who live very closely with their grandparents, aunts, uncles and cousins, and see these wider family members as equally significant in their lives as their parents and siblings because they share the care of the children amongst them.

- Many children have parents who are not married to one another, even though they live together in committed and strong relationships.

About one in four families with dependent children in the UK are single-parent families. It is still common for single parents to be stereotyped and their children labelled as automatically deprived by their parents' single status. This sort of prejudice may be increased by some people's negative attitudes to divorced parents, step-parents and unmarried parents.

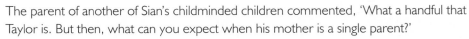

WHAT IT LOOKS LIKE IN PRACTICE

The parent of another of Sian's childminded children commented, 'What a handful that Taylor is. But then, what can you expect when his mother is a single parent?'

Sian pointed out that while Taylor is a lively boy, his behaviour is not a great concern. She thinks his mother is bringing him up with good values and lots of love, and he sees his Dad regularly.

It is true that *on average* children from single-parent families experience lower income levels (over 45 per cent of single-parent families are below the poverty line) and are over-represented in the statistics for young offenders. However, it would be a misinterpretation of these facts to make generalisations about the difficulties lone parents face, since they don't apply to all single-parent families.

Families headed by same-sex parents are still quite rare, but likely to increase. Homosexual couples can now legally become foster carers or adoptive parents; some gay or lesbian people bring children from a previous relationship to their new partnership; some lesbians choose to conceive a baby by 'artificial' means and rear the child as a couple. Concern has been expressed about the well-being of children of such families, but a growing number of studies, mainly from the United States, indicate that children thrive just as well in the care of homosexual parents as they do with heterosexual parents.

Sometimes, there is resistance to the idea of referring to same-sex parents and their children as a family at all. Some people see such a group of people as a 'pretend family' which in some way undermines 'true' family values. This is insulting to the same-sex parents who provide their children with a loving and secure home, and can be damaging for their children's perception of themselves and their parents.

Homosexual parents often encounter considerable prejudice. They may experience harassment and abuse, and their children may be bullied. If your setting cares for children who have a homosexual parent, you should show them that you respect and value their parents as much as you do the parents of other children.

Families come in many forms

In your professional role, you must be alert to any prejudice and hostility towards families whose structure is different from the so-called 'norm', and avoid stereotypical views limiting expectations about children's abilities and potential. Children who live in these families may see few reflections of their family in public images in the media of television and books, and that could lead them to deduce that their family is in some way not normal or acceptable. You must be careful that this impression is not reinforced in your setting.

Disability

To be able to ensure the inclusion of all children in your setting, and promote equality of opportunity for them, it is necessary to understand the concepts of impairment and disability, and the medical and social models of disability.

Impairment and disability

Many people have **impairments**.

> **WHAT DOES THIS MEAN?**
>
> **Impairment** describes a condition which is different from what is usually expected from a child at a particular age or stage of development or an adult. (Talking about what is 'usually' expected is more helpful than saying 'normally'. It avoids the connotation of someone who develops differently from what is considered usual being labelled as 'abnormal'.)

An impairment may be:

- an impairment of the senses
- a physical impairment
- associated with a medical condition or disease
- a learning difficulty
- a difficulty with emotional or social development.

An impairment may give rise to **disability**.

> **WHAT DOES THIS MEAN?**
>
> The Disability Discrimination Act 1995 (DDA) defines **disability** as, 'A physical or mental impairment which has a substantial and long-term adverse effect on a person's ability to perform normal day-to-day activities.'

You will certainly work at some time with disabled children. 'Disabled children' include those with a wide range of impairments or conditions including 'hidden' ones. For example, a child's sensory impairment may consist of hearing loss (deafness) or restricted vision (blindness).

A physical impairment and/or learning difficulties may be the result of:

- a genetic inheritance such as:
  - cerebral palsy
  - muscular dystrophy
  - sickle cell and thalassaemia
  - haemophilia
  - cystic fibrosis
  - brittle bones
- events before or during birth, such as a mother's excessive drinking resulting in foetal alcohol syndrome, or shortage of oxygen during birth
- an accident (including a 'medical accident' such as the prescription in the 1960s of the drug thalidomide to pregnant mothers)
- a disease such as polio, meningitis, measles or rheumatic fever.

Medical conditions include:

- asthma
- epilepsy
- diabetes
- coeliac disease.

Some children's disability relates to learning difficulties, which may or may not have a specific title like Down's syndrome. For others, their difficulties are with emotional or social development, communication and interaction, and behaviour, including conditions like autism. No list of disabilities could include every impairment or condition, so you are likely to encounter children with impairments not referred to here. Furthermore, each child will be affected differently by their impairment or condition.

Some children have more than one medical condition. Sometimes, conditions are linked, for example diabetes can cause visual impairment. Sometimes, they are not directly connected, for example a child may have the unconnected conditions of asthma and autism. Some children have multiple impairments and are often described as having 'complex needs'. The development of medical techniques which keep very premature babies alive has led to the survival of more children with such complex requirements for their care.

An impairment usually brings some restrictions and limitations to a person's life, but there are ways of avoiding or reducing the consequent disability. It may be possible to remove or reduce disability for many people with impairments if the environment where they spend their time is adjusted and appropriate resources and facilities are made available to them.

- A person with a sight impairment may wear spectacles and/or use a strong light, or read Braille, be supported by a guide dog and be helped by announcements on public transport and audible signals at traffic lights.

◆ A person with a hearing impairment may use a hearing aid or a loop, communicate in sign language or be supported by a hearing dog.

◆ A person who uses a wheelchair can get into and move around in buildings and use public transport when ramps and lifts are provided, when sufficient space is available (e.g. wide aisles in shops), and when counters and lift buttons are at a height that can be reached from a wheelchair.

◆ A person who cannot use their hands may use a voice-activated computer to write or communicate by pointing to symbols on a board with a head stick.

Adjustments to the environment and provision of resources like these support people with impairments in leading a more independent life and reduce the impact of their impairment.

But impairment is not only turned into disability by the physical environment or lack of resources; people's attitudes are also significant. It is often the assumptions that are made about what a person with an impairment can and cannot do that result in restriction or limitation and which makes the person seem 'disabled'.

Social and medical models of disability

To ensure that practitioners promote equality of opportunity for disabled children and that such children are included in the setting, it is vital to appreciate the **medical model of disability** and the **social model of disability** as ways of understanding the effect of disability on individuals.

WHAT DOES THIS MEAN?

The **medical model of disability** treats the person as a sick patient and tends to focus on 'How can we make this person more normal?' The problem is seen as the disabled person and their impairment, and the solution is seen as adapting the disabled person to fit the non-disabled world, often through medical intervention.

The **social model of disability** recognises that discrimination against disabled people is created by society, not by disabled people's impairments. It focuses on addressing the issue 'What do we need to do to enable this person to achieve their potential and have a fulfilling life?'

The medical model is a traditional view of disability as something to be 'cured', even though many conditions have no cure. When medical labels are placed on the disabled person in order to define their needs (for example, referring to people with epilepsy as 'epileptics'), the individual is seen only as an impairment and not a person. This can prevent us developing a picture of the whole person, including their gender, ethnicity and culture, and social background. It can lead to too much focus on what is 'wrong' with a child and what they cannot do, rather than paying attention to what a child can do and is achieving and looking at their potential to develop, learn and progress.

The social model of disability is a more constructive approach to disability. It helps us to see that impairments are a fact of life – many people have impairments. However, the restricting effects of impairment can be reduced by appropriate:

◆ environment

◆ resources and facilities

◆ attitudes and assumptions.

These enable disabled people to have opportunities to make choices, develop their potential, become independent and play a full part in society.

The social model of disability puts the emphasis on the way in which society needs to change; the medical model expects disabled people to change to fit into society. The strength of the social model is that it identifies problems which can be resolved if the right resources are made available, whereas the medical model dwells on problems which are often insoluble. The social model asserts the rights of disabled people; it involves listening to individual disabled people to see what that person wants and, when there are barriers to their requirements, looking at ways of removing those barriers. The social model has been constructed and promoted by disabled people themselves, so it should be respected.

It is the social model of disability which provides practitioners with a guide in their work with children. You can help to remove or reduce the disability resulting from impairments by:

◆ finding ways to adjust the physical environment in the setting

◆ providing or adapting resources

◆ organising routines and the way you work in a different way.

Perhaps most important of all, practitioners can help by not making assumptions about what a child can do, or may be able to achieve. You will look at this more in Chapter 4.

'Special needs'

The term 'special needs' is often used to refer to disabled children. This is unhelpful because it implies that disabled children have different needs from other children. However, their needs are not 'special' – they have the same needs as other children. All children need:

◆ a safe and secure environment

◆ nourishing food

◆ love and attention

◆ acceptance and praise

◆ opportunities to learn and achieve

◆ to be in the company of other children

◆ to be able to move about in their environment and community

◆ to be accepted and valued by other people

◆ to have choices and learn to make decisions.

Disabled children's needs are the same as other children's needs – although they may have different requirements about how those needs are met. In Chapter 4 we will look at how you may have to meet their needs in different ways, adjusting the environment, resources, routines and your practice.

When you work with disabled children it is important, of course, to take their impairments into account. But impairments should not be taken as the defining characteristics of that child, or the centre of the focus of your work with the child. Your practice should be firmly based in your usual practice for working with all children, even if you sometimes need to adjust or extend it. Your aim should be to see the child as a child like all others.

If you use your observation and assessment skills, you will be able to find out about the needs and requirements of that particular child in the way you would for all other children. Talking about 'special needs children' could divert you from this approach, tempting you to think that you cannot use your existing knowledge and skills of working with all children – that you need some entirely alternative approach when you work with disabled children.

Instead of seeing disabled children as having needs so special that we make separate provision for them, the emphasis of policy has become integration – aiming to adjust mainstream settings as far as possible so their requirements can be met and barriers to **inclusion** are removed.

WHAT DOES THIS MEAN?

Inclusion *is a process of identifying, understanding and breaking down barriers to participation and belonging (definition developed by the Early Childhood Forum).*

Unfortunately, the term **special educational needs** is embodied in legislation so we have to live with it at present.

WHAT DOES THIS MEAN?

The legal definition says that a child has **special educational needs (SEN)** *if they have a learning difficulty that requires special educational provision to be made for them. This might be because:*

◆ *they have a significantly greater difficulty in learning than the majority of children of the same age, for example a child may have language, learning or behaviour difficulties*

◆ *the child is disabled and is prevented or hindered from making use of educational facilities provided for children in their area; in other words, they need additional or different provision to enable them to learn.*

A child must not be seen as having a learning difficulty solely because their home language is different from the one used in educational provision in the area.

In England and Wales, the Special Educational Needs (SEN) Code of Practice (2001) sets out the guidance about the provision that should be made for children with special educational needs. The principles of the Code of Practice include the following:

◆ The special educational needs of children will normally be met in mainstream schools or settings.

◆ Children with special educational needs should be offered full access to a broad, balanced and relevant education, including an appropriate curriculum for the Early Years Foundation Stage in England or the Foundation Phase in Wales, and the National Curriculum.

Every setting must have a **SENCO**.

WHAT DOES THIS MEAN?

A **SENCO** is a Special Educational Needs Co-ordinator who is responsible for:

◆ ensuring liaison with parents and other professionals concerning children with special educational needs

◆ advising and supporting other practitioners

◆ ensuring that appropriate Individual Education Plans are in place

◆ ensuring that relevant background information about individual children with special educational needs is collected, recorded and up-dated

◆ taking the lead in assessing a child's particular strengths and weaknesses

◆ planning future support for the child

◆ monitoring and reviewing any action taken

◆ making sure that appropriate records are kept.

SENCOs liaise with parents

The SEN Code of Practice sets out a step-by-step approach to what should be done if a child may have special educational needs.

◆ About 20 per cent of children at some stage are likely to appear not to be making progress either generally or in a specific aspect of learning. The first step should always be to discuss this with parents.

◆ The setting and the parents can make plans together, and see if the child then begins to overcome the difficulty and to progress.

◆ Often the difficulty will be overcome this way, but if, after a while, this doesn't seem to be happening, the setting's SENCO should put together an Individual Education Plan (IEP) for the child to help them progress. This plan might outline the provision of different learning materials or special equipment, or training to help practitioners introduce new strategies for the child's learning.

◆ For most children, the help given through an IEP will be enough to enable them to progress satisfactorily. For about two per cent of children, however, a statutory assessment which can lead to a **statement** of special educational needs may be necessary.

Since 1981 local authorities have had a duty to provide a **statement** *for a child who is thought to have special educational needs. The authority should:*

◆ *assess the child's special educational needs*

◆ *issue a 'statement' which sets out the child's specific learning needs*

◆ *identify the provision required to meet these needs and what the authority will do.*

This is the process of statementing. Parents have often found the statementing process difficult and long-drawn out. Problems can arise if the statement includes vague references to 'access' to services, as access is likely to depend on what is available within the authority's budget, rather than what the child requires.

Early Support

Perhaps the most positive development in recent years for young disabled children and their families in England has been the Early Support Programme, which aims at early identification of children's impairments and better co-ordinated, 'family focused' services. The programme provides parents with information about living with a disabled child and 'the system'. It explains which professionals they may meet and how health, education and social services can provide support, as well as giving information about sources of financial help and childcare. Its most innovative feature is a family file, which the family holds and which professionals involved with the child and family use to record information. In this way, information can be shared effectively with the family and with other professionals. This is a great boon to parents who do not have the frustration of having to 'tell their story' from the beginning every time they encounter a different professional or service. It also prevents professionals from working in a vacuum – they are aware of the advice and support being provided elsewhere and are able to identify priorities for their contribution as part of a whole strategy for the child, planned jointly with the family. You will find more information about Early Support at www.earlysupport.org.uk.

Stereotypes about disability

In the past, many disabled people were put into care homes. This meant being separated from their families and community, sometimes at birth. This resulted in their segregation from the rest of society and exclusion from the everyday life of other members of their community. Of course, this meant that they met and knew very few non-disabled people, and non-disabled people met and knew very few disabled people. In this way, stereotypes and prejudices about disabled people were reinforced and perpetuated.

Stereotypes about disabled people are widespread in the media, and even in charitable appeals for funds. Local newspapers especially are often full of stories about disabled people who are either presented as 'tragic' victims to be pitied, or as 'courageous', 'heroic' and 'cheerful in the face of adversity'. These stereotypes undermine the concept of disabled people as individuals who deserve respect. Seeing disabled people in this way fails to acknowledge that they may also have negative feelings such as anger about the way their impairment disables them in a society and an environment which does not adapt to their requirements.

Disabled children have a right to express their frustration about the way their impairments limit them

REFLECTING

Over the next few weeks, observe closely how disabled people are represented:

◆ on television and in films

◆ in magazines and newspapers

◆ in books (for children and adults), puzzles and toys (such as play people).

Are disabled people portrayed on television soaps, sitcoms and advertisements in active roles and as part of everyday life? In children's stories, if disabled children appear at all, are they playing an active part central to the story or just on the margins, the edge of a picture?

Probably the main prejudice about disabled adults and children focuses on them as helpless and dependent. The 'does he take sugar?' approach assumes that disabled people are unable to speak for themselves and make their own requirements known. People using wheelchairs are often ignored, and shop assistants speak to the person pushing the wheelchair instead. Even the organisations which work on behalf of disabled people are rarely run by or even truly involve disabled people.

Prejudice based on such stereotypes can lead to the expectation that a disabled person always needs to be taken care of, that they cannot manage to be independent. Some settings have in the past been reluctant to accept disabled children because they thought a disabled child would create extra work and would always need more adult attention. These assumptions were often based on lack of knowledge about disability and insufficient information about the individual child: many disabled children do not need constant attention and do not create extra work. (As you will see in Chapter 5, it is now unlawful to exclude a child from a setting simply because he or she is disabled.)

Your role

Working with disabled children requires you to see past the stereotypes and prejudices, and ensure that they are fully included in your setting. As you will see in Chapter 4, there are various aspects of resources and practice to consider, but your attitudes should be guided by the social model of disability. Avoid the medical model approach of focusing on the child's impairment and seeing the problem as getting the child to fit in to the environment and routine of your setting – or being marginalised when that proves impossible. Instead, think in terms of how the environment can be adjusted, what resources can be used, and how you can adapt routines and your practice to be sure of offering disabled children equality of opportunity. Although you may have to adapt your practice to suit the needs of disabled children, that doesn't mean working in an entirely different way; continue to have confidence in your usual practice in working with children. The key factor is to observe the child and assess their stage of development, just as you would with any other child, so you can plan how to support their development and learning. Your focus should be on the child, not their impairment.

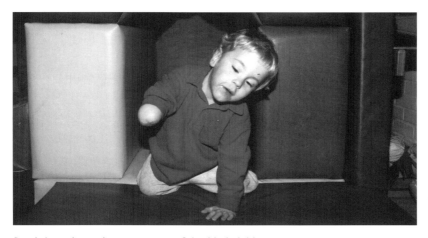

Don't have limited expectations of disabled children

Low expectations of the potential of a disabled child, or being over protective of them, can limit what they achieve. You should always keep a balance between being realistic about the way a child's impairments result in limitations and at the same time having high expectations for their progress and achievements. Because the development of disabled children is often more delayed in one or more area than in others, it is easy to fall into the trap of saying things like, 'He's eight years old, but developmentally he's like a three-year-old.' It may be that the child's cognitive development is at a stage usually associated with a younger child, but his chronological age remains eight years, and he is likely to have other aspects of development in which he is like other eight-year-olds. Most significantly, his interests are likely to be similar to other children of his own age, so it is important not to treat him as though he was only three years old. His self-esteem will be damaged and his development held back by talking to him in a babyish way or keeping him only in the company of younger children.

Sexuality

Attitudes to **homosexuality** have changed enormously in the past 40 years, but it is still surrounded by many stereotypes and prejudices.

WHAT DOES THIS MEAN?

Homosexuality *refers to being attracted by and having sexual feelings towards people of the same sex as oneself. It is most often used to refer to men, but it can be applied to both men and women – the 'homo' part of the word means 'same'. Homosexual men are usually referred to as gay, and homosexual women are usually referred to as lesbian. People who are attracted to people of the opposite sex are referred to as heterosexuals, and those who are attracted to both sexes are referred to as bisexual.*

It is thought that between six and ten per cent of the population is homosexual, but gay men and lesbians are often 'invisible' in the communities they live in, and many people think that they do not know anyone who is homosexual. The stereotypes are of gay men being 'camp' and lesbians being 'butch', but most homosexual people do not conform to these stereotypes. Most often, their sexuality is concealed from the people they work with or their neighbours, or even their families. It is understandable why so many homosexual people prefer to hide their sexuality. The price of being open about your sexuality can be high – gay men and lesbians continue to experience prejudice and discrimination, despite huge changes in recent years.

A mistaken but widespread prejudiced belief is that homosexual people do not form long-term relationships. One reason for this is because gay men and lesbians, especially those who are famous for some reason or another, often prefer to keep their stable, long-lasting and loving relationships out of the public eye. This is not surprising, considering the way the media has so often presented same-sex relationships and the sometimes vicious comments that have been made about the partners of celebrities.

One issue which is sometimes raised is the suggestion that children brought up by parents of the same sex will inevitably become homosexual themselves, because their homosexual parents are offering them the 'wrong' role model of how to behave as an adult. Yet most homosexual people grow up in heterosexual families and do not 'learn' to be heterosexual. It is not possible to 'teach' children sexuality – it is part of their nature.

Some parents, especially fathers, seem to be concerned that boys will grow up to be gay men if their pretend play includes activities like ironing, cooking, dressing up or playing with dolls. There is no evidence for this, and boys and girls benefit from acting out what it is like to be grown up, including the nurturing and domestic roles of both genders.

You may find that some people are very hostile towards homosexuality because of their religious beliefs or cultural traditions. This may even amount to **homophobia**.

WHAT DOES THIS MEAN?

Homophobia *means a fear of homosexual people. This fear leads to some of the more extreme and violent opposition to gay men and lesbians.*

Another mistaken belief is that gay men are more likely than heterosexual men to abuse children and should therefore not be permitted to work in roles which bring them into contact with children.

Appearance and accent

We all make instant assumptions about people based on their appearance and the way they speak, and some of these assumptions lead on to inequality of opportunity. It is widely recognised that personal presentation is what is most effective at job interviews, often carrying more weight than what is said in reply to questions. Assumptions are often made that someone who dresses in a certain way and does their hair in a particular style is going to be efficient at their job. Studies have shown that tall men are more successful financially than short men. Some regional accents seem to be more accepted in other parts of the country than others. Having grown up with the soft and – to some people, comical – tones of a Cornish accent, when I left home I soon learned how to speak differently when it suited me and I wanted to be taken more seriously as an intelligent person. Similarly, some foreign accents, such as French, seem to be regarded as charming, while others, such as those of the Indian sub-continent, are often mocked and referred to as 'jabbering'.

For some people, their appearance becomes the focus of prejudice and discrimination. The Victorians thought you could tell whether someone was criminal by the shape of the bones in their head. We may have moved on from this prejudice, but others have replaced it. Job opportunities for women in particular can still depend on their 'attractiveness'.

For children, their appearance and accent can be the cause of bullying and unhappiness, and they need adult protection and support to deal with this.

REFLECTING

What examples have you encountered of children being bullied or excluded from play or activities with other children because of the way they look or speak? Think about children who are overweight, have red hair or prominent teeth or ears, have scars or birthmarks, are very tall or very short, or speak with an accent from another part of the UK or from outside the UK.

Children affected by HIV/AIDS

A source of discrimination and prejudice towards children and families may arise because they are affected by **HIV** or **AIDS**. A child or a parent may be **HIV positive**.

WHAT DOES THIS MEAN?

HIV *stands for Human Immunodeficiency Virus and* **AIDS** *stands for Acquired Immune Deficiency Syndrome. A person who has the virus in their blood stream is said to be* **HIV positive***. They may develop AIDS, which depresses the body's immune system so the person becomes very susceptible to infections and has little resistance to disease of various kinds.*

Much of the prejudice against those who are HIV positive has arisen because of lack of knowledge and understanding about the virus. Fear of catching HIV is usually caused by misunderstandings about how it is transmitted from one person to another. The only ways HIV can be transmitted are:

◆ through unprotected sexual intercourse – anal or vaginal

◆ sharing infected needles or syringes

- receiving a transfusion of infected blood or blood products
- from mother to baby.

HIV has been found in amounts sufficient to cause infection in:

- blood and blood products
- semen and vaginal secretions
- breast milk.

But HIV has not been found in amounts sufficient to cause infection in:

- saliva and tears
- sweat
- urine and faeces.

It is very unlikely that HIV will be transmitted from one person to another in a setting for children. HIV is a fragile virus. Outside the body, it deteriorates rapidly and is easily destroyed by the digestive enzymes in saliva, the toxins in urine and faeces, and heat, water and detergent. Good hygiene precautions remove any slight risk of becoming infected through contact with the blood of someone who is HIV positive. First aid precautions emphasise using gloves to deal with cuts that are bleeding, and clearing up any spilled blood with disinfectant. These precautions should always be adhered to, less for the fear of transmitting HIV than from the much greater risk of hepatitis.

These precautions must be taken in all circumstances because you may not know the HIV status of the person whose blood you are in contact with. Remember that this applies not only to children in your setting, but also to their parents, to colleagues and to anyone visiting the setting. No one may have information about a particular person's HIV status since no test may ever have been carried out, or perhaps the person (or their family) may be aware that the individual is HIV positive but may not have told the setting. Indeed, there is no reason why the setting should be informed since the risk of transmission is so minimal and virtually non-existent if proper hygiene is adhered to.

When these simple facts are known about HIV, fear of it is diminished. But for those who do not yet know these facts, their fear of the virus can lead them to great prejudice and discrimination against those who are HIV positive. When information about HIV first emerged into the public domain in the 1980s, many myths developed, such as that HIV could be caught from sharing a cup, glass or toothbrush, from kissing, in swimming pools or from toilet seats.

Prejudice has been most intense against homosexual men, who have been blamed for the spread of the virus, even though much of the transmission has been as the result of heterosexual intercourse and drug use. Children and people with haemophilia who have been infected as the result of blood transfusions have been seen as 'innocent victims'. However, they have still experienced some discrimination, as attempts were made to exclude children from various settings.

This seems to have diminished as accurate information about how the virus is transmitted has become more widespread.

Advances in the development of drugs mean that fewer children in Britain are likely to develop AIDS, and those who are HIV positive should be able to lead a normal life, including taking advantage of all that settings for children have to offer them. Although they present a very low risk to other people, they may be more susceptible to childhood diseases such as whooping cough, measles, mumps and rubella. It may be possible for them to be immunised against these diseases, but if there is an outbreak of any of such infections, or chicken pox or diarrhoea, they may need to be withdrawn from a setting for a while.

PUTTING PRINCIPLES INTO PRACTICE

If you become aware that a child (or a member of their family) is HIV positive, you should maintain your usual standards of professional confidentiality. The golden rule of confidentiality is never to pass on information about a child or family without the permission of the parents, unless it is in the interests of the child to do so, when the information should be shared with an appropriate professional.

Different but of equal value

It is important to explore differences in detail, as we have done in this chapter, but we should always return to our shared humanity – that which we have in common with one another as human beings.

Too many divisions and conflicts arise because of differences – or perceived differences – between groups of people and individuals. When groups or individuals see other groups or individuals as so different that they feel unsettled or fearful, they tend to lash out, in words or deeds. This is how violence towards others, civil conflict and wars begin.

You can play a role in helping children to grow up understanding and respecting people who are different from themselves, so their fears and suspicions are allayed. If they can avoid perceptions of themselves as superior to people of the other gender, or another ethnic, cultural or social group, or people with a disability, or those who look or sound different from themselves, they will be able to live in harmony with their fellow human beings, and not want to attack or vilify them. Their futures will be happier and more productive and there will be hope for a more peaceful world.

Chapter 3

Every one an individual

In this chapter, we look at the importance of seeing each child as a unique individual. We consider:

◆ how stereotyping can prevent practitioners from seeing a child as an individual

◆ ways of getting to know individual children well

◆ the likely effect of prejudice and discrimination on children's self-esteem and the damage this can do

◆ feeling good about your own individuality

◆ respecting and valuing others as individuals

◆ how children develop stereotypical and prejudiced views

◆ helping children to learn about differences in a positive way.

'Every child is a unique individual with their own characteristics and temperament' (EYFS)

A *unique individual*

To say that every one of us is a unique individual is so obvious that it has almost become a cliché. But this is perhaps the most important principle to grasp when thinking about issues of inclusion, equality and diversity – it is the basis of anti-discriminatory practice.

We began to see in Chapters 1 and 2 that one of the keys to offering children equality of opportunity is to see each as an individual, and to avoid categorising and stereotyping them.

Each one of us is different from all other individuals. Each of us has a set of physical and psychological characteristics that makes us distinct as a person. Some of those characteristics may be similar to other people's, but your own collection of characteristics is unlike anyone else's. You may look similar in colouring, height and shape to other people in your family or ethnic group, perhaps even your voice sounds similar. But your ways of thinking, your responses to emotions like joy or fear, your sense of humour, your sense of responsibility and standards for behaviour may all be very different. In fact, all those psychological features may be more similar to people who look and sound very different from you.

We all know families where siblings look alike but have different personalities, or have similar personalities but look entirely different. In my husband's family there are two men who are identical twins. They still, in their 50s, look remarkably alike, but their talents and skills are entirely opposite: one is a mathematician and the other an artist.

REFLECTING

Next time you pick up a bag of potatoes, have a good look at each potato individually. You will find that each one is slightly different from all the others. Some have little knobs, some have pits or scars, some are mottled, and they are all different sizes and shapes.

Think about how much more varied people are from one another than potatoes are – yet even each potato in your bag is an individual!

Besides these physical and psychological differences, each of us brings together our own individual combination of ethnicity, cultural and social background, gender, age, sexuality, and perhaps impairment/disability. Taken together, this is what gives each person their unique identity. As the Early Years Foundation Stage (EYFS) says, 'Every child is a unique individual with their own characteristics and temperament'.

REFLECTING

Think of two or three children you work with, or have worked with, who are all the same age. In what ways do they differ? Think of their gender, ethnicity, height, appearance, skills, family members.

Now think of two or three children of the same gender, and reflect on their differences, including their age.

Repeat the exercise once more for a group of children of the same ethnicity.

Consider the huge range of permutations of characteristics which makes each of us a unique individual.

Many characteristics combine to make us an individual

At the heart of good practice in providing inclusive, non-discriminatory provision for children is the ability to recognise each child's uniqueness, and to respond to them as an individual. This means avoiding making assumptions about a child based on your previous experience of children who were similar to this child in some way.

WHAT IT LOOKS LIKE IN PRACTICE

'Never assume that because, in your experience, many or most two-year-olds or nine-year-olds behave in a certain way or like or dislike certain things, the same will be true of the two-year-old or nine-year-old you have just met. You must focus on getting to know that two-year-old or nine-year-old and finding out what makes them unique, different from everyone else.'

Sarah, experienced nanny

'It's easy to pick up information, like lots of children with Down's syndrome are affectionate, or love music, or have heart problems, and then assume that the child with Down's syndrome who has just joined your setting will be affectionate, love music and have heart problems. I find I must avoid this sort of assumption because none of this may apply to that child. You've got to get to know the child as an individual and find out whether any of this is true of that particular child.'

Manjit, pre-school worker

'You can read statistics that show that children who grow up with an absent parent experience higher levels of poverty, have poor educational attainment and are more likely to be in trouble with the law. I have had colleagues who had low expectations about children from single-parent families because they took in information like this. But I have worked with many children from single-parent families who make great strides in their learning and grow up with sound values about ways to behave.'

Andy, teaching assistant

In Chapters 1 and 2 we began exploring **stereotypes** and understanding how, if you fall into the trap of stereotyping children according to their gender, age, ethnic, cultural or social background or impairment, you are likely to hamper your ability to meet their needs and support their development.

WHAT DOES THIS MEAN?

Stereotypes *are generalisations about a person, assumptions (usually inaccurate) that because he or she is part of a particular group, that individual will:*
- *have certain characteristics*
- *have the same needs as all other members of that group*
- *will or should behave in a particular way.*

When adults have stereotypical views about children and families, this often has the negative effect of limiting expectations of what those children can achieve, or how their families can support their development. Even so-called positive stereotypes can have a limiting effect. Suggesting that black people are natural athletes or that Chinese children are naturally good at maths, or that a disabled child is 'brave', may appear to be compliments, but they put a label on the individual and distract from what that person may or may not be able to achieve. Thus, an academic, unsporty black child may be diverted from aiming high in exams; an artistic or musical child from a Chinese family may not have the opportunity to develop their creative skills; a disabled child who is feeling angry about being restricted by their impairment may have their right to these feelings denied. In these examples, the children are entitled to be seen as themselves, not as 'typical' of black, Chinese or disabled children.

To be able to include all children in the setting and offer them opportunities on an equal footing with one another, you have to be able to see past the stereotypes and focus on the individuality of each child.

Getting to know you

Your strategy in really seeing each child as an individual should be to get to know them as well as possible, understanding the ways they differ from children who may appear to be similar to them. This process begins before they join the setting, and it is important that you set aside time for gathering information about the child and their family, either when the parents visit the setting or when you visit the family at home.

PUTTING PRINCIPLES INTO PRACTICE

Think about how you gather information about children joining your setting so you can get to know them as an individual. Consider these points and think how you can improve your own practice for the future.

You may have a form which is completed by the parent together with someone in the setting, listing basic information such as name, address, parents' contact details, immunisation status, health issues and so on. But how do you, as a practitioner, take that information on board and how do you use it? For example:

◆ if a child has a known food allergy such as sensitivity to milk products or wheat, how is every person in the setting made aware of this and of its significance (food allergy can be a matter of life or death for some children)

◆ if a child should not be given into the care of a particular person, what precautions does your setting have to ensure this can't happen?

What other sort of information do you gather from parents and family members, both before and after the child joins the setting?

How do you find out about:

- any aspects of the child's ethnicity or the family's cultural, religious or traditional background that have implications for caring for their child, such as dietary requirements

- what language is spoken at home and any special words, names and other vocabulary specific to the child

- for a disabled child, whether they use communication or other aids (such as a hearing aid or walking frame) or specific eating implements

- for a young child, information about nappies and/or toilet training, whether they still have a nap and any routines which help them to sleep, any special object or toy they find a comfort, and their likes and dislikes, including anything they find alarming or unsettling (for example, dogs or people in spectacles)

- any new factors or special problems in the child's life?

Some information is available to you from your colleagues. If your setting caters for young children, there should be a key worker system so one person is responsible for direct contact with parents and for the day-to-day care of the child. If you work with disabled children or children with special educational needs, the Special Educational Needs Co-ordinator (SENCO) for your setting will hold information about a child's impairments and requirements. In a school, a class teacher or tutor may be aware of significant personal information about a child. How do you gain information from these people which helps you to understand the child as an individual and be sure you are meeting their needs?

How do you gather information directly from the child? Depending on their age and stage of development, they may tell you about themselves and their family, adding to information you have gathered from parents. This can be from:

- what the child tells you verbally (for example, who is important to them in their family, including grandparents and pets)

- your observations of the child.

Listening to parents

It is important that practitioners give high priority to gathering information from parents and family. Parents are central to their children's lives and they know their own child better than you can. Working in partnership with parents is a cornerstone of working with children, especially young children, and partnership involves two-way communication – not just telling parents about their children but listening carefully to what they have to tell you. The information they share with you will enable you to care for their child according to that child's individual characteristics and requirements.

Listen to what parents tell you about their child

WHAT IT LOOKS LIKE IN PRACTICE

Natasha described how when Precious joined the nursery she was just a baby and her mother, Tanisha, spent a little time with Natasha and her colleagues showing them the cream Precious needs to have massaged into her skin. Natasha admits that they hadn't realised how important this was for black children. They have now been learning from Tanisha how to look after Precious's thick curly hair and keep it free from tangles.

It is important that you begin to learn about and understand something of the cultures of the children you work with. However, this is not a question of becoming an expert on a whole range of cultures and learning details about languages used, food and dietary customs and rules, elements of belief systems and festivals. What matters is that you find out about the individual children you work with and their families, and how they live and experience their culture. This will help you to avoid making assumptions about members of a cultural group and ensure that you have accurate information which is relevant to the specific child and their family.

Similarly, by listening to what parents can tell you about their child, you can avoid making assumptions about a child because of the nature of their impairment. Parents of disabled children are often the greatest experts on their child's disability and the specific effects an impairment has on their particular child. This may be different from the way in which children you have previously encountered with a similar condition were affected by it.

WHAT IT LOOKS LIKE IN PRACTICE

Tom, a classroom assistant, admitted that he was very anxious when Phoebe joined the class because she has asthma. But Phoebe's mother explained to Tom exactly what the early warning signs of an attack look like for Phoebe, and went through the details of what he should do if that happened. Tom felt much more relaxed about it, was able to spot when an attack was beginning, and was able to take the right action promptly before the attack became severe.

Observation

Actively observing a child is perhaps the most important way of developing your understanding of them as an individual.

WHAT DOES THIS MEAN?

Active observation *means consciously watching and listening to children, really paying attention to them, and asking yourself questions such as the following:*

◆ *What are they doing and saying?*
◆ *What are they trying to do?*
◆ *What do they almost have the skill to do?*
◆ *What can't they manage yet?*
◆ *What do they need help with?*
◆ *What are they interested in?*

The EYFS sums this up as, 'Observe children to find out about their needs, what they are interested in and what they can do.'

Observation like this will help practitioners gain more information about each individual child, pin-pointing their stage of development and getting insight into what fascinates and intrigues them. You need to know all of this if you are to be able to help each child learn and develop, offering experiences and activities suitable to help them progress. It will help you to avoid making assumptions about their potential capabilities based on stereotypes. Rather, you will develop realistic and accurate expectations for each child's progress and you will not be held back in aspirations for them because of their gender, ethnicity, impairment or family and social background.

Active observation helps practitioners know each child as an individual

This strategy is especially relevant to helping you overcome any anxieties you have about needing special knowledge before you start working with disabled children.

WHAT IT LOOKS LIKE IN PRACTICE

Nina has worked with disabled children for some years.

'When the nursery I was working in first began to admit disabled children, I was very apprehensive. I thought I would need a lot of theoretical knowledge about all sorts of impairments and conditions before the first child arrived. What I have learned is that I need to focus on the child first and foremost, not their impairment. I have to put my energies into getting to know each one well as an individual. The best way I can help them is by being ready to learn about each of them and the effect their impairment has on them. It's different for every child.'

Knowing each child well is the way to see them as the unique individual they are and your starting point in making sure they have equality of opportunity.

Self-esteem

You saw in Chapter 1 that one of the reasons practitioners should oppose prejudice and discrimination is the harmful effect they can have on children's **self-image**, **self-esteem** and **self-confidence**.

> ## WHAT DOES THIS MEAN?
>
> **Self-image** *is the picture we have of ourselves – who we are and what we are like, and how we fit into the world.*
>
> **Self-esteem** *is valuing ourselves, and seeing ourselves as having value in other people's eyes.*
>
> **Self-confidence** *is feeling able to do things and capable of achieving.*

Self-esteem derives from a positive self-image, and gives us self-confidence. Low self-esteem can have damaging results for children's emotional well-being and future life-chances, limiting their achievements and affecting their behaviour into adulthood. People with a clear self-image and high self-esteem are confident enough to tackle new activities and experiences, to take responsibility for themselves, to care for others, and to make choices and decisions for themselves. Strong self-esteem is the basis of sound emotional well-being and resilience.

As children develop, they formulate their self-image based on what people around them say to and about them, and how others behave towards them. If a child is consistently encouraged and praised, told that they are good, strong, clever and lovable, listened to and shown respect and love, they formulate a positive self-image. They see a picture of someone others want to know and like to be with. They develop strong self-esteem because they feel sure that other people admire them and value them. They grow to feel that they are capable of tackling challenges and reaching new achievements. They are confident in encountering new situations and meeting new people, and become able to take on responsibilities (for themselves and others) and run their lives autonomously. They have the inner strength to cope with stress and difficult situations.

The opposite of all this happens for children with low self-esteem. If children constantly hear themselves or their family members criticised or insulted, or meet with disapproval or find themselves shunned or treated with lack of respect, their self-image will be poor. Stereotyping and prejudice can lead to, for example, girls or black children starting to see the world as consisting of the hierarchy of male over female or white over black, and this can put the self-esteem of black and female children at risk. Prejudiced attitudes and remarks can make children feel ashamed, inferior or abnormal, which may erode their self-esteem and shake their self-confidence. A child may feel that they are not being truly included in a setting because it seems to them that some aspect of their individuality – who and what they are – is not valued by the people around them. They feel marginalised and even alien in the setting.

Prejudice and discrimination
can damage self-esteem

Children with a poor self-image are likely to develop negative feelings about themselves, and their self-esteem will suffer, affecting their behaviour and the progress of their development. Because their unique combination of characteristics is not acknowledged and valued, they are denied equality of opportunity. They may begin to feel that they can never succeed at anything, and they may not develop the ability to be either independent or dependable. They may become depressed or anxious, and are more likely to be abused or bullied and to abuse or bully others. They may feel a sense of injustice or resentment, and this may have a negative effect on their behaviour.

WHAT IT LOOKS LIKE IN PRACTICE

A group of experienced practitioners shared examples of children they had encountered who had been affected by messages about their lack of value.

◆ Marcia told a heart-rending story of a little four-year-old black girl who tried very hard to pretend she was white like the other children in her nursery, even scrubbing her arms and legs with a stiff brush to try to get the 'dirt' off. She only wanted to play with white baby dolls and drew herself like Cinderella in the story book – blonde and blue-eyed.

◆ Josie told about the eight-year-old boy who had just been diagnosed as having dyslexia, after a long struggle to learn to read and write and a lot of bullying from others in his class. He usually referred to himself as 'thick' and had become withdrawn and uncommunicative, even though he had a wide spoken vocabulary and great skills in making models.

◆ Marc told about a four-year-old girl at the children's centre who was causing everyone a lot of concern in her behaviour – scratching and soiling herself, rarely joining in play with enjoyment and at times crying inconsolably. When she did play, it was always with cars and trains, or kicking a ball or climbing as high as possible (sometimes too high for safety). She never took part in the home-corner play, or painting and drawing. She was the youngest of five girls, in a family desperate for a boy, and had heard her parents and grandparents say many times that they wished she had been a boy.

These children's self-esteem had been eroded because they felt that an important aspect of who they were was not valued by the people around them.

For some children whose parents are of different ethnic groups, developing a clear self-image can present some difficulties. A child who has one black parent and one white parent, for example, is likely to find they are seen by others as black. Some people of mixed ethnic origins resist the labels that others put on them in this way, feeling that this denies them the right to claim the other part of their ethnic heritage and choose their own definition of their ethnicity. They know they are a unique individual, of mixed ethnic origins like so many others, yet some people are defining their identity by putting them in a category which relates to only part of that identity.

Some of the children you work with will grow up to be homosexual. It is important that they grow up in an atmosphere of acceptance of homosexuality as a valid part of a person's individual identity. They should be able to retain their self-esteem, and not see themselves as abnormal and their sexuality as something to be ashamed of. They have the right to feel that they are as entitled to their way of life as heterosexual people, and to expect that the children who grow up to be heterosexual will respect homosexuals and treat them without prejudice.

Practitioners have an influential role to play in acknowledging all aspects of a child's individuality and demonstrating to the child that they respect and value all those aspects. Working in a context of inclusion and equality, you can contribute a great deal to children's development of their self-image by the way you interact with them and the way you talk about them to others. Never underestimate your role in building and sustaining children's self-esteem and the part that is played by your practice in respecting and valuing their individualism.

In Chapter 6, we will look at the importance of helping children who encounter situations where they feel that they are not valued. You will consider how to support them to deal with experiences of prejudice and discrimination, to build their resilience in the face of prejudice, and to be 'empowered' to resist the negative effects of discrimination.

Feeling good about ourselves

As you get to know children and their families, you will inevitably encounter people who are different from yourself and your own family. In your professional role, you must ensure that you show that you respect these differences and value each person as an individual. To be able to do this well, you also need a clear self-image and strong self-esteem.

A person's self-image and self-esteem come from many sources. We may feel good about ourselves because we are part of an ethnic, social or faith group which we feel has good values or status and a past history based on achievements. For some people, a pride in their 'roots' is significant – holding a certain nationality or belonging to a particular country or region, having ancestors from a specific area or region, or tracing origins to an ethnic group. For others, it is a matter of the social class they grew up in. Still others derive such feelings of belonging from their membership of a religious group. And for some people, their gender, sexuality and physical make-up is part of this feeling of positive self-image. Educational, sporting, musical and artistic talents and achievements and qualifications also play their part.

FOOD FOR FURTHER THOUGHT

Over a period of time, think about what gives you *your* sense of self-image – who and what you are – and forms the basis of *your* self-esteem. Consider the part your ethnicity and culture, social class, gender, sexuality, faith, appearance, talents and achievements, life-choices and other factors play.

This will be a difficult and sensitive process for you, but if you have a sound concept of what contributes to your own self-image and self-esteem, you will be better able to respect the individuality of other people. It is important, therefore, that you are honest with yourself. You may want to enrol the support of a close friend, family member or your partner to help you think this through.

The aspects of our individuality that make us feel good about ourselves are important to us all, since they form the basis of our image of ourselves and so our self-esteem. To have these perceptions of who and what we are undermined, threatens our emotional well-being.

Our gender and sexuality, physique, natural talents, nationality or ethnicity and social origins are not something completely under our control. They can have either positive or negative effects on our self-esteem. People who come from a family which values children of one gender more highly than another may have low self-esteem if they are of the gender less valued in their family, whereas others may have high self-esteem because they are their parents' 'little princess' or 'son and heir'. It is sad to hear of people whose self-esteem is lowered by their homosexuality when, influenced by prevailing attitudes in their society, they develop negative feelings about themselves, sometimes as extreme as revulsion and disgust. Black people have a long history of being regarded by white people as inferior, and this has eroded the self-esteem of many. Working-class people share this experience to some extent, feeling that, whatever they achieve in life, they don't quite 'fit' – they will always be looked down on by upper- and middle-class people.

Some people derive feelings of superiority and pride from their nationality or ethnicity or social position, even though this is something they were fortunate enough to be born with, rather than achieving through their own efforts. Other aspects of our life, such as our educational and career achievements, *are* the result of our own efforts; and some are dependent on our decisions and choices – our life partner, where we live and how we create an environment for our family to live in, how we dress and enhance our appearance, how we speak (our accent and vocabulary), the pattern of our daily lives and routines, and how we rear our children. It is important for our self-esteem that we value our own achievements and think the choices we have made in life are the right ones – self-doubt weakens self-confidence.

Unfortunately, what happens for some people is that their pride in their origins and life-choices makes them feel that those are the only ones that matter and are 'correct'; that others' origins and life-choices are of less value or even 'wrong'. To accept that other people's origins and life-choices are equally valid feels to some people like a betrayal of their own origins and choices. But this is not true. Taking pleasure in our own ethnicity, culture and religion, gender, sexuality, social background or appearance and achievements, should not lead inevitably to regarding them as superior to other people's. We don't have to belittle other people's origins and choices to maintain pride in our own.

If you encounter people who condemn other people's traditions or faith, or put down their gender or sexuality, or dismiss their achievements, or sneer at their social class or accent, or make fun of their impairment or appearance, you may feel you can draw the conclusion that they have a poor self-image. People who think badly of themselves and have feelings of weakness are not secure in their own emotional development. To boost their shaky self-esteem, they feel they have to present other people in a negative light. They try to prove their worth and avoid their feelings of inferiority by exercising power over other people, to demonstrate that they are superior to them. Such people may express prejudices and are likely to discriminate or resort to **bullying**.

> ## WHAT DOES THIS MEAN?
>
> **Bullying** *is:*
>
> ◆ *deliberate – it sets out to hurt*
> ◆ *persistent – it is repeated over time*
> ◆ *exercising power over another person – the bully gains satisfaction from their ability to manipulate and intimidate others.*
>
> *It may be:*
>
> ◆ *physical – punching, slapping, kicking, pushing, poking, damaging belongings*
> ◆ *verbal – teasing about appearance, ethnicity, disability or sexual orientation; taunting about family or friends; threats; spreading rumours (in person or by text or email)*
> ◆ *exclusion – from activities, the group; by ridiculing, humiliating*
> ◆ *extortion – demanding money or possessions with threats of physical attack.*

Putting others down and hurting them helps bullies to feel better about themselves; they build their own self-esteem through getting a 'hit' from seeing others unhappy and put in a weak position – 'I know I'm pretty useless, but I'll prove I'm better than *you* by hurting you.' Bullies bully again and again to maintain their own feelings of worth, which are very shaky.

A child or adult who expresses racist prejudice is trying to prove that someone of their ethnic background is in some way more important than people with a different colour skin or cultural practices. This is part of constructing their own identity as superior. The same applies to men who put women down or women who belittle men, and to anyone who ridicules someone because of their impairment, appearance or accent, or mocks someone of another social class or disparages homosexual people.

A good self-image and strong self-esteem is what determines how comfortable you feel about the value of your own identity, and that is what will enable you to be effective in anti-discriminatory practice and inclusive of all children and families, respecting and valuing their individuality.

Respecting and valuing each individual

Anyone who works with children must take the need to value differences between individual children and their families very seriously, and must show them respect because of the potential effects on children's self-image and self-esteem.

Showing respect is about demonstrating that you may lead your life differently from others, but you accept that they have a right to conduct their lives in ways they think appropriate, according to their values and traditions. You can show children, by your genuine interest in them and their families, that you have positive opinions of their home life, and don't regard it as peculiar or strange just because it is different from your own.

WHAT IT LOOKS LIKE IN PRACTICE

Julie tells of an event in the school where she works.

'For a project we were doing with Year 2, one teacher asked the children to bring in a photo of their parents' wedding. I knew from the class records that several of the children, as you might expect, lived in families where the parents hadn't had a wedding. I saw this as suggesting to those children that their families were not quite 'right', maybe not 'moral', and it certainly showed insensitivity and lack of respect for the parents' choices. I know one little boy brought in a photo of his aunt and uncle's wedding, but one little girl was very upset about it all.'

Saying that we value differences can be superficial, consisting of gestures of 'multi-culturalism' focused on sharing food and festivals. We will look in Chapter 5 at some 21st century debates about integration and assimilation, which highlight how far people feel able to go in 'valuing' cultural differences when such differences seem to hinder the development of coherence in society. However, in your professional role, you should show that you value the individuality of children and families and the ways in which they differ from others.

PUTTING PRINCIPLES INTO PRACTICE

'One way we show how much we value having a variety of cultures and ways of life represented in our school is to involve parents and ask them to contribute to the school in many ways. We've had Malathy's father playing his sitar, Parminder's older brother came to show us how to put on a turban, Zofia's mum taught us all some Polish nursery rhymes, and Leah's mother cooked us some gorgeous food at Hannukah. We want all the children to know about the different ways people in our community live their lives, and we show that we think everyone is important to us.'

Viv, teacher

'We've been systematically working our way through our resources of books, puzzles and other materials with pictorial representations of families. We found what we suspected: families are all shown as having a Mummy and a Daddy, and we haven't any examples of single parents, mixed-race families or extended families. We're now looking for materials that are more representative of the families in our setting. We have found a book with two Mummies – our first step. We want to be sure that we show that we think all sorts of families matter and are welcome here.'

Marian, pre-school worker

A setting which has a diverse staff team can contribute to the equality and diversity agendas by showing respect for various cultures in practical and real ways, such as:

- supporting staff members' compliance with dietary practices by, for example, keeping certain foodstuffs separate
- negotiating breaks at appropriate times and providing a quiet space for prayers
- being understanding about colleagues doing less strenuous activities on their fast days
- not imposing a uniform which cannot be adapted to traditional styles of dress
- ensuring that all members of the staff team have equal chances to take leave for the festivals or holy days of their religion. The Christian festivals of Christmas and Easter are public holidays in the UK, but Hindu workers should feel they have as much right to time off for Diwali, Muslims for Eid, Jews for Yom Kippur and so on. This may need planning in advance, especially for festivals that fall on different dates each year, to ensure that ratios are maintained and, if necessary, supply staff are brought in.

Workers with cultural requirements such as these should not be made to feel that they are being unreasonable or causing unfair burdens for their colleagues. A setting which declares its intentions to respect and value a range of cultures must address these issues relating to the staff it employs.

Names

Showing respect towards children and their families is largely a matter of courtesy; being alert to what is regarded as polite by others and what would give offence. An element of this is to pay attention to names and how individuals prefer to be addressed.

WHAT IT LOOKS LIKE IN PRACTICE

Susan, who works in an after-school club, talks about using people's names.

'I am very particular about getting people's names right. I check how to pronounce and spell names that aren't familiar, especially if they are from a language other than my own. I was very unhappy about a colleague who made a big fuss about pronouncing an Eastern European surname that had a lot of consonants. All she had to do was to listen carefully to how the parents pronounced their family name and practise saying it. I think it is lacking in respect to use another name just because it seems easier to pronounce. I had another colleague who called Asian children 'Ben' and 'Sam' because she claimed she couldn't get her tongue round their real names. Names are an important part of who we are, our individuality – I hate being called Sue and get annoyed when people think they can shorten my name without my permission.'

The systems used for names and titles vary across ethnic and social groups. The naming pattern which has been traditional in the UK for many centuries is for a person to have one or more personal names or forenames (which Christians call Christian names), followed by a family name or surname. Most personal names are associated with one or other gender, and names that can be used for either gender are often spelled differently (Leslie/Lesley, Francis/Frances). Women often adopt their husband's surname on marriage, although this is less frequent now than in the past. You may find that a child's parents have different surnames, whether or not they are married, or parents may combine their surnames into a new family name.

You are likely to encounter several other ways of constructing a person's name associated with specific ethnic or religious groups. However, it is essential not to make assumptions that because a person belongs to such a group, they will use the system widely used in that group. It is helpful to understand some of the principles that underpin various naming systems but *always* check when you meet someone how they prefer and expect to be addressed. This is a basic factor in developing a respectful and courteous relationship.

Systems of naming include the following:

◆ *Hindu*: usually a personal name, some of which are not gender specific (they can be used for a boy or a girl), so it may be followed by a second name which may indicate gender such as Lal/Bhai (male) or Devi/Bhen (female), and a family name; most married Hindu women take their husband's last name.

◆ *Sikh*: many first names are not gender specific so they are followed by the religious gender title Singh (male) or Kaur (female), and then possibly a family name, although these are not always used. A woman may continue to be known by the name of Kaur after marriage, and the name Singh or Kaur may be used for children, according to their sex, without a family name.

◆ *Chinese*: traditionally, the family name is placed first, followed by the personal name(s), most of which are gender specific. However, many Chinese people living in the UK have reversed this order. It is always best to ask a family what system they use.

WHAT IT LOOKS LIKE IN PRACTICE

'I only recently found out about traditional Chinese naming systems when I started to look after Mei. Her mother had put 'Mei' second when she wrote her name down, and I thought that was her family name. It was only when I was talking to her about names that I realised the family sticks to the old ways and puts personal names last. I'm so glad I found out – I would have hated to be impolite and said 'Mrs. Mei'.'

Linda, childminder

◆ *Muslim*: because this religion spans so many countries and cultures, there are great variations. The personal name may be more than one word, which should always be used together. The first of these personal names for boys may be religious (Mohammed or Syed) and should not usually be used on its own. Most personal names are gender specific but in some parts of the Indian sub-continent, a middle name is added to indicate gender – Miah/Agha for male and Begum/Bibi for female. These names are usually but not always followed by a family name.

◆ *African*: there are wide ranges of systems across this vast continent, but traditionally, in sub-Saharan Africa, gender-specific personal names only were used, but no family name. Religion and colonisation has affected African naming systems so a family of African origins may use Muslim or Christian personal names and a family name. In some parts of West Africa, names are given to children according to the day of the week they were born on, such as Kofi and Kwame for boys born on Friday and Saturday.

◆ *African Caribbean*: the influence of slavery means that 'family' names are in fact often the names of slave owners who forced their slaves to adopt European names, including their own surname, to show their ownership.

PUTTING PRINCIPLES INTO PRACTICE

To be sure you are pronouncing and spelling names correctly and using an appropriate naming system, just ask parents to confirm all of this for you. They will be much happier being asked than seeing you struggle to guess what is correct. The often quoted rule is 'Don't assume. Ask'.

Children learning stereotypes and prejudice

Not only do children experience **discrimination** and have **prejudice** and stereotypes expressed against them, they may also learn to express prejudice and stereotypes themselves, and begin to behave in discriminatory ways towards individuals who are different from themselves.

WHAT DOES THIS MEAN?

Prejudice *is a judgment or opinion of a person or group, often negative, which is made without careful consideration of accurate relevant information. It normally leads to the view that some people are inferior to others, and of less worth and significance.*

Discrimination *means treating someone less or more favourably than other people because they or their family are seen as belonging to a particular group in society. Discrimination obviously has a positive side for some – the people who are not discriminated against benefit from an unfair advantage. However, it is the negative side of discrimination that needs our attention because it limits the opportunities that some people have in life.*

Some people are reluctant to accept that children – especially young children – learn prejudice. They prefer to think of childhood as a time of innocence, free of negative influence, but this is not an accurate picture. Many adults take comfort in the mistaken view that children – especially in their early years – don't 'notice' differences, don't 'see' skin colour or impairments in others. They claim that children cannot be prejudiced because they think of everyone as 'the same'. This isn't true – children do notice differences and, sadly, they do learn prejudice.

Even the youngest children are sharp observers – that is one of their key assets in learning about the world they find themselves in. Their natural curiosity drives them to watch and listen to other people, look carefully and wonder about what they see. In fact, we encourage young children to look and think about what they see because we want them to explore and question their environment. We want them to build up interest in people and develop understanding of others, so these skilled observers certainly do 'notice' differences. Observation of children shows them developing perspectives on gender differences and skin colour differences by the age of three years.

WHAT IT LOOKS LIKE IN PRACTICE

'I have noticed that children learn very early (by the age of three years) to pick up the clues that tell them if someone is a boy or a girl, a man or a woman. And just as they learn to recognise and name red, blue and yellow, they recognise differences in skin tone. When they meet a new child or adult, they don't take long to spot if that person has difficulties with mobility or hearing. They are fascinated with wheelchairs and other aids because we have taught them to be fascinated when they encounter something new and interesting.'

Val, experienced practitioner who works in a children's centre

Noticing differences doesn't automatically lead to prejudice, but the experience of practitioners like Val and research findings, such as those of David Milner (*Children and Race: Ten Years On*, 1983), have shown that not only do young children notice these differences, but they also begin to form stereotyped views very young. Where stereotypes are learned, prejudice is often not far behind.

Even by the age of two years, some children are beginning to develop stereotyped ways of thinking, seeing certain objects and tasks as being linked to men (tools and mending things) or to women (vacuum cleaners and cooking).

WHAT IT LOOKS LIKE IN PRACTICE

'I find it quite depressing, the way even little children have already learned what is supposed to be 'proper' or 'correct' for girls and boys – you know, all the stuff about 'boys don't cry' or 'be a good girl'.'

Val, experienced practitioner who works in a children's centre

Children may develop assumptions such as:

◆ black people cannot and do not take on responsible and leadership roles in society – that black men are singers, boxers, athletes or criminals, but not doctors, lawyers, teachers or politicians

◆ disabled people are helpless, cannot look after themselves, do not have jobs, cannot take on responsible or active roles in society, and should be pitied

◆ men cannot and do not take on caring or domestic roles.

For some children, these stereotypes persist, even when they see and hear about black lawyers, disabled politicians or men who work with children.

By the age of four years, some children start to attach different values to those differences; they may see men and white people as preferable, more important and higher up in the scheme of life. This was powerfully illustrated in comments from young children in the television series 'Child of Our Time', in which both black and white children described their preferences for white friends.

Recent research in Northern Ireland has shown that pre-school children can identify the symbols of Republicanism and Unionism, and prefer the ones which belong to their community. By the age of seven or eight years, children are developing negative and antagonistic attitudes to children from the other side of the sectarian divide (Paul Connolly and Julie Healy, *Children and the Conflict in Northern Ireland* 2004). Even young children can behave in discriminatory ways by making hurtful comments and excluding certain children from their play.

It is not difficult to pinpoint how and why children learn such attitudes and begin to behave in these ways. Like all other aspects of their learning, they gather clues from their observations of what adults and other children do and say (both verbally and through body language) and from television and other media. In Chapter 2 you saw how the way adults treat children may give them subtle but powerful stereotypical messages about what it is possible for them to do and achieve. The effect of visual images that bombard us from the media is powerful, providing perceptions and misconceptions about ethnic and social groupings. One form of prejudice that children are often exposed to at school and through the media is homophobia. Even when they are too young to know much about sexual relationships, whether heterosexual or homosexual, children may develop various misconceptions which can lead on to prejudice.

REFLECTING

Over the next week or so, give some time to looking out for examples of stereotypes and prejudice related to gender, ethnicity, culture, disability and sexuality in your environment and in the media. These may consist of images or the behaviour and conversation of other people.

Think about how these can affect the development of children's attitudes.

Be honest with yourself and identify stereotypes and prejudice you have held in the past that you may have learned in your childhood. Question whether you still hold some of those attitudes and how they affect your practice.

It is alarming to discover that prejudice begins to develop so young, but practitioners must be prepared to accept this uncomfortable truth if they are to make a difference for the future of society.

As we saw earlier in this chapter, the self-esteem of children who experience prejudice and discrimination is likely to be harmed, but you also need to consider how prejudice harms the development of children who acquire prejudiced views. Such children will have a false and distorted view of the world if they think that:

◆ certain ethnicities, cultures, religions or social classes are superior to others

◆ white or able-bodied people are of more value than black or disabled people

◆ only heterosexual people and certain family groupings are 'normal'.

Prejudical views can have a negative effect on children's cognitive development because they become used to starting from false premises when they are thinking and reasoning about other people. The basis of their thinking is faulty, but if it goes unchallenged and uncorrected, they do not learn to question what they have grown up to assume. Their social and emotional development is also hampered because they may lack appreciation of the feelings and perspectives of other people, and they may grow up with feelings of suspicion, or even hatred, fear and aggression.

A crucial part of your role is to support children in overcoming or 'unlearning' the stereotypes and prejudices they have already learned. An essential way of approaching this is to help children learn about differences in positive ways that prevent them developing stereotyped or prejudiced views. Besides showing that you respect and value each unique child and their family, you can help the children you work with develop respect for individuality and difference.

Exploring differences with children

Because children notice differences between people from an early age, the role of the practitioner is to help them understand that such differences are what make everybody an individual, and that we are all entitled to respect from one another. You want children to develop a sense of their own worth and have strong self-esteem, but not to the point of feeling that they are superior because of their:

◆ gender

◆ ethnicity and culture

◆ social, economic and family background

◆ physical abilities and ability to learn more easily and quickly than others do

◆ appearance or their accent.

Feelings of superiority inevitably lead to the view that other people are inferior. Negative attitudes to diversity can become prejudice and lead to discriminatory behaviour; if practitioners are to prevent such prejudice and discrimination, they need to help children look at differences in a positive way.

Understanding our feelings about differences

To be able to support children's thinking about differences, you need to understand the reactions of both children and adults to difference. Meeting a person from an unfamiliar ethnic group or with a visible disability, or even from a very different social group, seems to produce a mixture of fascination and suspicion in many of us. I remember realising that the person standing next to me, waiting for the train to stop so we could get off, was Princess Anne. I was quite thrown – should I make eye contact and smile, as I might have done with someone else – or not?

REFLECTING

Think about some of your own experiences of encountering people very different from yourself. Then consider how you might respond to being in some situations you haven't yet encountered.

Try to recall childhood memories of meeting someone from a different ethnic background for the first time: how did you feel and what did you do? For many years, few western people were seen in China (this is still the case in some rural parts of the country) and when they did appear, they were openly and blatantly stared at on the street. Older black people sometimes recount similar experiences when they first visited less urban parts of the UK, including some instances of small children who had never seen a black person before being alarmed. People of mixed ethnicity sometimes describe how they and their parents were abused in public.

Can you also recall early memories of seeing people dressed differently from the way you and your family dressed? It is shocking for people from cultures which expect women in particular to dress modestly to observe the way some young women reveal so much of their bodies in western fashions. Those who wear the traditional clothing of their culture in the UK may be stared at and called racist names, even in areas with a rich mix of a variety of ethnic groups and cultures.

Observe reactions to disabled people in public places, especially if the person's impairment involves looking different in some way such as missing limbs or scars, difficulty in controlling head movements or speaking clearly, or restricted stature. Do people stare openly or steal furtive glances of curiosity?

How might you react to meeting a person from a different social position, such as someone with a noble or royal title or the holder of high political office? Would you react differently if you met in some grand ceremonial occasion as opposed to just spotting them in a public place?

Prejudice and discrimination often result from feelings of being uncomfortable about people who are different, or from fear of the unfamiliar or unknown.

Some people feel it is inappropriate to dwell on differences when talking to children, especially young children, because they feel it just 'makes things worse', drawing attention to differences and setting children apart from one another. But it doesn't help to pretend that differences don't exist. Because children notice difference, and this can become the basis for learning prejudice from an early age, practitioners can't just ignore the matter. It is better to be open and honest, and above all consider differences in a positive way as something to enjoy and be interested in. By exploring with children aspects of being different in positive and up-beat ways, you can help them to see difference as something interesting, something to enjoy – not something that prompts abuse or teasing. In this way children can grow up avoiding the suspicion of difference, which can lead on to prejudice and discrimination. Talking about differences, giving information and showing how you value diversity helps children to develop understanding and respect for people who look, sound or behave differently from themselves.

Celebrating diversity

Presenting differences in a positive and enjoyable way is often known as **celebrating diversity**.

WHAT DOES THIS MEAN?

Celebrating diversity *involves presenting a positive attitude and approach towards the differences between individuals and groups in society arising from gender, ethnic origins, social, cultural or religious background, family structure, disabilities, sexuality and appearance. It sees these differences as enriching society by making it varied and interesting rather than something to be fearful of, or to be a source of suspicion or dislike.*

Children are fascinated by people who are different from themselves. The EYFS recommends that you 'Encourage children to recognise their own unique qualities and the characteristics they share with other children'. The Pre-school Learning

Alliance's publication *Equal Chances* (1991) said, 'Children need opportunities to discuss and acknowledge the similarities and differences between themselves and their friends and neighbours. Discussions which take place in a positive way result in children having good feelings about themselves, feeling neither inferior nor superior to others.'

Some adults feel uncomfortable in dealing with children's natural curiosity about people who are different from themselves and talking about variations in skin tone, hair texture, shape of features, physical abilities and impairments. Yet these are the very characteristics which make us what we are as individuals. Part of your practice should be to:

◆ discuss such differences openly with children

◆ provide information and answer their questions

◆ show your pleasure at their individual characteristics.

This can help children to see the diversity of human beings as fascinating and enjoyable, and help them to avoid developing prejudiced views and discriminating against others.

Practitioners should respond readily to children's questions and comments about differences in gender, ethnicity, culture and family, physical appearance and so on. This will help them to grow up with accurate information and help them avoid stereotypes and prejudice. The EYFS puts it simply: 'Give children accurate information which challenges cultural, racial, social and gender stereotypes.'

PUTTING PRINCIPLES INTO PRACTICE

When you talk about differences with children, try the following:

◆ Don't ignore a child's question or comment, and don't change the subject. Talk to children openly and honestly. So, if a child says, 'That man is riding in a buggy like a baby,' explain that maybe he finds it difficult to walk and the wheelchair helps him to get around.

◆ Respond in a direct way, tailored to the child's stage of development. If a three-year-old says, 'Myfanwy speaks different from me,' it may be more sensible to just say 'Well, her family come from a place called Wales,' rather than rushing off for an atlas which is unlikely to be at the right level for a child of that age.

◆ Keep it simple. If you're asked, 'Why are Jamila's arms browner than Molly's?', it's better to say something like, 'Because Jamila's mum and dad have darker skin than Molly's parents,' than trying to go into a long explanation about skin pigment and sun levels in tropical countries.

◆ Give some factually accurate information and introduce appropriate new vocabulary. For example, respond to 'Parvati's mummy wears a funny long dress,' by explaining that it's called a sari.

◆ Help children to learn that they have to temper their desire to look, observe and comment with courtesy and thought about other people's feelings. Small children are likely to show their fascination in differences by staring. This is not surprising because we encourage them to look carefully at new and interesting things. In some contexts, their fascination is not a negative issue, but it can be very uncomfortable and annoying for disabled people to experience constant staring. You may want to encourage the child to keep the volume down when asking about personal characteristics, explaining that some people might have hurt feelings when they are talked about in this way. However, you should not discourage them from asking questions and seeking information about what they observe in the people they meet – just explain that it's best done in a quiet voice.

◆ Don't be embarrassed. When a child says, 'That man's got no hair,' or, 'That lady's hair is all white,' just be matter of fact about what happens to people's hair as they get older.

◆ Offer reassurance if you think the child is anxious or concerned in some way. If a child says, 'I don't like that thing on Leo's leg,' explain that it's called a calliper and is very helpful to Leo by making his leg stronger.

◆ Remember that when children pursue their natural curiosity and see and comment on differences, this does not automatically lead to prejudice. As you have seen, valuing some people more than others is learned by children from the adults around them and other sources of inaccurate information such as parts of the media.

Don't wait for children to remark on differences – be pro-active in getting them to consider the ways they are different from other people. Some practitioners find it helpful to use dolls (especially Persona dolls) or puppets to help these discussions by encouraging the children to express their ideas and feelings, show empathy and challenge unfair treatment.

Dolls with a difference, to make a difference: it can be helpful to use Persona dolls to discuss differences

PUTTING PRINCIPLES INTO PRACTICE

Talk with a group of children about the ways they are different from one another. Who is tall, who has freckles, who has the darkest hair or the brownest skin? What colour eyes does everyone have? How does their hair grow? What sort of clothes do they and their families wear? What language(s) can each of them speak? Do they say words the same way, or do some of them have different accents? What are they each good at? Guide the conversation so the differences are brought out as interesting and enjoyable, not something to laugh at or be wary of.

Think of other ways you can hold positive conversations with children to explore differences between them. Topics for conversations might include:

◆ the food they eat at home

◆ their families

◆ special events their family celebrates.

Your conversations with children can help them appreciate that although people may look and behave differently from themselves, all people are interesting and valuable. The way you talk about the diversity of humanity can help a child to understand that just because someone looks or sounds different to them, or behaves differently, or expresses different views about how to live, this is not something to be worried about or to avoid. You have seen the early age at which young children start to develop stereotyped perceptions and even prejudice, so from the early years practitioners need to help them avoid the fear and suspicion which can lead on to dislike and hatred.

Learning about people who are different

Practitioners in all settings with children can contribute to helping children to understand that being different is not threatening, and what we have in common as human beings binds us together. Ideally, this could be achieved through children establishing and maintaining friendships with children of different ethnic, cultural and social groups.

Supporting children in making such relationships can be challenging – whether you work in an ethnically and culturally diverse area or not. In an area where minority ethnic groups live, differences may already be the source of disharmony and some families may not be enthusiastic to see such friendships: some parents remove their children from schools because of ethnic variations. In predominantly white areas, children are likely to have few opportunities to form such friendships. It is also difficult to promote friendships across social classes, since – especially in urban areas – people of different social strata tend to live in different areas and some choose deliberately not to mix with families of a different social class. Policies for greater integration and inclusion for disabled children are having some effect, and disabled people are much more commonly visible in public places than as recently as twenty years ago. However, many disabled people are still segregated into special provision which limits their contacts with the wider community.

All of this means practitioners may have to make considerable efforts to help children learn about people different from themselves who are not part of their setting, and perhaps not part of the local community. White children living in white British families need to learn about the ways that black, Asian, Chinese and other European families live their lives, and vice versa, whether or not they meet such families in their setting or in the local community. Non-disabled children need to learn about disabled people, whether or not they meet disabled people in their setting, and vice versa. In the area of learning Knowledge and Understanding of the World, the EYFS says 'children need regular opportunities to learn about different ways of life'.

In Chapter 4, you will look at children learning about their own and other cultures, but a starting point for learning about differences can be the provision of resources in a setting.

PUTTING PRINCIPLES INTO PRACTICE

Consider how your setting provides and uses resources which reflect the diversity of society as a whole. Look at the following:

◆ Puzzles, books, dolls, puppets and small world figures – do they show a wide range of people:

- from a variety of ethnic and cultural backgrounds

- with a range of impairments

- in a variety of family groupings?

Are they used regularly and do you talk with the children about them?

◆ Pretend play materials – do they represent everyday items used in a range of cultures? If the children are unfamiliar with cooking utensils and forms of clothing, do you make sure they treat them with respect and learn, for instance, how a sari is draped and how a wok is used?

◆ Books – do you have some in dual language or script? Even if you and they can't read the language, children can learn that English is not the only language spoken and written.

◆ Paint or crayons – do you offer a full range of skin tones so children can portray people from a variety of ethnic backgrounds accurately? Do you make sure they're always available, not just as part of a special 'project'?

How would you like to improve the provision of resources for diversity in your setting?

Providing resources like those listed above widens children's knowledge of humanity beyond their immediate experience of their family, the setting and the local community. They can begin to see that people come in many and varied forms; that:

- their skin and hair may be a whole range of tones
- they may dress in a variety of ways, eat a variety of food and speak or write in a variety of languages
- they may have impairments of some kind
- they may live in families made up in a wide range of groupings.

Alongside showing children all this diversity, if you are going to make a real difference, you should help them to explore their reactions to difference in a positive way. You need to talk with the children about what is on offer, and monitor the use of these resources to ensure that children are developing understanding. It is important to make these resources available regularly and routinely in your setting. If you reserve certain resources for special projects, you will limit children's chances to learn.

This aspect of children's learning is essential for the future if we are to live together in a more harmonious and cohesive society, and avoid the dangers of division, prejudice and discrimination.

Chapter 4

Including all children: more than black dolls and Diwali

In this chapter, you look at practical issues related to inclusion and consider:

◆ identifying, understanding and breaking down barriers to inclusion

◆ creating an inclusive environment for children

◆ using resources for inclusion

◆ making routines inclusive

◆ issues in including all children in play and learning experiences and activities, such as:

 – offering all children the full range of play and learning experiences and activities

 – expectations about children's participation in play and learning

 – adjusting your practice

 – children's behaviour and their emotional development

 – providing positive images

 – supporting bilingual children

◆ including parents and families

◆ offering the services of a setting in an inclusive way

◆ learning about other cultures, including a few warnings about potential pitfalls.

Inclusion

You saw in Chapter 1 that even when settings have good intentions about including all children and families, some children and families may encounter barriers to their inclusion or they may perceive that such barriers exist. Either way, they feel excluded. Although the practitioners who work in the setting may be entirely unaware of these encounters, perceptions and feelings, and their failure to include certain children and families may be completely unintentional, practitioners need to identify any barriers to inclusion they are unwittingly allowing to persist, so they are in a position to start removing those barriers.

If a certain group is not being included on an equal footing with other groups, the result is **discrimination**.

WHAT DOES THIS MEAN?

Discrimination *means treating someone less or more favourably than other people, because they or their family are seen as belonging to a particular group in society. Discrimination obviously has a positive side for some – the people who are not discriminated against benefit from an unfair advantage. However, it is the negative side of discrimination that needs our attention because it limits the opportunities that some people have in life.*

Because discrimination has negative and unacceptable results:

◆ each setting should regularly review and evaluate ways in which it is achieving, and ways in which it may be falling short of, its aims and intentions about **inclusion**

◆ all practitioners should be constantly aware of how their practice promotes or limits inclusion.

WHAT DOES THIS MEAN?

Inclusion *is a process of identifying, understanding and breaking down barriers to participation and belonging. (Definition developed by the Early Childhood Forum.)*

The Early Years Foundation Stage (EYFS) says, 'All families are important and should be welcomed and valued in all settings.' To fulfil this aim of all children and families being able to participate in your setting and feel they belong there, your setting should:

◆ identify the policies / procedures, resources and practices of the setting that are resulting in barriers to inclusion

◆ understand how these barriers have arisen and what issues are influencing them

◆ take action to change the policies / procedures, resources and practices which are having a negative effect on inclusion.

If you can make progress with this process, you will be contributing to a more inclusive environment in your setting and helping more children and families to participate in it. In recent years, the phrase 'hard-to-reach families' has come into use by government and policy makers. This phrase carries undertones which suggest that some families are hiding away and unwilling to respond to 'outreach' from settings, such as home visiting schemes. It may be more productive to think in terms of whether, from the perspective of those families, it is the setting that is 'hard to reach'. This doesn't just mean in a physical sense of being within easy travelling distance, but in the more subtle sense of looking and feeling like a place where:

◆ the whole family will be made welcome

◆ their needs and requirements will be catered for sensitively and effectively

◆ they feel they can belong and take part equally with other families.

PUTTING PRINCIPLES INTO PRACTICE

Look back at the barriers to inclusion that Dalvinder identified in Chapter 1 (page 18) and consider whether some of these barriers (or others) may exist in your setting. Which of the barriers could you do something about reducing, either in your own daily practice or by working with colleagues?

Identifying, understanding and breaking down barriers to inclusion

Barriers to the inclusion of certain children and families in a setting may arise because of:

◆ the adoption of a particular policy

◆ a procedure put in place by the setting

◆ resources used there

◆ the working practices of the setting's practitioners.

Any of these may have the effect of excluding children and families or creating barriers to their joining and taking part.

WHAT IT LOOKS LIKE IN PRACTICE

Consider the following examples of barriers to inclusion:

◆ The Little Treasures Pre-school decided to introduce a policy that it would not accept children who still wear nappies. This had the result of excluding some children, who needed to wear nappies longer than most children do because of either physical impairments or learning difficulties.

◆ The Olympian Sports Club required all young people using its facilities to wear clothes and use equipment bought from a particular local retailer. This meant that young people from low-income groups were not able to join because they could not afford the kit.

◆ The Daisy Chain Nursery used resources like dolls, books, cooking utensils in the home-play area and dressing-up clothes which only reflected a white Western European culture. Children and families from minority ethnic groups did not feel they belonged or were welcome in the nursery.

◆ Sutton Hall School for Girls provided one communal changing room for games lessons. Muslim families who visited the school, when considering a place for their daughters, felt this was inappropriate and would not protect their daughters' dignity and modesty.

◆ The St Theresa's School only celebrated Christian festivals and only served traditional British food. Families from non-Christian religions and minority ethnic groups did not feel the school was the place for their children.

There is a wide range of potential barriers to inclusion, and it can feel daunting to look at them all at one time. You and your setting may want to tackle a few at a time, prioritising the areas of policy and procedure, resources and practice which are most in need of change.

PUTTING PRINCIPLES INTO PRACTICE

The staff and committee of the Puddleducks Pre-school decided to carry out a critical review of how inclusive the pre-school really was, and what barriers existed to inclusion. They defined three phases for their work, and agreed they wanted to start by focusing on the experiences of the children in the pre-school.

◆ *Phase 1*: They started by looking at the provision they were making for children, and asked themselves to what extent they were actually providing an environment, resources, routines and activities which truly included all children.

◆ *Phase 2*: Their next step was to look at how well they included the children's families.

◆ *Phase 3*: Lastly, they looked at how they told families in their local community about their inclusive practice and their aims to provide for all, and how they attracted them to the pre-school.

At each stage, they worked towards breaking down the barriers they identified.

Creating an inclusive environment for children

When you think about providing an inclusive environment for all children, begin by thinking about what it would be like to be a child coming to your setting for the first time and looking around it. What visual clues would they get that they are welcome, that they 'belong' there?

WHAT IT LOOKS LIKE IN PRACTICE

The Puddleducks team thought about how the setting would look from the point of view of a black child and then a disabled child. They looked around at the visual representations of black people or disabled people these children would find in the pre-school, starting with pictures on the walls. They saw for the first time that there were few such pictures, and discussed how this could make a black or disabled child feel.

The practitioners came to the conclusion that the message of the initial visual impact was likely to be that the pre-school did not provide for black or disabled children, that they were not really welcome there, and that they were in some way less significant than the white and non-disabled children who could see reflections of themselves in the pre-school's environment. The staff realised that this very simple aspect of the environment was giving out messages contrary to their intentions to include all children.

The visual impact of the environment is important because the absence of inclusive signals can make children feel insecure and uncomfortable. If they feel their presence is less welcome than the presence of other children, the impact on their self-esteem will be negative, and could undermine their self-confidence. This in turn will have a negative effect on their readiness to learn. The way a setting looks can represent a barrier to some children being able to fully participate in it.

Visual messages are not only carried by pictures on walls, but also by many other resources such as books and puzzles, dolls, puppets and 'small world' figures, and role-play area materials including dressing-up clothes. In Northern Ireland, pre-schools have introduced jigsaw puzzles which show aspects of cultural life (such as sport, dancing and flags) from both sides of the sectarian divide (an example is shown overleaf). This is part of a strategy to build respect and tolerance amongst young children.

Puzzles used in Northern Ireland depict diverse cultural symbols

PUTTING PRINCIPLES INTO PRACTICE

Consider the first impressions made by your setting. Are there visual images in wall displays and resources which reflect the lives of the children who come to the setting? Do you observe representations of:

◆ people of both genders

◆ the ethnic and cultural groups of the children in the setting and reflections of the way of life of these groups (including the written scripts of the children's home languages)

◆ people with impairments similar to those of the children who come to the setting

◆ different sorts of family groupings (such as lone parent, mixed ethnicity, large extended, same-sex parents) like those of the children who come to the setting?

How far do you think the visual impact of your setting's environment and resources makes it clear that all children are welcome and included? How would you like to improve this?

Sound can be a significant part of an environment, especially for people with visual impairments. You can also think about whether you could provide a welcoming environment by playing certain types of music from a variety of cultures that the children who come to your setting might be familiar with.

If you work with refugee children, part of your task will be to help them adjust to life in a new country with unfamiliar environments, language and customs. As we saw in Chapter 2, everything they see and hear, and even smell and taste, may be strange and unsettling. For these children, it is especially important to provide home-play materials, such as pretend food, cooking utensils, furnishings and dressing-up clothes, which are familiar to them from their homeland. By using

Providing a visual welcome

resources which are familiar to them and playing music that they recognise, you can help children to begin to feel that your setting is a safe place to be.

Other aspects of the environment may be especially significant for making it inclusive for disabled children. As we saw in Chapter 2, the social model of disability involves adapting the environment to meet the child's needs, not expecting the child to change to fit into the environment. For example, a child with a visual impairment may be helped to find their way around a setting and to identify an area or activity by:

◆ different scents or smells in certain indoor areas

◆ different scented plants or plants with interesting textures to touch (bark, 'furry' or smooth leaves, pine cones) and wind chimes in various parts of the outside area

◆ variations in textures on floor coverings and panels on walls, and rough or smooth stones and bricks outdoors

◆ white strips along the edges of steps.

Avoiding shiny surfaces and having adjustable window blinds can prevent visually-impaired children from being dazzled, and intense, focused light from small lamps will help them make the best use of their sight in their play and learning activities. Reducing hard surfaces and increasing carpeting and soft furnishings may assist hearing impaired children by diminishing the noises which their hearing aids pick up, thereby helping them to concentrate on voices.

You cannot plan in advance an environment which will suit the needs of every disabled child – the requirements of a child with visual impairment are different from those of a child who uses a bulky walking frame. Also, the requirements of two children with the 'same' impairment is unlikely to be identical since their impairment may affect them in different ways or to a different extent. What matters is that the layout of the setting's environment has the potential to be flexible and adaptable – and, perhaps even more important, that staff are willing and ready to contemplate making changes to the layout of the setting in order to remove any barriers to disabled children's inclusion. To be inclusive, the environment you provide in the setting must take into account the individual requirements of children.

PUTTING PRINCIPLES INTO PRACTICE

The Puddleducks review of the pre-school's environment revealed that:

◆ the layout of furniture was creating narrow pathways which were preventing Daniel, who uses a walking frame, from getting access to several areas of the pre-school so he was excluded from certain sorts of play

◆ play equipment was often left lying in thoroughfares and this was a hazard to Billy who has a sight impairment

◆ a lot of the equipment and materials was kept on open shelves so the children could have access to what they wanted to play with. Qiang, who is unable to walk, gets around by bottom shuffling. He often found that the resources he wanted were out of his reach, too high up.

The staff discussed how to make the pre-school's environment more inclusive for all the children and decided to:

◆ re-plan the layout to make sure that there were pathways from one area to another, wide enough for Daniel's walking frame

◆ organise a rota of staff and volunteer helpers to check regularly that toys and equipment were cleared up, and explain to the children how important it is to help Billy by being tidy

◆ take the short-term step of re-arranging materials so Qiang could reach the materials he especially liked, and plan for a long-term aim of new storage to provide lower level accessibility. They also encouraged the other children to understand that Qiang might sometimes need their help to reach things on shelves.

Resources for inclusion

The resources practitioners use in the setting also play a powerful part in ensuring that it is inclusive and caters for the individual needs of each child. As you have seen, these play a crucial part in contributing to the visual welcome of the setting. Some of the resources we looked at in Chapter 3 as helping to reflect the diversity of society are also valuable in creating a welcoming visual environment.

PUTTING PRINCIPLES INTO PRACTICE

Kay describes the resources which are used in the nursery where she works.

'Our home-play area includes a wide range of domestic pretend-play equipment, so that all the children can play out their imaginative ideas with what is used and worn in their own families. We've got a wok as well as saucepans, and the play food includes all sorts of vegetables eaten by lots of families in our area as well as food packaging in a range of home languages. The dressing-up clothes and dolls' clothes include saris and shalwar kameez, skull caps, headscarves and turbans, and we've just added some wrappas (long robes worn by Muslim women in Africa) and dashikis (colourful shirts worn by African men). We provide a variety of things to sit on – not just chairs, but also mats and cushions, including some gorgeous satin ones a traveller family has contributed.

   We use musical instruments from a variety of cultures and several of our books are dual script, with English and other home languages alongside one another. Our paint or crayons includes a range of skin tones so the children can draw and paint pictures that really look like themselves and their families.'

It is not enough just to have appropriate resources – they should be used regularly, not just brought out for special occasions and when 'we're doing multicultural activities'.

You want to communicate to children that they are included in the setting and that their identity and background are valued there, so you must make the resources that give this message an integral part of daily activities. Make sure the small-world figures showing black or disabled characters are used always, alongside the other materials for small-world play, and that the full range of home-play equipment and dressing-up clothes is always available. You must also make sure that resources are used in respectful and inclusive ways.

WHAT IT LOOKS LIKE IN PRACTICE

Kay describes an incident that made her aware of how important it is to support the children in using the resources offered, so that proper respect is shown for the culture involved.

'We had hung some lengths of sari material with the dressing-up clothes. A couple of the children whose mothers wear a sari had tried to use them properly, but the other children had used them for Batman cloaks. We realised we had to explain what a sari is and how it is put on.'

The use of 'disability toys' has caused some concern and shown that children need explanations and support in playing with dolls and small-world people who have wheelchairs, crutches, hearing aids and other equipment. In the 1990s, Save the Children carried out some observations of children using these resources. They found differences between the way children who were familiar with a disabled person played with the resources and the uses made of them by children who did not have first-hand experience of disability. The latter group used a wheelchair as a roller-skate and crutches as guns, and thought the hearing aid was a Walkman tape player. Merely providing resources does not increase children's understanding of disability.

PUTTING PRINCIPLES INTO PRACTICE

Kay also describes how 'disability toys' are used in the nursery.

'We discuss ideas about disability with the children, posing questions like the following:

◆ The doll who uses the wheelchair can't get upstairs in the doll's house – how do people who use wheelchairs get upstairs?

◆ If the doll falls out of the wheelchair on the ramp to the doll's house, how can we stop that happening again?

◆ How can we help the disabled doll join in with everything the others are doing?

We also have some books which feature disabled people and we act out the story with the dolls. Then we leave the dolls out afterwards, so the children can carry on with the story for themselves.'

In Chapter 2, we learned how good practice with disabled children arises out of your usual good practice with all children, and this also applies to use of resources. There are many imaginative resources such as hand-propelled trikes on the market, which are liberating for some disabled children. However, you should also think about how you can use your usual resources with disabled children. You may find that with some imagination and some simple basic materials, you can adapt some resources or improvise with what is usually at your disposal, in order to use them with children with various impairments.

PUTTING PRINCIPLES INTO PRACTICE

Nick read about using Velcro and rubber suction mats to keep toys and dishes fixed and steady. He got some for the nursery and it transformed the way Chloe, who has cerebral palsy, was able to use puzzles. She even began to feed herself. Nick also stitched bells onto some gloves so Chloe could join in music-making sessions.

Nick's colleague, Fran, made a shape and texture lotto game which Helen, who has visual impairments, can play with other children. She made pieces of various shapes (circles, squares, triangles) with different textured surfaces, using bubble wrap, fur, foil and sandpaper.

Hasan uses a wheelchair and was finding it difficult to join in with painting because he couldn't reach. Fran brought in some long-handled rollers (which are used for painting behind radiators) to overcome this barrier to his participation in this activity.

In these simple ways, Nick and Fran helped Chloe, Helen and Hasan to participate in more of the nursery's activities and be included alongside the other children.

However, some children can only participate fully in the activities in a setting if they make use of specialist aids or equipment. These might include:

◆ spectacles or a reading light

◆ a hearing aid or hearing loop

◆ a Makaton board or electronic communication aid, perhaps with a head stick or mouth stick, or a voice-activated computer

◆ a wheelchair, crutches or a walking frame or roller

◆ a prosthetic limb or a calliper

◆ a feeding tube or a catheter.

Just as practitioners don't need a mass of theoretical knowledge about forms of impairment before they start to work with a disabled child, so you don't need to have extensive theoretical knowledge of this sort of equipment. What matters is that you are prepared to learn how to use such aids if necessary when working with a particular child, listening to advice from the child's parents and other professionals like occupational therapists. You may have to learn how to maintain the equipment, or keep it clean, and be able to use it safely and effectively in ways best suited to the individual child. Even if you become accustomed to using an aid with one child, you may find that you have to adjust your practice with another child whose impairment requires that the aid is used in a slightly different way.

You also have a role to play in helping non-disabled children understand the importance of such equipment to disabled children, and how to treat the equipment with respect.

PUTTING PRINCIPLES INTO PRACTICE

Fatima describes what happened when Leroy, who uses crutches, and Luke, who uses a wheelchair, joined the holiday play scheme.

'The other children were fascinated – which is understandable because they're curious and enquiring. Several of them wanted to 'try out' the wheelchair and the crutches. We had a discussion about how these items of equipment are not toys. Leroy and Luke depend upon their equipment and need it to be available for use at all times. We said it was up to Leroy and Luke to decide if someone could share their aid briefly, but they were to be returned immediately Leroy or Luke asked for them back.'

It is important that the resources you choose to create an inclusive visual environment represent people accurately. For example, if you have dolls, puppets and small-world figures to represent a range of ethnicities, do they have features and hair which are an accurate depiction of such ethnicities? Having a baby doll which has been painted black but still has the features and straight hair of a white child will not communicate a clear message to either black or white children about how black children are a valued part of the setting. The same principle applies when choosing books. Do the pictures show realistic representations of people from a range of ethnic backgrounds and not just 'white' faces shaded in?

Practitioners should also check that books:

◆ do not show black people living only in 'primitive' conditions ('mud huts') and poverty but in the reality of modern high-rise urban areas

◆ show disabled people, black people and females as main characters, taking an active and positive role in the story, being 'in charge' and making decisions, not just standing passively on the sidelines and clearly only included as **tokenism**.

WHAT DOES THIS MEAN?

When a story or picture includes a person who is marginalised within society, for example a black person or a disabled person, but places them on the margins of the action and plot instead of making them a main character who is essential to the story, this is known as **tokenism**. *The inclusion of the marginalised character is only done as a gesture, to comply with some sense that they ought to be there, but does not contribute to, for example, the black or disabled children's feelings of being valued and included.*

Much has been said and written about golliwogs, and some people's feelings run high about this. Some black people remember as a child being called 'golly' in an abusive way in the playground. Some white people remember their childhood toy or collecting labels from Robertson's jam jars to get badges and models of golliwogs with nostalgic affection; they feel a lot of fuss is being made about nothing. Whatever your own opinions, it has to be accepted that many black people find the exaggerated features and woolly hair of the golliwog an offensive caricature of black people. Seeing a golliwog, or a picture of one, in a setting would give the immediate message that that setting was insensitive to black people's feelings and concerns, and not a place where they would find a truly inclusive welcome.

Making choices about resources means both avoiding inaccurate, tokenistic or potentially offensive materials as well as choosing equipment and materials which make a positive and creative contribution to inclusion.

Inclusive routines

The routines of the setting also play a part in making sure it is open to all children and capable of including each individual. Routines, by their very purpose and nature, can become fixed and unchanging. This can make it difficult for practitioners to challenge ourselves in thinking of ways of adapting them. Changing a routine needs careful thought and gradual introduction.

Children benefit from a consistent pattern to their days, and young children in particular find security in the predictable routines of meal times and other fixed times in the day. However, it is easy to let this need for consistency lead to establishing a rigid routine for the day, with everyone doing the same thing at the same time.

There is a balance to be found between the value of consistency and the importance of keeping routines flexible enough to ensure that each individual child's needs for personal care and food are met appropriately, according to their stage of development and their individual requirements. As in so much of practice which promotes equality, this is a matter of treating each child as an individual, and not letting the convenience of fixed routines and ways of carrying out routine activities dominate our thinking.

PUTTING PRINCIPLES INTO PRACTICE

'In our nursery, we take the attitude that babies should not be subjected to a rigid routine for feeding and nappy changing. Even though they need to be fed fairly regularly throughout the day, babies' feeding routines should be flexible because each baby is different. We consider that it is not good practice to wake a baby up to feed them or to make a crying baby wait just because it fits in with a routine the nursery has established for its own convenience. Babies wake up when they need to be fed and they soon communicate to us that they are hungry. If we tried to wake them up, we would have a sleepy baby, and if we made them wait, we'd have a distressed baby – and neither would feed well! Each baby has an individual pattern for needing to be fed, and this changes as they grow and develop. Similarly, we don't have fixed 'nappy times' – we change nappies when it's necessary. A baby should never be left in a wet or soiled nappy.'

Susheela

'In the after-school club, our usual routine is to put out a different activity at the beginning of each session – modelling one day, painting another, and so on. We think this offers the children variety and keeps them interested. But when Connor joined us, he found it bewildering. He has autism and he gets agitated and angry when things change – he likes a very set routine and without it, he feels insecure and frightened.

We thought about changing the practice of having varied activities each day, but we felt that would have a negative effect for the other children. Penny came up with a great idea. She made Connor his own chart with a picture for the activity starting each day. As each session starts, she gets out his chart so he can check which activity is available today. He has slowly adjusted to the feeling of a weekly routine and is much more settled.'

Paul

'We have several disabled children at our holiday play scheme. We do our best to be sensitive to each child's dignity when we provide personal care routines. Jack wears nappies, but he's 9 years old and we're really careful about his privacy when he's being changed.

Jade and Leon need to have their clothing protected while they are eating. We were quite shocked to find that another setting had put them in bibs with pictures of baby toys like teddies and rattles on them. We thought that didn't show much respect for Jade and Leon – they're 8 and 10 years old, not babies. We've made some bibs ourselves. We got hold of some material with pictures of characters from their favourite TV programmes and logos of football teams, stuff that interests them, and asked them to choose which material they would like us to use.'

Shelley

Make your routines flexible so you can respond to children as individuals

It is also easy to slip into carrying out routine care and other activities in exactly the same way for all children at all times. However, just because you have always given a baby a bottle in a particular way or potty trained a child using a particular method, this does not mean the approach will be best for all children. You may have to adapt your practice for even these apparently simple aspects of childcare to suit each individual child. Practitioners will be ready to use a different technique to bottle-feed a baby with a cleft palate, and such readiness to adapt should be extended to all babies. Each baby will do best if held in the way they find comfortable – some like to be cuddled in close, others feed best when held more upright. Older disabled children may need longer to complete personal care routines than their peers of the same age. They should not be treated like toddlers but offered the help and support they want – follow their lead.

Listen to what parents have to tell you about what each child needs and wants, to enable you to maintain continuity in their care from their home to your setting. One of the advantages of a key worker system is that one person can relate closely and continuously to young pre-verbal children, getting to know them really well and adjusting care practices to individual requirements.

Part of the routine for some disabled children is working through a specified programme such as:

◆ physiotherapy

◆ speech and language therapy

◆ activities suggested by a **Portage** worker

◆ specialist programmes such as **patterning.**

WHAT DOES THIS MEAN?

Portage *is a system of helping children to learn by breaking down skills into a series of small steps. It is based on home-visiting, which enables parents and a Portage worker to develop a programme which suits the individual child. See www.portage.org.uk, the website of the National Portage Association.*

Patterning *is an intensive system which involves adults repeatedly moving the limbs of a child with brain damage, with the aim of stimulating other parts of the brain to take over physical movement. Patterning is carried out several times a day, sometimes for quite lengthy periods.*

As we saw in Chapter 2, a child in England and Wales with special educational needs may have an **Individual Education Plan** as set out in the SEN Code of Practice (see pages 69–71).

WHAT DOES THIS MEAN?

If there are concerns about a child's development, a setting may initiate a stepped approach to deciding how to provide additional support for their learning. This may include an **Individual Education Plan** *setting out:*

◆ *the short-term targets for the child (focusing on three or four key targets)*
◆ *the strategies used and provision made for the child*
◆ *when the plan is to be reviewed*
◆ *the outcome of the action taken.*

These programmes have an important part to play in supporting the child's development and well-being, but it is important not to let them dominate the child's day or displace opportunities for play and activities which all children need for healthy development. Creative thinking will enable you to integrate these programmes into the child's play as much as possible, and physiotherapists, speech and language therapists and Portage workers will be able to advise you how to do this. In particular, you need to think about ways of making sure that disabled children do not spend a disproportionate amount of their time engaged in activities which are initiated by adults, depriving them of opportunities to pursue play which interests them and which they control for themselves. Disabled children can become very dependent on adults if too much of their time is spent on adult-directed activities, and this can have an adverse influence on their long-term development.

Most settings have settling-in routines for children new to the setting, but it is important to be flexible about this. Some children (and their parents) may take longer than others to feel relaxed and secure in a setting. For example, the previous traumatic experiences of a refugee family and their abrupt relocation to a new country may make the children reluctant to separate from their parents, and the parents may need longer to build enough trust in you to feel they can leave their child with you. An effective first step can be to learn and use greetings and some basic vocabulary in the children's home language.

Food and mealtimes

A major part of a setting's routine is mealtimes. The food that is offered and the way it is prepared and served should take account of the cultural and family backgrounds of the children who attend the setting.

How food is prepared and served varies from one culture to another

Various cultures and religions have rules and customs about food.

◆ Adherents of several religions such as most Hindus, Buddhists and Sikhs are vegetarian because their religious beliefs forbid the taking of life; they eat neither meat nor fish. Many do not consume alcohol or smoke tobacco and they may avoid tea and coffee because these are also stimulants.

◆ Those Hindus who do eat meat do not eat beef.

◆ For Muslims, certain foods are halal (permitted) and some are haram (forbidden). Pork is haram, and for other meat to be halal, it must be slaughtered in a particular way. Alcohol is forbidden.

◆ Jews do not eat pig meat, shellfish or game, and only eat the meat of animals with cloven hoofs which chew the cud (sheep and cows) that has been prepared in ways which make it kosher. Mixing milk foods and meat is not permitted and so should not be offered at the same meal. An orthodox household will extend the principle of kosher to having separate sets of cooking utensils, crockery and cutlery for use with dairy products and meat.

◆ Some Christians, especially if they are Catholic or Orthodox, do not eat meat on Fridays.

Remember that you should never assume that because a child is a member of a particular ethnic group, they and their families will stick to the dietary rules and traditions associated with that group. Always discuss what a family wants and clarify with parents which religious practices they want their child to follow – 'Don't assume. Ask.'

There may be other reasons for parents requiring a particular diet for their child. Some families choose vegetarianism on the grounds of conscience (not necessarily linked to religion) about the rearing of animals for slaughter, or for health reasons arising from concerns about methods of animal husbandry (such as giving too many antibiotics to animals being reared for meat). Some children need to avoid certain foods for medical reasons, for example an allergy to nuts or coeliac disease, which results in intolerance of gluten. When a child joins your setting, you should always discuss with parents the sort of food they should eat, both at meal times and snack times, and record these requirements. If a child with diabetes needs small amounts of food frequently throughout the day, not just at mealtimes or set snack times, the setting could establish a more flexible approach to the times when children can have snacks. If a child has to be fed by tube, you may need some additional training to become confident.

REFLECTING

Think about the food served in your setting for meals and snacks. How are the requirements of children from certain cultural and family backgrounds taken into account? Do some avoid pork or beef – or not eat meat at all? Are there issues about food allergies or the timing of mealtimes for some children?

What is the attitude of practitioners in your setting towards these food requirements? Do you detect that some colleagues regard the provision which is made for some children as a burden or a nuisance for the setting? If all children were expected to eat the same food, regardless of their cultural/family background or medical condition, what effect would this have on the inclusive nature of your setting in ensuring the well-being of all the children?

How can the children's families be involved in identifying sources of suitable food and recipes?

Having ascertained the wishes of a family for their child's diet, it is essential to comply with what is agreed with parents. It would be lacking in respect for the family's religious beliefs and values to be disregarded and the child given a food which is excluded by the traditions the family follows. In cases of allergy, of course, it could cause the child serious illness (or even death) if they were given a food which should be excluded from their diet.

Devout followers of many religions may fast – abstain from eating from certain foods or at certain times.

◆ Muslims fast from sunrise to sundown for a month during Ramadan, leading up to the festival of Eid ul-Futr.

◆ Jews fast at Yom Kippur.

◆ Some Christians fast during Lent, the 40 days leading up to Easter.

◆ Hindus may fast on holy days and on Saturdays.

Usually children are not expected to go without food and drink until they reach puberty, so if you work with young children this will not affect the food you usually give them. However, if you work with older children and young people, you will need to be aware of their changed needs during their period of fasting, even if just for a few hours each day. They may, for example, get tired more easily, or find it more difficult to concentrate.

Once again, including all children involves treating each as an individual, 'with equal concern', and making sure that the routines of the setting can accommodate all children's needs.

Including all children in play and learning experiences and activities

To avoid discrimination, you want to give all children equal chances to get involved in opportunities to learn through the experiences and activities offered in the setting. As discussed in Chapter 1, to treat children equally, you often have to treat them differently. If you want to offer all children equal opportunities to learn and develop, you mustn't treat them all the same. The phrase 'with equal concern' is a good way to think about how you need to work with children, adapting your practice to suit the characteristics and needs of each individual child. This is a basic principle of working with children in an inclusive and **anti-discriminatory** or **anti-bias** way.

> ### WHAT DOES THIS MEAN?
> **Anti-discriminatory** (or **anti-bias**) *practice means:*
> ◆ *taking positive action to counter discrimination*
> ◆ *identifying and challenging prejudice*
> ◆ *being positive about the differences and similarities between people.*

To ensure all children are included in the play and learning opportunities offered to them and are able to take advantage of such opportunities, it is essential to avoid **stereotypes**.

> ### WHAT DOES THIS MEAN?
> **Stereotypes** *are generalisations about a person, assumptions (usually inaccurate) that because he or she is part of a particular group, that individual will:*
> ◆ *have certain characteristics*
> ◆ *have the same needs as all other members of that group*
> ◆ *will or should behave in a particular way.*

We saw in Chapter 1 the danger of making judgments or assumptions about what a child can, or may be able to, achieve, and how this can limit expectations about what each child may be capable of. In Chapter 2, we considered the tendency to stereotype people according to their gender, ethnic group or cultural/social background. Practitioners have to avoid seeing children as defined only by, for example, their gender or ethnicity, disability, or cultural or social background.

Stereotypes can influence many aspects of your practice in working with children. To be sure you are offering each child equality of opportunity, you have to be critical of your practice and how far stereotypes are limiting what you do and what you expect.

Offering children play and learning experiences and activities

Most settings would claim that they give all children – girls and boys, children of all ethnic origins, disabled children – equal opportunities and encouragement to join in all play and learning experiences and activities. But a critical review of what is actually happening may reveal some startling unintended stereotyping and discrimination.

WHAT IT LOOKS LIKE IN PRACTICE

Puddleducks pre-school carried out their review of how far all children were genuinely offered equality of opportunity to benefit from the experiences and activities on offer. They began by monitoring which activities were more popular with boys and with girls – how much time each gender spent on certain types of activity. They found that boys spent more time than girls on the climbing frame, kicking balls, using the ride-on toys and building with the construction sets. The girls spent more time drawing, dressing-up or playing in the role-play area and doing puzzles or looking at books.

However, when they took their analysis a step further, they found that when a boy was apparently uncertain about what to do next in the session, the adults' suggestions to boys were more frequently to go and do something physical, whereas girls were more often pointed towards creative or imaginative play or quiet activities.

Stereotypes linked to gender relate partly to expectations about what girls or boys will want to do, and partly about what they will be good at. As we saw in Chapter 2, successive generations have expected that girls will naturally be interested in the domestic, creative and caring end of the spectrum, ready for their role as home-maker and mother, whereas boys will be interested in the adventurous, physical and construction range of activities, linked to their expected adult role as breadwinner. This was hard on girls who enjoyed climbing trees and were called 'tomboys' or were interested in science and maths, and were even seen as not being feminine. It was equally hard on boys who were creative and drawn to caring roles, who might be seen as 'cissy'. These assumptions about what will interest the developing male and female have direct and obvious links to what boys and girls are most likely to succeed at.

Even though we have seen significant changes in these attitudes over the last few decades, some of the underlying assumptions are hard to throw off. It is the role of practitioners who work with children to be acutely aware of how attitudes are influenced by long-held assumptions. They need to prevent stereotypical approaches to children's learning from limiting their opportunities and narrowing their horizons.

If the sort of differentiation of play and learning like that observed in Puddleducks Pre-school develops and persists, it is likely that such differences would be reinforced and gender differences in learning skills could be self-perpetuating. The girls absorbed in make-believe play in the role-play area, in their dressing-up clothes and in playing out stories they see in books, are likely to strengthen their communication and negotiation skills and develop their imagination. The boys building elaborate constructions or becoming more confident at physical play will strengthen their logical thinking and planning skills, learn to understand size and shape, and experience risk taking.

However, both girls and boys need both sets of skills, so if their play falls exclusively within one set of categories (physical/constructive or imaginative/creative/co-operative), their learning is being limited. It may be that a child chooses a particular type of activity because they truly prefer it to others and get the most satisfaction from it. But they may be basing their choice on thoughts that they 'ought' to engage in a particular sort of activity because it is 'right' and 'proper' for their gender, and is what is expected of them. If the latter is so, children will benefit from sympathetic adult support in thinking again about the opportunities open to them.

Encouraging a child to take part in a balanced range of activities will help them to develop a balanced set of skills. You cannot compel a child to participate in an activity. However, your role as practitioner can be to gently but persistently support children to make a variety of play choices, trying out the whole range of what is on offer and not limiting themselves by not venturing into the activities they less frequently choose.

Girls will benefit from:

◆ experiencing the achievements of climbing

◆ developing physical confidence through jumping

◆ extending their spatial awareness through building and construction projects

◆ becoming more familiar with mechanical and electronic devices.

Boys will benefit from:

◆ the satisfaction of being creative

◆ exploring ideas and emotions through make-believe play

◆ discovering the information and interest that books can provide.

Encourage boys to participate in make-believe play

Practitioners can help both genders to benefit from a full range of play activities by, for example, making sure that the role-play area and the dressing-up clothes include props for 'male' roles as well as 'female' ones, or encouraging boys to engage in make-believe play with small-world people or puppets in the place of dolls. We saw in Chapter 2 that there are particular concerns that boys have come to see reading as a female activity. If boys are reluctant readers, this can have serious implications for their future literacy skills.

PUTTING PRINCIPLES INTO PRACTICE

To encourage boys' interest in books, you could try:

◆ building up a collection of books to include content which you know especially interests the boys in your setting, such as non-fiction and information-giving books, not just those with stories

◆ placing books in the play areas that boys favour which are connected to those forms of play. For example, put books about buildings and bridges in areas where you have construction play.

If children develop stereotypical views of what constitutes appropriate roles and activities for males and females, they may begin to impose their expectations on other children, teasing any who step outside the stereotypical gender role and reinforcing their own and others' stereotypes.

PUTTING PRINCIPLES INTO PRACTICE

The staff of Greenways Crèche became concerned when they realised that some areas of the playroom were becoming 'no-go' areas for each gender. The girls had begun to see off any boys venturing into the role-play area, and the boys weren't letting girls near the road and train layouts.

The staff discussed ways of talking this through with the children. They also decided to set up girl/boy buddy pairs for part of the session, encouraging each pair to play with the same activity at the same time. If this didn't improve things, they considered the possibility of having single-sex sessions, when only the girls could play with the cars and trains and only the boys could go in the home-corner, with the aim of gradually introducing mixed-sex play again. However, they were reluctant to go down this route since they feared that banning either sex from specific play activities would build up resentment and be counter-productive.

There is another side to this issue, however. We saw in Chapter 2 that there do appear to be some differences in the way many boys develop from the ways many girls develop. The differences in their play are not all derived from the pressures of stereotypes. Practitioners should acknowledge these differences and organise provision for children's learning to take this into account. This is largely a question of thinking critically about whether settings are more suited to the ways most girls learn than to the way most boys learn (perhaps because they are mostly run by women). In particular, young boys (under the age of six or seven years) may have their learning opportunities limited if they are required to spend too much of their day indoors, engaged in adult-initiated activities in which physical activity is restricted. They may just switch off and not participate in activities which require them to sit for lengthy periods under the direction of an adult.

REFLECTING

Think about what is known about the natural learning styles of many boys – exploratory, physical, involving movement. Consider the attitude which is widespread that learning is only really happening when children are sitting quietly. Is boys' boisterous play valued or are there attempts to control and suppress some of it? What is your own attitude to boys' fantasy games involving super-heroes? Do you see it as mostly about fighting and exerting power over others? Or do your careful observations reveal a lot of imagination and creativity in the play? How do you feel about the inclusion of guns (made from Lego or imaginary ones) in adventure play?

There is a danger in seeing boys' play and learning styles as noisy, disruptive and generally undesirable, and not acknowledging the value of their games in supporting the exploration of ideas and understanding. When practitioners in various settings have observed one another's interactions with boys and girls, they have been surprised and dismayed to find that the boys take up more of their time and attention than girls, and also that such attention is largely negative, telling the boys to stop doing something.

Expectations about the relative abilities of girls and boys to achieve academic success have diminished in the face of girls' consistent higher achievement at every level of the curriculum at school. However, we have a long way to travel in terms of assumptions about children's potential to learn based on their ethnicity and social class background. Black children, especially boys, frequently seem to experience low expectations about their potential to achieve from those who should be supporting their learning. Many black young men tell stories of being encouraged at school to put their efforts and energies into sport, which they were expected to be good at, rather than into academic subjects, which they were expected to be less successful at. Similarly, many working-class children continue to have low expectations of their access to higher education. Low expectations are often self-fulfilling; if educators or parents or children themselves are convinced a child cannot be good at a subject, or pass an exam, or get a place at a university or on a vocational training course, the chances are that the resulting low self-esteem of the child will ensure the predicted outcome becomes reality. Pessimistic expectations about an independent future for a disabled child can have a similar result.

Practitioners who work with children have a responsibility to look carefully at how much they encourage all children to set their sights high and aim for academic and career success. While it would be irresponsible to support unrealistic or inappropriate aims, vigilance is needed to check that it is not a stereotype that is diminishing support for high aims.

Expectations about children's participation in play and learning

Apart from ensuring children's equal and fair access to equipment and activities, you need to explore expectations about how children will play and participate in learning and activities.

WHAT IT LOOKS LIKE IN PRACTICE

The staff team at Roundabout Children's Centre discussed some common assumptions about children's participation. Jamila recalled how a fellow student at a course she had attended had revealed some stereotypical assumptions, as follows:

◆ African Caribbean boys just want to run around and not sit down to concentrate on quiet activities

◆ Asian girls are quiet and biddable and do not want to join in physical games.

Jamila felt that the danger was that these attitudes could mean that this practitioner would not be pro-active in supporting African-Caribbean boys to engage in quiet, focused activities or in supporting Asian girls in developing their physical skills. In either case, a child might be limited in their access to play and learning activities.

Sally talked about when she had worked in a school and how the staff there had assumed that an eight-year-old with physical disabilities would not be able to join in PE lessons. He made it clear that he wanted to and he could, rather than just sit on the sidelines and watch from his wheelchair. His physical strength and confidence was much greater than they had realised. Sally said it was a valuable lesson for her, and had made her much more ready to have an open mind about what a disabled child might try and achieve.

Keep an open mind about what disabled children are capable of

To ensure that all children have equal opportunities to participate in particular activities, you may have to give some children positive encouragement by making it clear that it is entirely proper and acceptable for them to engage in certain activities. For example, you may need to give 'permission' or reassurance that it is perfectly OK for a disabled child to climb or for a girl to play with technological gadgets, or for a boy to wash up. The most effective way of doing this is likely to be the role model of a male practitioner reading a book or mending dressing-up clothes, or a female practitioner playing football or mending a broken chair, demonstrating the acceptability of breaking away from gender stereotypes.

Adjusting your practice

Anti-discriminatory practice may require you to adjust some of the ways you present play and other learning experiences and activities, and the way you support children as they take part in them. Caring for children and including all of them in activities and experiences is often as much to do with careful thought and planning as it is to do with having specialist resources.

WHAT IT LOOKS LIKE IN PRACTICE

Amarjit describes the care they take of Ngozi at pre-school.

'Ngozi has tight curly hair which she wears in braids close to her head. If she gets sand in her hair, it's a nightmare for her and her mum, so we keep a careful eye on her when she's playing in the sand. She's very good at remembering not to put her sandy hand up to her hair, and so far we haven't had any problems. We want her to enjoy that part of pre-school play just as much as the other children do, and gain from the learning opportunities it offers.'

Tina, a childminder, describes how she made a difference for Ethan who has cerebral palsy.

'I bought some chunks of foam on the market and created shapes which helped Ethan to sit more upright and securely so he could play with equipment on a table. It's transformed his days with me – he can join in so many more things with the others, and it was such an easy thing to do.'

Lisa describes the support they offer Bushra in the holiday playscheme.

'Bushra is from a Muslim family, and wears traditional clothes, covering her limbs modestly. At first, she was reluctant to get up on some of the climbing equipment because she was concerned that her clothes would get in the way. We've worked with her to help her find ways of overcoming this, tucking her clothes securely so they didn't get caught up or torn, and still keep her covered, and she has become more confident.'

Sharon describes strategies for encouraging Chelsea at the children's' centre.

'Chelsea's family don't have much spare money, but she's their only girl after four boys and they like to dress her prettily. They send her to play sessions in the best clothes they have for her. I know they can't afford to have them torn or stained, and

I can see that Chelsea's mum gets anxious about her taking part in messy play and playing outdoors. We are very careful about gently reminding Chelsea to pop on an overall before she starts painting. We have thought about letting her use some of the spare clothes we keep for emergencies for outdoor play, but we don't want her to feel she's wearing shabby clothes when her family are so proud of dressing her nicely.'

Leila describes some of the ways the dance class includes disabled children.

'We play parachute games with all the children sitting on chairs rather than standing so Kwasi, who uses a wheelchair, can take part. He joins in the dancing by wheeling his chair around or using streamers of ribbon to dance with his arms and hands. Aidan, who has a hearing impairment, dances in bare feet and picks up the rhythms and pulsations of the music through the vibrations of the floor.'

Simon describes a scheme for assessing children which was previously used in the school.

'We use an assessment scheme to help us plan our teaching of the children. One of the indicators for assessing a child's manipulative skills was 'able to use a knife and fork'. We stopped using this when we realised that it was culturally biased. Some children could eat very skillfully with chopsticks or their fingers, so we were assessing their manipulative skills as 'poor' when they were actually very good.'

The key to inclusive practice is to be ready to be flexible and open to new ideas for developing ways of working, whether that means learning some Urdu rhymes or acquiring new skills like using an epi-pen or sign language.

Be prepared to learn new skills like signing

Children's behaviour

Stereotypes about children's behaviour are just as common as expectations about what sort of activities and learning they will want to engage in and succeed at. Stereotypes about what behaviour is appropriate or relevant for a child may have a limiting effect on their social and emotional development.

REFLECTING

Think about how gender stereotypes about children's behaviour might be influencing your own practice and leading you to have different expectations about the behaviour of boys and girls (be honest!).

Do you accept more aggressiveness and noisiness in boys' behaviour than in girls'? Do you emphasise controlled and quiet behaviour more to girls than to boys? Do you expect girls to be able to sustain quiet concentration more effectively than boys? Do you let things go further with boys before you intervene in a dispute than you do if girls have fallen out? Do you think that boys won't talk with you about their feelings?

Have you observed such varying expectations based on gender in other practitioners?

What do you think might be the outcome of different expectations such as these about behaviour on gender lines?

As we read in Chapter 2, not all boys are aggressive. However, society does seem to expect males to be more aggressive than females, and to some extent more aggressiveness is tolerated from boys and men than from girls and women. This is a major issue for society since such a high proportion of those engaging in antisocial behaviour is male. People who work with children should never accept that boys will be aggressive and girls won't. Practitioners thus have a key role to play in helping boys to find non-aggressive ways of settling disputes and dealing with strong feelings. Equally, of course, not all girls are reasonable and cooperative, and they, too, need help to find more acceptable ways of relating to others.

Many children's behaviour stems not from their gender, but from their life experiences – whether of variable and unpredictable limits being set for their behaviour at home, or discord and even violence within the family, or the experience of abuse or trauma of some kind. Such experiences can make a child either aggressive or withdrawn and quiet. For these children, putting their behaviour down to the mere fact of being male or female can mask the true causes and may deprive them of the help they need in the face of the destructive influences on their lives.

In the same way, boys with concentration problems need recognition of the possibility of a condition such as Attention Deficit and Hyperactivity Disorder (ADHD). A child with such a condition is likely to need a lot of support and may

Help children to find non-aggressive ways of settling disputes

be helped to overcome their problems by taking medication. Just accepting that boys are more active and less able to concentrate on quiet activities than girls may delay their getting the help they need.

The flip side of society's apparent tolerance of male aggression seems to be the expectation that females will more willingly embrace responsibilities – for themselves and others. These assumptions, like so many others, run deep in the psyche. Practitioners have to be alert to the effect such expectations might have on children's development of ideas about the roles men and women should play in society.

REFLECTING

Some settings still seem to have different expectations about children's behaviour and role. For example, the boys may be asked to set out the chairs and the girls to serve the drinks or food. Or there may be differing expectations of girls and boys about clearing up after activities. Perhaps boys are rarely encouraged to be sympathetic and to help younger children.

What sort of messages do you think these approaches give to boys, and to girls? What effect might these expectations of behaviour have on children's perceptions of their future role in society? How do these issues affect your practice?

All practitioners need to be aware of perceptions about the behaviour of black boys. There is great concern that black boys are excluded from school up to six times as frequently as the average for the school population as a whole. In some schools, there seems to be generally low expectations about how black boys will behave, and their behaviour is often interpreted as defiant and uncooperative. It seems that black boys get into trouble for behaviour that is tolerated in other ethnic and gender groups, and when they react to harassment or bullying, they often carry the entire blame for the situation.

WHAT IT LOOKS LIKE IN PRACTICE

Beverley was very upset when her son Jermaine was excluded from the under-13s football team he had played for last season. When she spoke to the coach, he explained that he had to impose the ban because at the end of the last away match, Jermaine had suddenly set upon the captain of the opposing team and punched him.

Beverley was angry with Jermaine because she had worked hard to impress on him how much she disliked fighting. Reluctantly, Jermaine told her the full story. Whenever they played this particular team, he and the other two black boys on his team were subjected to constant muttered racist abuse throughout the match from members of the other (all-white) team. The captain was the worst, egging the others on. The referees and the coaches never seemed to notice what was going on and at the end of the last match, Jermaine just lost his temper.

The referee had demanded that Jermaine was banned from his team, and had said 'That's the problem with that sort, they're so bloody aggressive.'

Jermaine says he doesn't want to play football anymore – it just gets him into trouble.

A vicious circle can be set up when adults' low expectations and over-assertive control feeds children's resentment and lack of desire to comply. There may also be an element of cultural body language – many black families teach children that it is disrespectful to look an adult straight in the eye, while some white adults see this as shifty behaviour indicating a failure to focus on wrongdoing. Whatever the complex explanations, there is clearly a worrying issue here and practitioners should be critical of their expectations of black boys' behaviour and consider whether their responses are always justified and proportionate. In any aspect of managing children's behaviour, it should always be your practice to be ready to investigate the background of an incident to find out what is causing the behaviour. Avoid jumping to conclusions or just accepting that certain groups of children, such as black boys, will behave badly.

We saw in Chapter 2 that you should always see a disabled child as a child first and foremost, and not stereotype them according to their impairment. Your work with disabled children should be based on your usual good practice with all children. When you approach issues related to the behaviour of disabled children, hold on to the same basic principles and expectations and use the strategies you would usually employ with any child, disabled or not. There is a temptation not to be 'too hard' on disabled children, but this is misguided. It does disabled children no favours to be allowed to behave in unwanted ways when they have the capacity to learn positive patterns of behaviour. They have the same need as every other child to learn to behave in ways which will not harm others or damage things or make them unwelcome.

PUTTING PRINCIPLES INTO PRACTICE

Eight-year-old Rhiannon, who attends the primary school where Leanne works, has diabetes and requires regular injections. Her family have been very protective of her since the diabetes was diagnosed and often let poor behaviour pass unchallenged. Rhiannon and Huw were having a fierce argument in the playground – Rhiannon grabbed Huw, hit him and kicked him.

Leanne intervened immediately to stop the assault and reminded Rhiannon that that sort of behaviour was not accepted in the school. She gave her time to cool down in 'time out' while she made sure that Huw was all right. Later she talked to Rhiannon about not hurting other people and discussed calm ways of sorting out differences and conflicts. She used exactly the same approach to the situation as she usually used with children of Rhiannon's age, making no concessions because of her diabetes.

Oliver, who has cerebral palsy, is nearly 9 years old and attends the after-school club where Geeta works. When Geeta overheard him using racist language to Parvinder, she intervened and immediately made it clear to Oliver that this sort of behaviour was not acceptable in the club. She showed Oliver that she disapproved of what he had done and explained how much he had hurt Parvinder's feelings. She made it clear to Oliver that she didn't like the way he behaved, but she still liked him. She subsequently developed some ways of introducing Oliver and the other children to information about Sikh families and their way of life. She arranged for Oliver and Parvinder to take part in some activities together, and supported them to talk and cooperate. As with Leanne and Rhiannon, Geeta challenged Oliver's racist behaviour as she would have done for a non-disabled child.

Although there is usually no reason to set different expectations for behaviour for children with physical impairments, children with learning difficulties may not learn patterns of behaviour at the same age as other children. If this is the case, you may need patience and persistence in encouraging their positive behaviour.

PUTTING PRINCIPLES INTO PRACTICE

Three-year-old Daisy spends time in the crèche at the local college, where Neil works. Daisy has learning difficulties, her communication development is considerably delayed and she has little sense of danger. She has had several attempts at getting out of the playroom, despite being told that she mustn't go out near the stairs.

When – yet again - Neil spotted Daisy trying to climb over the safety gate, he picked her up to remove her from the danger and distracted her by taking her to play with the dollies, which she loves, talking to her all the time about how she could hurt herself on the stairs. He had to do this consistently many, many times over the term. He would more usually use this distraction technique with younger children, but it suited Daisy's stage of development and understanding.

Moira childminds Molly, who is four-and-a-half and has Down's syndrome, and is only just beginning to learn how to share. Two-year-old George wanted a turn on the trike Molly was using. She seemed to be about to push him away as usual, but then hesitated and got off and handed the trike over to him.

Moira praised Molly for sharing, telling her that it was a kind thing to do, and giving her lots of attention and smiles. She told Molly's parents about her good behaviour when they came to collect her. Like Neil, this was the approach she usually took with younger children, but she knew that it was right to reward Molly with explicit praise for sharing, as she was just reaching that stage in her development.

Similar issues emerge when there are low expectations that disabled children will do things for themselves, let alone take responsibility for doing things for others. Disabled children need adults to have a positive attitude to what they may be able to achieve and should encourage them to try to expand their capabilities to new limits. Don't be afraid of letting disabled children 'have a go' for themselves. Permitting and encouraging disabled children to attempt to do things which contribute to their own well-being, such as looking after their own aids like spectacles and walking frames, helps them to become more self-reliant. They also need to be encouraged to respond to the needs of others. If this doesn't happen, the perception of disabled people as dependent and helpless will be perpetuated, both for the disabled children themselves and for other children.

PUTTING PRINCIPLES INTO PRACTICE

Before Kofi joined the after-school club, Becky had explained to the other children that because of Kofi's sight impairment, he would need their special consideration and help. The children responded well by helping Kofi to find his way around and learn where things were kept. However, after a while, Becky became aware that Kofi was being waited on by two of the girls, rather than beginning to fetch materials for himself. She gently discouraged the girls from being so attentive and made sure that Kofi did more of what was within his capabilities. Kofi became more independent and soon children new to the club began to ask him for assistance, seeing him as an equal member of the club.

Children's emotional development

Children's healthy emotional development depends upon:

◆ developing high self-esteem

◆ recognising and being able to deal with their feelings

◆ developing independence and self-reliance.

Children need opportunities to take leading roles and assume responsibilities. They need praise, encouragement and compliments. They need opportunities to express their emotions and learn how to talk about how they feel. Learning about risk and how to keep yourself from harm is an essential part of growing up which children can't learn if they are over-protected. They need to learn how to take care of themselves and take initiatives.

Stereotypical assumptions can get in the way of this. When adults respond to children in stereotypical ways, they may:

◆ encourage white children, boys and non-disabled children to take leading roles in play and activities, allowing black children, girls and disabled children to be subordinate and marginalised

◆ describe a boy who organises other children as 'a born leader' but describe a girl who does the same thing as 'bossy'

◆ praise boys for succeeding at 'male' things and girls for being good at 'female' things, or express surprise when boys show the sensitive and considerate side of their character, or when girls are adventurous and courageous

◆ tell girls how nice they look, but don't focus on boys' appearance, or avoid commenting on the appearance of some disabled children whose looks are affected by their impairment

◆ tell boys that they should be brave and not cry when they are hurt or upset but acknowledge girls' fears and mop up their tears sympathetically

◆ give boys and non-disabled children more opportunities to be independent and take risks than they make available to girls and disabled children.

This sort of practice does not contribute positively to the emotional development and well-being of black children, girls or boys and disabled children.

REFLECTING

Think about your own practice (be honest!) and how you could do more to ensure children's emotional development free from stereotypical expectations.

Do you encourage black children, disabled children and girls to take leading roles in play and activities? Do you praise girls for being confident and strong? Do you praise boys for being gentle and kind? Do you compliment boys on their appearance? How do you think you could do more to avoid stereotypes in nurturing the development of children's self-esteem?

Do you discourage boys from expressing feelings of fear or distress? Or do you communicate the message that it is OK for boys to be afraid or to cry? Do you respond more quickly to a boy who is crying or to a girl who is crying, or respond in a different way according to gender? How could you be more effective in non-stereotypical ways of supporting children's ability to cope with their feelings?

Do you give boys and non-disabled children more opportunities to be independent and take risks than girls and disabled children? Do you have different views about boys and girls getting dirty? Do you tend to over-protect girls or disabled children? What differences in children's development of confidence, self-reliance and the ability to understand and overcome risk do you feel might result from such practice? How could you improve your practice?

Practitioners need to be wary about giving more attention to boys who shout out answers than to girls who put up their hands and wait their turn to speak. Constantly being ignored will have a detrimental effect on the girls' self-esteem and does not help boys to learn self-control.

If you work with refugee children, you may be able to contribute to the process of their recovery from the trauma of leaving their former homes suddenly and in frightening circumstances. You could help to repair some of the emotional damage they are likely to have suffered.

PUTTING PRINCIPLES INTO PRACTICE

Cassie and her colleagues support the emotional development of the refugee children they work with by:

◆ playing music from the children's home culture

◆ telling stories, reciting rhymes and singing songs which they have learned from the children's families

◆ providing activities which are soothing and relaxing, like water play and fragrant dough

◆ supporting the children in role playing, which helps them to work through some of their feelings of fear, anger and hatred towards those who have harmed them and their families. The children find masks, puppets and small-world figures especially helpful in providing a safe structure for the expression of these strong emotions (but they never put pressure on children to talk about or play out their experiences).

They also make parents very welcome, being aware that some of them are themselves traumatised by their experiences and need support to rebuild their confidence and provide their children with feelings of security in their home environment and routines.

Positive images

Many of the images children see around them can influence their expectations about their own future and the future of their peers. For example, many media images show black people, especially children, as malnourished and in need of charitable aid. Charities seeking funding to support disabled people still use images to promote their appeals that show disabled people as helpless and as victims. Local newspaper stories frequently focus on the 'tragic' story of some 'brave' disabled individual.

An important way of counter-balancing such images and helping to overcome stereotypical expectations about children's potential and possible future roles is by providing **positive images** amongst the resources in your setting.

> ## WHAT DOES THIS MEAN?
>
> **Positive images** *are visual and other representations which show people who are sometimes marginalised or discriminated against in roles and activities which go against stereotypes.*

Even very young children can be influenced by messages about what roles are appropriate for adults who are white, male and non-disabled, as well as for adults who are black, female or disabled. Practitioners can reverse these messages by providing positive images of a diverse range of people which show that black, female and disabled people can take on responsible, active and prominent roles in society, and that men can take on creative, caring and domestic roles. This helps children to develop strong expectations about their future potential and what they will be able to achieve in life, including the positions of influence and responsibility in society they will be able to take, whatever their ethnicity, gender, cultural or social background or disability.

PUTTING PRINCIPLES INTO PRACTICE

Carry out a thorough review of the resources and activities provided for children in your setting, looking at:

◆ pictures, posters and photographs

◆ books

◆ puzzles

◆ DVDs and video tapes

◆ computer games

◆ board games.

Do they include positive images, showing:

◆ girls and women as strong and independent

◆ boys and men as emotional, creative and caring

◆ disabled children and adults playing active roles, for example as the 'hero' of a story

◆ black people, women and disabled people taking responsible, challenging and influential roles?

What would you like to add to extend the range of positive images in the setting? It is not difficult to find puzzles and books with black doctors and female fire fighters, but you may have to search for materials which portray disabled people in active roles. A good source is www.letterboxlibrary.com.

As we saw on page 134, in the context of reassuring children that they do not have to comply with stereotyped expectations, perhaps the most powerful positive image is a real live adult. A male practitioner cooking or a father showing how he cares for his small baby, or a female practitioner using a hammer or screwdriver, will offer children a version of the world which challenges gender stereotypes.

Male carers provide a positive role model

Supporting bilingual children

At some point in your career, you are likely to work with children who are learning English as their second or subsequent language. If you work in areas where there are significant minority ethnic groups using a range of languages, including refugees, you are more likely to have the support of advisory staff and access to suitable resources than if you work in a largely monolingual area. However, you should feel confident in your ability to contribute to support for bilingual children, starting from your knowledge of how a child learns their first language. There are some factors involved in acquiring a second or subsequent language which have much in common with the way a child learns a first language, and you can use many of the same or similar techniques which you are already familiar with.

PUTTING PRINCIPLES INTO PRACTICE

To help a child acquire a new language, you can use some of the techniques you use with a child using language for the first time. These include the following:

◆ Introduce new vocabulary naturally through 'running commentary' on children's play, events and objects in the environment – don't try to teach long lists of words or give grammar instruction out of context.

◆ Back up what you're saying with non-verbal communication – the body language of facial expressions and gestures like pointing – which will help give clues to the meaning of your spoken language.

◆ Use rhymes and songs to introduce the rhythms of the English language.

◆ Engage the child in conversations about things that interest them .

◆ Repeat words and phrases consistently to allow children to become familiar with them. Also, read and tell stories like 'The Enormous Turnip', which children can join in with.

◆ Be aware of the child's passive vocabulary (the words they understand), which is much larger than their active vocabulary (the words they use).

◆ Use open questions which will elicit an answer that involves the child putting phrases and sentences together, not closed questions which simply lead to 'yes' or 'no' answers.

◆ Speak clearly and use language in ways which make its meaning apparent.

◆ Don't rush the child – give them time to think about what they want to say and to finish their sentences.

◆ When they make a 'virtuous error' of adding '–s' to a noun to make a plural or '–ed' to a verb to make a past, even in cases where that is not correct (*childs*, *goed*), don't point out the mistake but repeat the phrase back to them with the correct word.

◆ Praise success and progress.

Conversations will help a bilingual child develop their second language

When you work with a child who already has a spoken home language, there are additional issues to be aware of.

PUTTING PRINCIPLES INTO PRACTICE

Bilingual children acquiring English need you to:

◆ understand that they may spend some time being silent, listening and tuning in to the unfamiliar sounds of English and the patterns and construction of the language

◆ provide them with lots of play opportunities (outdoor physical play, sand and water) which enable them to adjust to the setting, free of the pressure to be talking to others

◆ find out about characteristics of their first language, such as the lack of definite and indefinite articles (*the*, *a*) or personal pronouns (*he/she*, *him/her*) – some languages of the Indian sub-continent and Eastern Europe do not include these, so you will need to demonstrate and emphasise their use in English

◆ encourage children to interact with one another, even if they have little shared language – they are likely to be able to play together, communicating in various ways

- understand that children will acquire English more effectively if they continue to develop their skills in speaking their home language, and include their first language in your setting by:
    - learning and using greetings and a few phrases
    - using dual-language textbooks (take a look at www.milet.com) and story tapes in the first language of the children in your setting
- make it clear to the child and their family that your intention is not to replace their home language, but to support their learning of English alongside their home language, valuing and encouraging their use of their first language
- as far as possible, keep consistency in the person who speaks each language to the child, since it can be confusing if an individual swaps from one language to the other
- use resources which are appropriate to the age of the child – don't use 'baby books' in English with an eight-year-old, even if their vocabulary level seems to be reflected in the text.

Using dual-language books gives the message that children's home language is valued in the setting

Be aware of the strain of speaking a new language and the relief of being able to relax into speaking one's first language. When my Danish friend (who is multilingual and fluent in English) comes to stay, from time to time she needs to spend time alone in order to have a rest from the effort of speaking English.

Ideally, all children learning English as an additional language would be greatly helped by spending time in a setting with a practitioner who spoke their home language. Some settings which cater for a specific local community are able to achieve this, but in some areas, so many languages are spoken this would not be possible. Even if you are bilingual yourself, you are likely to be in a position where you support children whose home language you do not share.

Including parents and families

When you work with children, it is always important to work in close partnership with their parents because parents:

◆ are central to their children's lives

◆ are a long-term and permanent part of their children's lives

◆ know their own children better than anyone else does

◆ usually have the children's interests most at heart – they care deeply about their own children.

This means that practitioners have to identify and overcome any barriers to parents' inclusion in the setting, in similar ways to ensuring the inclusion of all children.

Just as you focus on getting to know each child, so you should aim to get to know their families. To be able to work in partnership with parents, you need to be aware of what they want for their children and their expectations of you and the setting. This will involve you in listening to parents, respecting their way of life, valuing what they tell you, and establishing trust.

PUTTING PRINCIPLES INTO PRACTICE

Aim to include the parents and families of the children in your setting, to demonstrate that they are welcome there and that their presence and that contribution is valued. You may include parents in your setting by:

◆ asking them to help regularly in play sessions, after-school activities or sports training

◆ asking them to share their knowledge of their child with you

◆ asking them to contribute their specialist knowledge or skills to the setting, such as playing a musical instrument or demonstrating a technical or craft skill

◆ sharing with them some of your expertise – your knowledge of ways of supporting children in their play and learning or sport

◆ in the case of parents of disabled children, inviting them to visit the setting when specialists and therapists are present, so they can increase their knowledge of particular techniques and the use of specialist equipment.

We saw earlier in this chapter (pages 113–4) the importance of initial visual impressions of a setting in making children feel welcomed and included. The same is going to be true for their parents. Besides the adjustments to the environment and resources necessary to make children feel included, some other simple steps may make it clear to parents from minority ethnic and cultural groups that the setting wants to include them and their children.

PUTTING PRINCIPLES INTO PRACTICE

The Ship Street Children's Centre decided to get a new sign made for the entrance, saying 'welcome' in as many of the languages spoken in their area as possible. Staff at the centre spoke some of the languages, but for languages not represented on the staff team, they made contacts with some local community groups to make sure they got it exactly right. All members of the staff team began learning how to say these forms of welcome.

They also set about becoming more knowledgeable about naming systems in the cultures represented in the locality and how to address parents in ways they would perceive as courteous.

Making these sort of changes deals with some of the barriers to inclusion identified by Dalvinder in Chapter 1 (page 18), but he also identified:

◆ no one in the setting could speak the languages spoken in the area

◆ all the staff were from an ethnic background that was different from that of most of the families in the area.

These barriers are likely to be more challenging to tackle. It is valuable for practitioners to learn a few simple phrases of a language used by families in their setting, but more than that is needed to ensure effective communication between families and practitioners, which is essential in meeting the best interests of the children. Decisions and action will be needed at the level of management and budget-holders, such as to:

◆ arrange translation of information distributed to parents into appropriate languages

◆ gain the services of interpreters to be present at key conversations with parents

◆ recruit ethnically diverse and multilingual staff

◆ offer English language classes to parents.

It is especially important to include parents of disabled children in a setting because they are often the greatest experts on their child's disability and the specific effects of an impairment, which may be different from the way it affects other children.

WHAT IT LOOKS LIKE IN PRACTICE

A group of students on a course were discussing examples from their experience of how vital it is to gain information from parents of a disabled child.

◆ Rachel talked about how Wesley's parents were able to describe exactly how they knew that a sickle cell crisis was building up for him.

◆ Debbie explained how Poppy's foster carers had shared their knowledge about how to support and help her through an epileptic seizure.

◆ Tanya described how Jackson's father had explained the obsessions and fears he had as the result of his autism.

To be able to reach out to the parents of disabled children and establish an inclusive partnership with them, it helps if you have some understanding about how having a disabled child can affect a family. When a child's impairment is diagnosed, all the family's attention can become focused on the child as a 'problem', something to be made 'better', rather than a new human being to be welcomed, admired and enjoyed. It is not surprising that some families experience negative feelings connected to their child's impairment, such as those listed below.

Shock and anger. Most parents, when first told of a child's impairment, experience shock, which is likely to turn into anger – "Why me?" It may take them some time to move on from this feeling.

Blaming. Some parents are desperate to find a cause or reason for the child's impairment which they want to be someone's fault. They may blame their partner or their partner's family, or the medical practitioners who were involved in the pregnancy and birth or who gave treatment to a sick child, or an immunisation programme.

Guilt. Other people feel "it's my fault. What did I do wrong?" This can be a great burden for a parent to carry.

Grieving. There is a sense in which a family grieves for the able-bodied child they had expected or hoped for. They feel loss that their expectations have not been fulfilled.

Shame. Some people who have had negative attitudes towards disabled people may feel that to have a disabled person in the family is something to be ashamed of. Other people find that neighbours, friends, even members of their own family, make them feel that having a disabled child is shameful, through the opinions they express and the way they behave. Even some well-meaning people may express pity and refer to 'the tragedy' in a way which emphasises the negative aspects of the situation. This can lead to the family becoming isolated from their community, neighbours, even their own family.

Confusion. New parents may be swamped with medical information, as well as their powerful emotions. They may become bewildered with their situation and not realise or understand where they can find sources of practical help and emotional support.

Fear. Naturally, many parents of disabled children are fearful about the future. Parents of newborn children fear that the child will never be able to walk and talk. As children grow, their parents may see other children developing faster in some or many areas, and fear that their child will never be able to care for themselves, go to school, lead an independent adult life or be happy.

Rejection. Some families may even reject the child. At its most extreme, parents may refuse to take a new baby home from hospital after birth. Some families unconsciously reject the impaired child and find it difficult to feel love and affection for them.

Pressure. Some children's impairments lead to incessant hospital appointments, treatments, medication regimes and therapies, which can be very disruptive to parents' attempts to sustain their family and work life. This can be especially true following the initial diagnosis of the impairment, when efforts are being made to find a cure. It can be difficult to find time for other children in the family, and for parents to sustain their own relationship.

Reproduced by kind permission of the National Childminding Association

Not all families will experience all the negative emotions, but your communication with parents of disabled children should be sensitive to the possibility of a combination of such feelings.

When a child joins your setting, you always collect information about them from their parents. When you are doing this with parents of a disabled child, you must be careful not to give the impression that you have negative expectations – that you are expecting them to tell of a lot of difficulties and problems about, for example, diet and feeding. If they tell you of the need for their child to be given regular medication, show that you don't automatically see this as a problem but that you are willing to take a positive approach to learning about how to do this.

You can contribute to providing moral support to parents of children who are going through the process of assessment and **statementing**.

> ## WHAT DOES THIS MEAN?
>
> *Since 1981, local authorities have had a duty to provide a statement for a child who is thought to have special educational needs. The authority should:*
>
> ◆ *assess the child's special educational needs*
> ◆ *issue a 'statement' which sets out the child's specific learning needs*
> ◆ *identify the provision required to meet these needs and what the authority will do.*
>
> *This is the process of* **statementing**. *Parents have often found the statementing process difficult and long-drawn out. Problems can arise if the statement includes vague references to 'access' to services, as access is likely to depend on what is available within the authority's budget, rather than what the child requires.*

Despite having rights to be consulted and helped to understand the process, some parents find statementing depressing and demoralising. They may feel that the complicated and bureaucratic procedures do not involve them properly. They may have to deal with several different professionals such as educational psychologists and various medical practitioners, each one of whom seems to look at one aspect of their child, rather than the whole child. It may feel like re-living the trauma of the original diagnosis of the child's impairment. Your support may be as a listening ear or helping to check the meaning of written communications and encouraging parents to exercise their rights, or you may even be able to accompany them to a meeting.

You can also help parents of disabled children feel included in the setting by helping them gain access to specialised expert help, such as linking them to one of the many organisations that exist to support children and families. There is an enormous number of such organisations – the appendix on pages 227–9 gives contact details for some of them.

Be sensitive to making assumptions about parents' ability and readiness to be involved in your setting. For parents of some cultures and social backgrounds, the thought that their presence might positively be sought and valued may seem strange. They may see you as the expert professional and feel that they have little to offer, or feel shy or out of place in your setting. You may need to explain, in some detail but in non-patronising ways, the knowledge and skills you would welcome from them. Bilingual parents can be a great asset in teaching practitioners about their home language. But don't assume, for example, that they will be able to read and write the language they speak. Some will have been educated in Britain and only read and write English; others will have come from parts of the world where they had few educational opportunities and be unable to read and write in their home language.

If parents are disabled, the principles of inclusion and welcome should be extended to them. This isn't just a case of ramps for wheelchairs, but about your expectations of those parents. For example, don't assume that they won't want to or won't be able to be involved in your setting in the same way other parents are.

They may have many skills and interests to contribute and be very willing to come in and help with children's activities. We return again to the principle 'Don't assume. Ask.'

Offering the services of the setting in an inclusive way

A setting which has worked at becoming more inclusive for both children and parents has to be sure that it provides families with information that helps them to know about the services the setting can offer. It also needs to help the families gain easy access to the setting and participate fully in it. Advertising the service and admission procedures are therefore a part of inclusion, since they can present barriers if they are not thought about and planned carefully.

Dalvinder's barriers to inclusion in Chapter 1 also included:

◆ vacancies were not advertised in languages familiar to families in the area, or in places where they would see the information

◆ open days to 'come and have a look at what we do' were sometimes held on dates of festivals celebrated by cultures represented in the local community

◆ some parents with restricted literacy skills found the formal and complex English, used in the information that the setting distributed in the locality, difficult to understand

◆ practitioners in the setting projected nervousness about their knowledge and skills in working with disabled children, so parents of disabled children got the impression that their child could not be included

◆ some families could not afford the charges made by the setting

◆ admission forms asked for a child's 'Christian name', and families from other religions or who were not religious felt this meant they were not welcome in the setting.

PUTTING PRINCIPLES INTO PRACTICE

The Ship Street Children's Centre tackled this aspect of inclusion by:

◆ doing some research about the languages read by families in the area (they found some families did not read the languages they expected) and translating their information leaflet about the Centre's services into the appropriate languages (and setting up a system to check the value of this in attracting families to the Centre and whether other languages were necessary)

◆ distributing copies of the leaflet to a range of community and religious organisations in the area, using contacts of members of the staff team

◆ scheduling open days as a team, using knowledge of festivals and double checking dates of festivals of cultures not represented amongst the staff

- consulting the Plain English Campaign website (www.plainenglish.co.uk) about ways of making the style, language and layout of the leaflet as direct and accessible as possible (and moving on to revise other literature the Centre put out)
- redrafting the leaflet to include a paragraph making it clear that the setting welcomed disabled children
- getting a supply of information leaflets about Working Families Tax Credit to give to parents who enquired about places for their children
- redrafting the admissions form to ask for 'first name'.

A note of caution should be sounded about advertising in a language which no one in the setting speaks. An information leaflet welcoming families who speak a particular language can raise false hopes for a family that their needs will be fully catered for and they will find practitioners fluent in their home language. When distributing translated information, a setting should give thought to how to handle enquiries and how to overcome language barriers.

Learning about other cultures

In Chapter 3, emphasis was placed on the central role in anti-discriminatory practice of acknowledging and valuing the differences between individuals and groups in society, and ways of exploring differences with children were considered. Earlier in this chapter, you explored the significance of ensuring that the environment presents a welcome to all children and families in the locality of a setting. Taken together, this all represents **celebrating diversity**.

WHAT DOES THIS MEAN?

Celebrating diversity *involves presenting a positive attitude and approach towards the differences between individuals and groups in society arising from gender, ethnic origins, social, cultural or religious background, family structure, disabilities, sexuality and appearance. It sees these differences as enriching society by making it varied and interesting, rather than something to be fearful of or a source of suspicion or dislike.*

When you take the positive approach of celebrating diversity, you show children that you value and respect them and their family, whoever and whatever they are. You also encourage them to have positive attitudes towards the wide range of ethnic, cultural and religious groups that make up British society. This approach is central to ensuring the well-being and safety of all members of society.

One aspect of celebrating diversity which gets attention in a variety of settings is helping children (even quite young children) begin to learn about cultures other than their own and to show respect for the way other people lead their day-to-day lives. (See also page 48.) It is significant that one of the early learning goals for the end of the EYFS (when a child is five years old) is that children should, 'Begin to know about their own cultures and beliefs and those of other people'. One of the aspects of the area of learning about Knowledge and Understanding of the World is 'children begin to know about their own and other people's cultures in order to understand and celebrate the similarities and differences between them in a diverse society'.

With younger children, your focus is likely to be on such aspects of culture as food, dress, stories and music, and you can introduce other aspects of culture as children's understanding of the world develops. Don't feel you have to have details of all cultures at your fingertips at all times. The important thing is to explore sources of information available from books, magazines, the Internet and, most of all, the families of the children you work with.

PUTTING PRINCIPLES INTO PRACTICE

The Crossways Nursery includes in its storytelling time not only traditional European fairy tales like Red Riding Hood, but also Anansi stories.

At Chipping Hill Primary School, Year 3 were visited by a number of musicians who showed them their instruments and played them. The instruments included a sitar, bagpipes, a balalaika and South American pan pipes. The children also went to performances of a steel band and a gamelan ensemble, and listened to recordings of early English church music and Italian opera arias.

At the same school, Year 6 learned about how a range of festivals are celebrated in various religions and cultures – Eid, Hanukkah and Pesach, Chinese New Year, Holi and Diwali, Nanakshahi, Lammas and Harvest Festival, May Day and Hallowe'en. They found out what each festival celebrated and the associated traditional activities. They compared traditions of fasting such as Lent, Ramadan and Yom Kippur.

The after-school club at the school made their autumn half-term project sampling foods of various cultures. Local families helped to introduce the children to Indian, Caribbean, Chinese and Polish cuisines.

At Highmoor Secondary School, Year 9 found out about customs associated with birth, marriage and death in a range of cultures.

Learning about various cultures can widen children's horizons, making them aware of the wide range of ways in which people approach the events of everyday life. However, its real value will be lost unless they also learn that no single cultural group is better than another, or has a monopoly on the 'right' way to live. Children learn powerful messages from references to 'funny' food or 'strange' music, or to the suggestion that, for example, it is not very clean to eat with one's fingers. The greatest contribution you can make to help children grow up without developing prejudice is to show them respect for all cultures, not valuing one as better than or superior to another. Children will learn this if they see and hear practitioners showing as much respect for other people's culture as they do their own.

This is a tricky area since so many cultures have at their heart a religious faith, with its doctrines, values and customs. It is in the very nature of some religions to insist that theirs is the only correct way and that all others are wrong. This makes the task of promoting respect and tolerance more difficult, especially if your setting is associated with a particular religious group and you are expected to promote a specific faith. On the one hand, everyone should have the right to their own beliefs and traditions; on the other hand, everyone has the responsibility to respect the right of others to adhere to their own faith (including the right to have no belief system), and no one should try to impose their beliefs on others. This is a good example of a right bringing a responsibility in its wake.

A few warnings

Helping children to learn about cultures other than their own is not easy and there are some potential pitfalls to be avoided.

One trap is to introduce children to images and information about various cultures presented in an 'exotic' way. It is unhelpful if you talk only about people who live in 'far-away-lands' and present them as very different from people who live in the UK, perhaps as a bit strange and foreign with peculiar ways of living. This can easily create impressions of their ways being not quite as good or suitable as how things are done in our country. This can have the opposite effect to the one you are aiming for and increase **xenophobia**.

> **WHAT DOES THIS MEAN?**
>
> **Xenophobia** *is the fear or hatred of foreigners or strangers.*

People with many different cultural backgrounds and traditions now live in the UK, so it is more helpful for the children you work with to learn about their way of life than about people who live in other, far-off countries. Children need to know about the cultural traditions and practices of the people they will live next door to and go to work with when they grow up. Above all, they need to feel that cultures other than their own are not strange and alien, but are entirely valid ways of living and entitled to respect. If cultural variations are presented as what happens in other countries, this perpetuates the image of all people with ethnic origins in countries other than the UK as immigrants, not truly British and part of our society.

Another trap is to focus on the 'tourist curriculum', giving children information only about the festivals of various cultures, or the sort of 'souvenir' aspects of life that get presented to tourists – performances like Kandian drummers dancing in Sri Lanka, or costume like a Scottish kilt, or objects like carnival masks from

Venice. Remember that culture is not just about festivals and dress for special occasions – it is primarily about everyday aspects of life based on the patterns of tradition and custom, and that is what you should give priority to. The culture of an ethnic group or nation cannot be summed up in a few artefacts or garments.

REFLECTING

Some settings try to introduce aspects of cultures by using the 'interest table' approach – making a display which is intended to represent a culture. Think about your own culture. What objects or pictures do you think could be put on a display to sum up your culture? Would it in fact be possible to reflect the whole way of life, traditions and values of your culture in a respectful and honest way in such a display? Do you think it is possible to do so for other people's cultures?

You should not expect an individual family or child to represent or speak about aspects of their culture unless they feel happy and comfortable to do so. Some parents may be very willing to contribute, but others will be reluctant. Also, be aware that one family will reflect their own 'take' on their culture, which may be very different from other families' way of living in some of the traditions of the same culture. Remember that there is great diversity within cultures as well as between them.

Perhaps the biggest danger in exploring cultures different from one's own is to learn a little about a culture and then assume that everyone who appears to belong to that general grouping has the same beliefs, follows the same customs, eats the same food, and wears the same clothes. Within any cultural group, there is wide diversity. Not all Indian families are vegetarian or eat highly spiced food, any more than every English family always sits down together to a roast dinner on Sunday. Think how different the various groups within the Christian faith are, from the formal rituals of Catholic worship to the simplicity of Quakers; Judaism has many shades of orthodoxy from Hassidic to liberal synagogues with women rabbis; Buddhism has different traditions in Tibet and Sri Lanka; the Shia and Sunni traditions in Islam are distinctly different. You can never assume that a child who comes from a family which belongs to a particular religion will necessarily follow all that religion's laws, customs and practices in an orthodox way. You have considered several times in this book the need to get to know each child and their family as an individual and find out what parents want for the child, as well as the details of how their culture actually impinges on their daily life – 'Don't assume. Ask.'

If you bear these warnings in mind, your celebration of diversity can make a significant and positive contribution to helping children grow up with respectful attitudes towards cultures different from their own.

Celebrating festivals

Many settings for children have tried to explore various cultures through the festivals of a variety of religions. This needs to be approached with great care and sensitivity and carries another set of warnings. It is particularly important to give considerable thought to the idea of 'celebrating' the festivals of a culture which is not your own, especially if it is one based in a religious faith. Even more thought is needed if no one in the setting comes from the culture or religion involved.

If you work with children of a culture other than your own, you can show respect by finding out from the children's families about the festivals they celebrate and how you can contribute to the children's celebration by, for example, sharing celebration foods or telling traditional stories associated with the festival. It is important that you show the child and family that you are interested in their special occasion and welcome opportunities to be involved in some appropriate way. Even if you and your colleagues belong to the same broad cultural group as the children and their families, be sure to check that they celebrate in the same way that you and your family do – don't make assumptions.

However, if you, your colleagues and the children you work with have no connection with a particular culture, you should ask yourself whether you should be 'celebrating' something which may have great sacred significance for other people. It could be very disrespectful to claim to be celebrating a festival which has no personal meaning for anyone in the setting. If you have a religious faith of your own, you may have strong feelings about non-believers celebrating one of your religion's festivals and copying its sacred elements. This doesn't mean that you can't share factual information with children about the festivals of cultures they are not part of, simply that you should not act as though you and they were active participants in the festival.

If your setting is going to celebrate a festival, you must make sure you do so as thoughtfully and authentically as possible. It is worrying to see some suggestions made in books and magazines to use a festival simply as a theme for craft activities. This cannot be acceptable – making a Hanukkah or Diwali card has no meaning unless some of the symbolism is explained, and is lacking in respect for the significance of such a festival for Jews or Hindus. It can be argued that early years settings should give special thought to how far the children they work with are ready to explore the complex ideas of symbolism and belief which make up religion.

You may reach the conclusion that perhaps the aims of widening cultural awareness and respect are better achieved through focusing on the everyday aspects of cultural diversity rather than on festivals. However, although there are dangers to be avoided there are a number of festivals which your setting may find enjoyable to find out about and include in the experiences and activities you offer the children.

Birthday of Guru Gobind Singh

- Sikh festival in January.
- Celebrates birth in 17th century of prophet teacher who introduced many of the practices of Sikhism.
- Reading of holy book, Granth Sahib, by a team of readers over 48 hours; gurdwaras decorated with flowers, flags and lights; sweet warm food (karah parasaad).

Chinese New Year

- Chinese festival in late January or early February, for three days or more, each year named after an animal.
- Festival of renewal.
- Clearing out homes to get rid of bad luck and negative thoughts; drumming and dances such as the Lion (dragon) dance; decorating the home with colours of red and gold and lights; visiting family, giving flowers, cake and gifts; firecrackers to scare away evil spirit of Nin; young people receive red envelopes containing money and good luck messages.

Holi

- Hindu festival in March or April.
- Celebrates the arrival of spring and the death of the demon of winter, Holika.
- A time of mischief with bonfires and people throwing coloured water and bright powders over one another.

Easter

- Christian festival in March or April. Follows the 40 days of Lent (which begins the day after Shrove Tuesday); Holy Week begins on Palm Sunday and culminates in Good Friday and Easter Sunday.
- Commemorates the crucifixion and resurrection of Jesus Christ.
- Solemnity of church services on Good Friday followed by rejoicing on Easter Sunday.
- Overlaid with secular or pagan symbols of spring related to eggs, young animals and flowers.

Baisakhi or Vaisakhi

- Sikh festival on 13 April.
- New year festival, celebrating foundation of Sikhism and the wearing of the five Ks – kesh (uncut hair), kangha (wooden comb), kara (steel bangle), kirpan (small sword), kancha (underwear).
- Reading of holy book, Granth Sahib, by a team of readers over 48 hours; processions; new clothes (often yellow); bhangra dancing; special food such as yellow rice.

Pesach or Passover

◆ Jewish festival in March or April, lasting eight days.

◆ Commemorates the exodus of the Jewish people from captivity in Egypt with thorough cleaning of the house; reading the story of Moses leading the Israelites when there was no time to let the bread rise; eating unleavened bread (matza) and other symbolic foods at seder (meal).

May Day

◆ Pagan/secular festival on 1 May.

◆ Celebrates the arrival of spring.

◆ Many customs associated with rebirth and fertility, including dancing round the Maypole.

◆ Also an international day of celebration for the trade union movement and the employment rights of working people.

Vaisakha Puja or Wesak or Buddha Day

◆ Buddhist festival in May at the full moon, lasting three days.

◆ Commemorates the birth, enlightenment and passing to nirvana of the Buddha.

◆ Visiting temple, offerings to monks; decorating shrines and homes with flowers and candles; burning incense.

Summer solstice

◆ Pagan festival on 21 June.

◆ Celebrates the longest day in the year.

◆ Bonfires; watching sunrise.

Dhamma Day

◆ Buddhist festival, usually in July.

◆ Celebrates Buddha's first sermon, the Turning of the Wheel of Law, preaching the middle way in life between self-denial and self-indulgence.

Raksha Bandhan

◆ Hindu and Sikh festival in August.

◆ Celebrates the relationship between brothers and sisters, with stories of Krishna's sister binding his cut hand with her sari.

◆ Brothers visit sisters and take them gifts; sisters give brothers raki – decorated bracelets made of red and gold thread and sweets (barfi); painting hands with henna.

Rosh Hashana

◆ Jewish festival in September/October, lasting two days.

◆ New year.

◆ Often celebrated even by otherwise non-observant Jews.

Eid ul-Fitr

◆ Muslim festival at a time between October and January, lasting up to three days.

◆ Celebrates the end of fasting in Ramadan. Commemorates the revelation of the Qur'an to the Prophet Mohammed.

◆ Special prayers of thanksgiving in mosques; giving to charity (zakaat); visiting family and friends; new clothes; special food; women decorating their hands with henna (mehndi); exchange of gifts and cards (with greeting 'Eid Mubarak' – joyful Eid).

Yom Kippur

◆ Jewish festival, usually in October or November, ten days after Rosh Hashana.

◆ Solemn; the day of atonement, for seeking forgiveness and looking to the future; fasting.

Halloween

◆ Pagan festival on 31 October.

◆ In recent years, the Scottish tradition of children dressing up as ghosts (kelpies) and wearing masks, and the US custom of 'trick or treat' has spread to the rest of the UK, with children going door to door dressed as witches or ghosts, seeking sweets; light from pumpkin lanterns.

Diwali

◆ Primarily a Hindu festival, but also celebrated by Sikhs, usually in the last week of October or early in November, and lasting five days.

◆ For Hindus, beginning of new year and commemorates the story of Prince Rama's rescue of his wife Sita from a demon, Ravanna – on his return he was greeted by his people carrying a diwa, a small clay lamp. For Sikhs celebrates the release of leader Guru Har Gobind from prison.

◆ Festival of lights with prayers (especially to Lakshmi, goddess of wealth); lamps, fireworks; cleaning the house and making a pattern (rangoli) at the entrance with rice flour to provide a welcome and good luck; wearing new clothes; exchange of presents and cards (which carry the greeting Sal Mubarak – Happy New Year); visiting family and feasting (including special sweets such as coconut barfi).

Guru Nanak's birthday

◆ Sikh festival in October or November over three days.

◆ Celebrates the birth of the first Sikh guru.

◆ Reading of holy book, Granth Sahib, by a team of readers over 48 hours; gurdwaras decorated with flowers, flags and lights; sweet warm food (karah parasaad).

Hajj

◆ Muslim pilgrimage to the Kaba, the focus of Islamic worship, in the Great Mosque in Mecca. Two months after Ramadan, so any time from December to March, held over three days, culminating in Eid ul-Adha.

◆ Commemorates Abraham's willingness to obey God and sacrifice his son, Isaac.

Hanukkah

◆ Jewish festival in December, lasting eight days.

◆ Commemorates re-dedication of the temple in Jerusalem after its re-capture from the Syrians, and the miracle of a small bottle providing enough oil to light the temple lamp for eight nights until new oil could be purified.

◆ Festival of light; one of the eight candles in the menorah is lit each night until all burn; songs and prayers; special foods; exchange of gifts and cards; traditional games such as dreidle.

Christmas

◆ Christian festival, for most denominations on 25 December; also celebrated in secular ways as a mid-winter festival (which can be linked back to the pagan Yule, connected with the winter solstice) and by people of other faiths.

◆ For Christians, celebrates the birth of Jesus Christ in poverty in Palestine, with the nativity stories of 'no room at the inn', the birth in a stable, angels telling shepherds of the birth and wise men bringing gifts.

◆ For others, a time of symbolism of new hope, the turn of the dark cold winter months towards spring.

◆ Special songs (carols) and church services; homes decorated with lights and greenery; special foods; exchange of cards and presents; visits to family and friends; overlaid with newer traditions of Santa Claus, as well as ancient pre-Christian traditions of the mid-winter festival such as using greenery as decoration.

It is interesting to see the common elements in so many of these festivals – renewal, lights, exchange of gifts, spending time with family, special food and meals. There are many other festivals celebrated by various cultural groups throughout the year. By talking with parents of children in your setting, you will be able to find out what those families celebrate, when and how, and decide when it is appropriate to join in. You should give careful thought to how you will broaden children's understanding of the special occasions celebrated in cultures other than their own.

If you take a critical approach to constant reflection on:

◆ your setting's environment, resources, routines and policies

◆ your own practice,

you will be making a valuable contribution to ensuring inclusion for all children and families. You will be securing for them their rights to have equal access to and equal chances to benefit from the services provided in the setting.

Chapter 5

From there to here: history and law

In this chapter, we look at how the past has influenced the present, and trace some of the origins of the prejudice, discrimination and stereotypes that we face in our society today. We see how we arrived at the issues of today from the events of history and the attitudes which prevailed in the past. We look at the various laws which have been passed by British governments to try to promote the rights of both adults and children, in particular to prevent discrimination. We also explore some of the complex issues we face today in relation to inclusion and equality in our diverse society. We do this in the context of:

◆ ethnicity and culture

◆ gender

◆ disability

◆ sexuality.

We also look at legislation concerned with equality and discrimination in broad terms, and at the United Nations Convention on the Rights of the Child. Finally, we consider the issue of positive discrimination.

The **prejudice, discrimination** and **stereotypes** which exist in our society today have their origins in the past.

> ### WHAT DOES THIS MEAN?
>
> **Prejudice** *is a judgment or opinion, often negative, of a person or group which is made without careful consideration of accurate relevant information. It normally leads to the view that some people are inferior to others, and of less worth and significance.*
>
> **Discrimination** *means treating someone less or more favourably than other people because they or their family are seen as belonging to a particular group in society. Discrimination obviously has a positive side – the people who are not discriminated against benefit from an unfair advantage. However, it is the negative side of discrimination which needs our attention because it limits the opportunities that some people have in life.*
>
> **Stereotypes** *are generalisations about a person, assumptions (usually inaccurate) that because he or she is part of a particular group, that individual will:*
> - *have certain characteristics*
> - *have the same needs as all other members of that group*
> - *will or should behave in a particular way.*

Exploring some historical background can help you understand how stereotypes, prejudice and discrimination have developed, the progress that has been made in overcoming them, and what remains to be achieved. This can be a source of motivation to contribute in your own way to continuing this progress, and can encourage you to develop your practices in working with children and families. It can also help you understand why we need a framework of legislation to show the way that equality and discrimination issues should be tackled in our society, and appreciate what lies behind the issues we are still grappling with in the present day.

Ethnicity and culture

The origins of prejudice and stereotypical views of ethnicity and culture in British society today lie in the country's economic, social and political history. Laws have been passed to help prevent certain types of behaviour, but we still face some major issues which we all have a part to play in solving. Learning more about issues like imperialism and the slave trade, immigration and multiculturalism will help you to deepen your understanding of attitudes in Britain today, and support your determination to play a part in effective equality and anti-discrimination practice in your work with children.

Many of the roots of **racism** in the UK lie in the history of Britain's empire (imperialism) and its involvement in the slave trade.

Racism *consists of the attitudes and actions, often based on prejudice and deriving from stereotypes, that discriminate against certain people because they are seen as belonging to a particular 'race' which is seen as inferior to another.*

Racist attitudes include the view that people of some ethnic origins are less important or valuable than those of other ethnic origins, that they cannot be expected to benefit from education, or that they are not capable of achieving or of taking responsibility.

Imperialism

Over the centuries, several nations have created huge empires – Greece under Alexander the Great, ancient Turkey, Rome and, perhaps the most powerful imperial power of all, Britain.

As a group of islands, Britain has always been a sea-going and trading nation. The exploratory expeditions of adventurers like Walter Raleigh and Francis Drake in the reign of Elizabeth I in the 16th century laid the basis of an expansion of British trade with the world beyond Europe. The industrial revolution which took place in the 18th and 19th centuries stimulated this trade, as the demand for raw materials and markets for manufactured goods expanded. At this time, too, the British missionary movement stepped up its efforts to take Christianity to people of other faiths.

Britain began to colonise the countries where its trading interests had taken them, imposing its rule on the people of those countries. Other European powers, such as France, Spain, the Netherlands, Portugal, and later Germany and Italy, did the same in Africa, South America and Southern Asia. For example, the island of Sri Lanka was colonised in turn by the Portuguese, the Dutch and then the British. But none of these other countries' colonies was as extensive as the British Empire, which at its height covered 25 per cent of the world's land surface.

British colonial rule set out to impose British values and institutions on the populations of the colonies. The cultural and belief systems of the colonised countries in Africa, Asia and South America were largely ignored, despite the antiquity of their architecture and art and the contribution their knowledge of science and mathematics subsequently made to European learning. With few honourable exceptions, most British colonials took no interest in the daily way of life of the people of the countries that they settled in, and certainly did not adopt their customs or respect their religions. Native Americans in the United States and Canada, Aborigines in Australia and Maoris in New Zealand were driven from their ancestral lands, which were taken over by Europeans.

British rule did bring some advantages to the people of the Empire, such as the transport infrastructure of railways, but at a great cost. The people of the colonies were expected to learn to speak English and take on British values and ways of

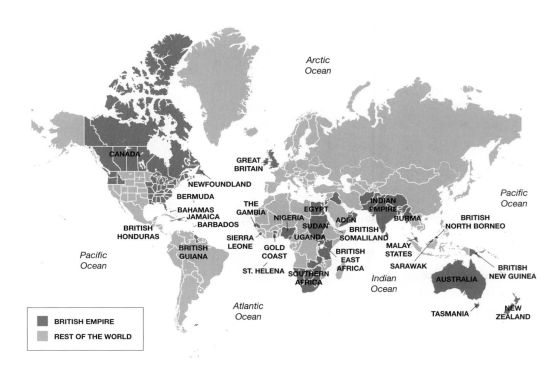

At its height, the British Empire was very extensive

living. Indeed, they were expected to be grateful to have been brought the opportunity to abandon their old 'heathen and primitive' ways. Everything British was regarded as superior and everything of the colonised people, 'the natives', as uncivilised. The Empire was seen as 'civilising' people whose own culture and achievements were valueless. Lord Macaulay, the historian, wrote that the British Empire represented the 'triumph of reason over barbarism'.

FOOD FOR FURTHER THOUGHT

Find out about the British Empire and the attitudes of the British people who went to live in the colonies. You will find websites useful; try www.learningcurve.gov.uk/empire. You may get some insight into prejudiced, arrogant and intolerant imperialist attitudes by reading novels set against the background of the British Raj in India, like *A Passage to India* by E.M.Forster or *The Jewel in the Crown* by Paul Scott.

The part played by black people from the countries of the Empire, fighting on the side of Britain in the two World Wars of the 20th century, has largely been underrated or even ignored.

The British Empire was dismantled in the second part of the 20th century, but its influence is still strong. The historical background of the Empire provides part of the explanation for the tendency, still apparent in Britain, to marginalise the culture, language and religions of black people. The certainty of the colonisers that British ways were the best, the only proper way to live, remains the basis of racist attitudes today. These live on in suspicion of and lack of respect for people who look, dress, eat and worship differently from those who are seen as traditionally British.

The slave trade

The slave trade is the greatest shame in the history of Britain's trade with the rest of the world. In the triangle of this trade, huge numbers of Africans were bought from African slavers who captured people, mostly in West Africa, and sold them for 'trade goods' manufactured in Britain, including firearms. The captives were shipped to North America and the West Indies in dreadful conditions and many died on the journey. Those who survived were sold to owners of plantations growing cotton, tobacco and sugar for export back to Europe. These slaves were the possessions of the plantation owners who could use them as they pleased. They were seen as animals to be put to work on the land; they were beaten, raped and murdered. Estimates of those who perished as a result of this appalling trade vary from 12 to 20 million (compared with 6 million who are thought to have died in the Holocaust during the Second World War in Europe).

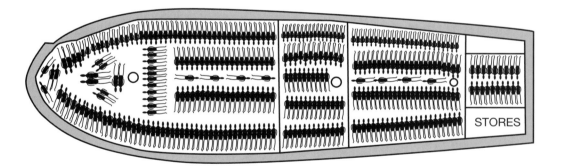

Slaves were shipped in dreadful conditions

Fortunes were made from the triangular trade, and citizens of Bristol and Liverpool accumulated wealth from the slave trade. The way those cities honoured slave traders can still be seen in the names of streets and public buildings; Penny Lane made famous by the Beatles was named after a slaver.

Find out about the slave trade and Britain's role in it. There are many websites to explore, such as www.nmm.ac.uk/freedom/. It can be harrowing to read about this grim trade in novels like *A Respectable Trade* by Philippa Gregory or *Sacred Hunger* by Barry Unsworth. Visiting Liverpool's museum concerning the slave trade is a moving and disturbing experience.

The slave trade ended in 1807 and slavery was abolished in the British Empire in the middle of the 19th century, but, like imperialism, its effects are still seen today. The belief that certain people can legitimately be treated inhumanely and bought and sold as commodities takes many generations to fade, and underlies some of the low expectations about the potential of people of African Caribbean origins.

FOOD FOR FURTHER THOUGHT

Imperialism and slavery together have left a legacy of racism in the form of seeing black people as incapable of contributing to human progress. Explore the history of black people which contradicts this, such as the contributions to medicine and science of Charles Drew, Garret Morgan and Mary Seacole.

Mary Seacole (1805–81) was a pioneering nurse

Guilt and apologies

The disadvantaged lives of black people in some countries is an aftermath of slavery, and some white families still benefit from the wealth their ancestors generated through the slave trade. This leads some white British people to feel distressed and guilty when they learn about imperialism and slavery.

Rather than feeling guilty, it is more productive to accept our responsibility to try to play a part in changing British society for the future. People who work with children have great power in achieving this. If today's generation does not recognise what has happened and become determined to resist the inequalities which are associated with racism, then we would be guilty and would fail the children who are the next generation.

There has been considerable discussion of whether Britain should apologise in some way for the slave trade. The bicentenary of its abolition in 2007 was marked by some leading politicians making public statements regretting Britain's role in the trade and practice of slavery. However, many people take the view that it is impossible to give a genuine apology for something that happened hundreds of years ago. It is argued that none of us can take responsibility for the actions of past generations; both they and those who were directly affected in such terrible ways are long since dead. Some people therefore see it as being more important to mark the horror of slavery by fighting the aftermath of racism it has left and the evils of the different forms in which slavery exists today, such as the trafficking of vulnerable women and children for sexual purposes.

European culture

Another way of beginning to understand (though not accept) the suspicion and fear of black people which often provoke racism is to look at European visual culture and the English language.

When we look at various forms of art, especially medieval and Renaissance painting, we find black and other dark colours being used to indicate evil creatures or unknown fears. This is probably derived from our basic human fear of darkness. I shall never forget the blazing anger of a black American woman who I stood next to in the Sistine Chapel in Rome over 40 years ago, as she looked at how Michelangelo had painted the devil as black. She interpreted the artist's choice of colour for the devil as saying that black people were evil; others would argue that he simply used the dark colour of night and fearfulness. Whatever the truth of this, dark colours are likely to have negative connotations for people who inherit the cultural visual images of Western European art.

We shall look in Chapter 6 at how the word 'black' in the English language has developed negative meanings, like 'black-hearted', and is used about things which are to be feared, like 'black magic'. This, too, adds to deeply ingrained perceptions of black as undesirable.

Immigration

Undoubtedly, much of the negative feeling towards people of other ethnic and cultural origins in Britain today is closely linked to continuing immigration to this country. Immigration to Britain is not new or recent; **immigrants** have been coming in sizable numbers to live in this country for over 2,000 years.

> ## WHAT DOES THIS MEAN?
>
> An **immigrant** *is a person who has come to live in a country, emigrating from the country where they lived previously.*

The Celtic and Pictish people who lived in Britain in 55 BCE saw the invasion of the Romans. In subsequent centuries, other invaders followed – the Angles, Saxons and Jutes (from Northern Europe), the Danes and Vikings (from Scandinavia) and Normans (with the invasion of William the Conqueror from France in 1066). There was also immigration of refugees like Huguenots (Protestants from France and the Netherlands in 1685), and Jews (from all over Europe and Russia, especially in the 19th century). Many of the UK's current inhabitants are of mixed ethnic origins because they are descendants of these invaders and immigrants.

The Empire and the slave trade resulted in black people coming to live in Britain several generations ago. Many more came to live here after the Second World War, when labour shortages led to people in the Caribbean being encouraged to come to work and live in the UK by employers like London Transport, which advertised in the West Indies in the early 1950s for bus drivers. In the late 1950s and 1960s, others came from India and Pakistan to work in the textile factories in the north west of England. The jobs these immigrants came to do were mostly jobs white British people were reluctant to do because of low pay and poor conditions.

In the 20th century, a sizable population of people whose origins were in the Indian sub-continent lived in Kenya and Uganda in East Africa, often running businesses and becoming prosperous, but in the 1970s many of them were persecuted and expelled. The colonised peoples of the British Empire had always been presented with the idea of England offering the best way of life, and they had a legal right to migrate to the UK, which many talked of as 'the home country'. It is not surprising that when they were forced to leave the country where they and several generations of their family had lived, they chose to emigrate to Britain. Shortly after, another group of immigrants were Vietnamese people fleeing the aftermath of the war with the United States.

At the end of the 20th century, refugees from countries at war, such as Somalia and the former Yugoslavia, or from countries where there is a persecuted minority, such as the Kurds from Turkey, sought a place of safety in the UK. In this century, the expansion of the European Community has brought **economic migrants** here from Eastern Europe, in search of employment.

WHAT DOES THIS MEAN?

Economic migrants *are people who migrate to another country in search of greater economic well-being. This is achieved through better employment and other opportunities than are available in their country of origin.*

Economic migrants often take unskilled manual and seasonal jobs, such as work on the land (in the UK this is especially true in East Anglia), for which employers struggle to recruit sufficient workers from the local workforce.

FOOD FOR FURTHER THOUGHT

What do you think about people who seek to be economic migrants, moving to another country where they hope prospects of employment and standards of living will benefit them and their family (whether that family remains in their country of origin or joins them in their new country)? Find out about the Irish and Scottish people who went to live in the USA and Canada in the 19th century as result of events such as potato famine and the 'clearances' of the Highlands.

Immigration is linked to negative attitudes and prejudice based on ethnicity and culture. Immigrants are, by definition, strangers, foreign and different from the people they come to live amongst, and people are generally slow to develop positive and welcoming feelings about those they see as 'other'. This inherent fear of outsiders who are different and unknown is played on by some politicians and journalists, who talk of immigrants 'swamping' Britain, or a 'tide' or 'flood'. The use of these words suggest that huge numbers of immigrants are entering the country in an unstoppable way which will demolish all before it. The large number of people leaving the UK to live elsewhere is usually not factored into this alarming imagery of an overwhelming influx.

Alarmist talk of how immigration threatens the 'British way of life' creates worries that those already living in the UK will in some way lose out to the newcomers. This anxiety usually centres around issues about employment and housing. These feelings are intensified by the rhetoric of right-wing political groups who peddle inaccurate information, such as exaggerating the proportion of the population in Britain which is made up of people from minority ethnic groups, and distorting figures about employment and housing in order to stir up racial hatred.

FOOD FOR FURTHER THOUGHT

Find out some accurate current facts about minority ethnic groups in the UK. For example, in the 2001 census, 87 per cent of the population of England classified themselves as white. Find out about comparative unemployment rates, housing and education for various ethnic groups. The Commission for Racial Equality (CRE) published free factsheets which are now available from the Commission for Equality and Human Rights at www.equalityhumanrights.com (look in the CRE legacy web pages).

Despite the facts about the lower employment rates and poorer housing of many minority ethnic groups, whether immigrants or second or later generations, immigrants as a group have been demonised in the public eye. Even the more responsible parts of the media rarely point out the positive side of immigration: how Britain benefits when people come from other countries to live and work here. The image (only partly a stereotype) of the hard-working, highly-skilled Polish plumber sits alongside the general recognition that the National Health Service would grind to a halt without the doctors, nurses and other medical professionals who have come here from abroad, providing the skills our country needs. (The downside of this is that their skills are lost to the countries they come from, which are often poor and deprived and which can ill afford to lose their highly skilled workers.)

Limits on the numbers of people migrating to live in this country ('immigration control') have been in effect for several decades. The Commonwealth Immigrants Act was passed in 1962, and between then and 2006, there were a further twelve Acts of Parliament seeking, in some way or other, to control the number of immigrants coming to settle here. However, desperate people will always find ways of getting into the country and their desperation is exploited by people smugglers who charge large sums of money.

Many economic migrants who come to the UK to work are exploited by unscrupulous employers, especially if they have come illegally. In 2004, several cockle pickers of Chinese origins were drowned in the treacherous currents and tides of Morecambe Bay, Lancashire. The subsequent enquiries revealed that they were hired by ruthless 'gang masters', who used the cocklers' illegal immigrant status to force them to work in dangerous conditions for very little pay. It seems that some employers are prepared to break UK laws about checking the credentials of the people they employ and paying the minimum wage, and often charge large sums for poor accommodation. Illegal immigrants are in a weak position in resisting this exploitation, unable to seek the protection of the law since they need to keep their presence in the UK hidden. Some immigrants are tempted by promises of chances to earn what they perceive as high wages in order to support their families back home, but find on their arrival that they are trapped in unending debt to the criminals who smuggled them into the UK. Probably the worst aspect of this is the young women who are brought here for purposes of prostitution.

The majority of immigrants settle in London and the south east, but there are sizable minority ethnic populations in areas of the north west of England, especially the old mill towns, and in the Midlands, particularly in Leicester, with smaller numbers in areas right across the UK. It is understandable that when people migrate to a country, they tend to settle in an area where there are already people with ethnicity and cultural traditions similar to their own. This offers them support and the familiarity of being able to find places of worship and others who speak the same language. However, minority ethnic populations are found in all parts of the UK.

Immigration is likely to continue to be high on political agendas. Many parts of Britain are densely populated, with great pressure on housing and the infrastructure of education, health and transport provision. There is understandable resentment from some UK workers who feel that wage levels are kept low by the supply of immigrants, especially those here illegally. Yet the UK needs to admit people from overseas who can contribute skills in short supply here. Unfortunately, the negative attitudes which have developed towards economic migrants have extended to **refugees** and **asylum seekers**.

WHAT DOES THIS MEAN?

*A **refugee** is someone who is fleeing from their homeland because they can no longer live there, possibly because of famine, war or natural disaster like floods, or because they are facing persecution (perhaps because of their ethnic group or religion, or support for a political cause). When a refugee tries to find a safe place to live, away from these dangers, they become an **asylum seeker**.*

It is important to remember that refugees seeking asylum are likely to have survived frightening and traumatic experiences, and need the sympathy and support of their fellow human beings, as well as a safe place to live. Difficult decisions are involved in ascertaining whether someone is a genuine or a 'bogus' asylum seeker – whether they have a 'well-founded' fear for their safety or are using claims of persecution to mask their intentions to be an economic migrant.

REFLECTING

If you had to flee your homeland because of some traumatic and frightening experience, and managed to find asylum in a safer country, how would you hope the people in your new country would treat you? What problems do you think you might have, and what help would you need?

More than skin deep

A lot of the issues surrounding racism are focused on differences in skin colour, but there are other forms of racism focused on issues of culture and religion, as you saw in Chapter 2. It is important, for example, to understand the history of anti-semitism, which is deep-seated in Britain, as in much of the rest of Europe.

WHAT DOES THIS MEAN?

Anti-semitism *is prejudice and discrimination against Jewish people.*

Anti-semitism still exists in all of Europe, including Britain; it has existed for longer than racism directed at black people. Persecution of Jews in Britain dates back at least to medieval times, when anti-semitism was an intrinsic part of Christian beliefs. The slaughter of the Jews in York in the 12th century is one example of violence against Jewish people in the UK, but there have been many other atrocities and a fundamental prejudice against Jews right across Europe for hundreds of years. The Holocaust in Europe during the Second World War is remembered with horror, but we have to recognise that its origins did not lie in Nazi Germany in the 1930s; rather, it was the extreme outcome of the persecution and exclusion of Jewish people that had been persisting for many centuries.

In recent years, since the terrorist outrages of 11 September 2001 in New York and 7 July 2005 in London, the UK has seen the growth of **Islamophobia**.

WHAT DOES THIS MEAN?

Islamophobia *is fear of Muslim people and the religion of Islam. This fear leads to prejudice and discrimination.*

The understandable revulsion against the motivation of those who were responsible for the death and maiming of so many people in those two terrible events led to a wave of feeling against all Muslims. The terrorists were a small number of extreme or fundamentalist young Muslim men whose views were not representative of the values of the majority of the followers of the Islamic faith. However, their actions affected attitudes to all Muslims. Women whose way of dressing marked them out as Muslim were abused, even spat at, in public places in Britain. Mosques were attacked and damaged. Muslim communities felt great hostility directed towards them, and some have responded by becoming more isolated from mainstream British society. Moderate, law-abiding Muslims have struggled to explain that the Qur'an does not exhort the killings of non-Muslims, and to root out the mullahs in some extremist mosques who have 'radicalised' some young men. Such men have often been vulnerable to extremist teachings because of the poor opportunities they have experienced and the barriers they have encountered in succeeding in British society. The resentment created by experiences like this has been a breeding ground for the thinking that resorts to violent acts and lashes out against perceived enemies. This has been a wake-up call for us all to re-commit ourselves to combating lack of opportunity and striving for greater understanding and respect across cultural groups.

Another cultural group that has suffered a long history of suspicion and persecution is gypsies, whose independent way of life has always provoked negative feelings from the majority population. Gypsies were persecuted and died in the concentration camps of Nazi Germany, along with Jews, homosexuals and disabled people. There is still open discrimination and even violence against gypsies in some parts of Eastern Europe, and much prejudice and discrimination against all travellers in the UK and Ireland (see also page 51).

Even within white British society, there is a certain amount of stereotyping and even prejudice and hostility between the English, Welsh, Scottish and Irish peoples, and even within England we see this between North and South.

Multiculturalism: integration or separatism?

In the last few decades of the 20th century, the response of several local authorities to the presence of minority ethnic people in some of the UK's main centres of population was to make efforts to support those people to retain their culture and hand it onto their children. The co-existence of groups of people with diverse cultural traditions was seen as a richness benefiting UK society. Much was made of the idea of 'multicultural Britain', and local authorities funded projects which involved activities such as language, music, dance and drama derived from the cultures of the ethnic groups in their area. Attempts were made to accommodate various religions and languages, and to show respect for them as being as valid as any traditionally British counterpart. These policies and practice came to be known as 'multiculturalism', and were seen as a sign of Britain's open, tolerant, liberal and democratic values. Events such as the Notting Hill Carnival, held each summer in London, were seen as enriching cultural life for everyone.

The Notting Hill carnival celebrates London's multicultural diversity

More recently, concerns are being expressed by political commentators and in the media that 'multiculturalism has failed'. It is thought that the good intentions of respecting people's cultures has actually hindered integration by perpetuating the development of isolated groups of minority ethnic people, with peoples of different ethnicities living parallel but separate lives in the same locality. The fear is expressed that this isolation of groups in society impedes the development of mutual understanding and respect for diverse ways of life, leading to divisions in society, and mutual suspicion and intolerance grows. This seems to be particularly marked in some of the towns of the north west of England.

The most extreme supporters of integration suggest that everyone who lives in this country should adjust to 'one culture, one framework' for living their lives. A more generally-held view seems to be for the need for everyone who comes to live in the UK to accept 'British values' and live in accordance with generally accepted standards of behaviour. This line of reasoning often runs into difficulties because of the challenge of defining 'British values' as distinct from anyone else's. Many of the suggestions for what the term means include ideas such as 'fairness', which are certainly not exclusive to British society (nor, indeed totally accepted and put into effect in British society).

There are various points of focus for the debate about multiculturalism versus integration. One is language: should everyone who lives in Britain be expected to learn to speak, and possibly read, English to the level they need to function in their everyday lives? Concerns have also been raised by some politicians that significant numbers of newly-arrived immigrants do not acquire even basic functional levels of spoken English. This can be especially true of many women in certain cultures which discourage them from participating in activities outside the home or their immediate cultural circle. There are two points to consider in this:

◆ On the one hand, there is concern about the amount of money spent by local authorities, education, health and justice services on interpretation and translation (bearing in mind that in some local authority areas, as many as 20 to 30 different languages may be spoken). It is suggested that the money spent on these services would be better spent on teaching English to more people.

◆ On the other hand, we must remember that even if someone can acquire enough English to get by with ordinary daily life, they may need additional help to understand and make themselves understood when in contact with officialdom.

It would be unreasonable to expect first generation immigrants to speak only English and become adept at reading and writing it. Also, it is understandable that later generations want to preserve some appreciation of the language of their country of origin, so they can retain understanding of the literature of their culture. In particular, refugees struggling to overcome past traumas and make a new life in a new country are likely to take a while to acquire even the basics of

English. However, we should also think about the implications for children who are born in this country but whose acquisition of the language they will need to succeed in the wider society – in this country, English – is delayed because the women folk (mother, aunts, grandmother) who care for them in their earliest years do not speak English. You saw in Chapter 4 the support needed to help such children become bilingual.

Another focus is dress. In the early days of multiculturalism, there was delight at colourful saris and the law recognised turbans as an alternative to helmets for motor cyclists (albeit after a struggle). However, the recent focus on the Muslim population has brought less warm feelings towards the wearing of the hijab (headscarf) and hostility to the niqab (veil). Again, it seems entirely reasonable that people should choose to dress in the way their parents and forbears did, to maintain customs and traditions. But the niqab hides a woman's face, and when something is hidden, feelings of suspicion and anxiety arise, which may explain some people's reactions to the veil. This issue is overlain, too, with suggestions of limitations of women's rights. Some people express concern that some women are put under pressure from the men in their families and communities to wear hijabs or niqabs. However, there are many Muslim women who publicly declare that they wear headscarves or veils from their own free choice and decisions, based on their own understanding of the traditions of their faith. This is a complex debate with no clear cut answers and you are likely to read and hear a great deal about it.

REFLECTING

Should minority ethnic groups be encouraged or even forced to blend in with British customs? Or should it be accepted that people will go on wanting to celebrate their cultural roots, and should such differences be tolerated or even encouraged?

How far can either approach be taken? Should public money be spent on translating official written materials or re-directed to teaching English as an additional language? Should a woman giving evidence in court be required to show her face, or a woman be required to remove her veil for identification purposes at passport controls? Should traditions and customs such as forced marriages, honour killings and female circumcision be permitted because of claims that they are long established and/or based on religious teachings?

The justice system in the UK has made it clear that forced marriages, honour killings (murdering a woman because it is claimed that she brought shame on a family, for example by choosing a partner outside her cultural group or sex outside of marriage – even rape) and genital mutilation (female circumcision) are illegal in Britain. Whatever the longevity of the tradition and whether or not such practices have foundation in religious teachings, the human rights of the individuals involved (primarily women) take precedence and mean that these activities are condemned by British society.

The part played by faith schools in the issues of separation or integration is contentious but must be addressed. It is argued that by segregating children into one school where they have little or no contact with children of other religious, cultural or ethnic groups, divisions in society are exacerbated. If children do not meet and interact and learn about one another when they are young, they are more likely to grow up with mistaken stereotyped and prejudiced views of 'the others'. In addition, the central aim of such a school based on one faith is likely to be to promote one religion as superior to all others and that tends to reinforce separatist views. The perpetuation of the sectarian divisions in Northern Irish society has been underpinned by separate schooling for Protestant and Catholic children.

This may be a difficult issue for you to tackle in your working life if you are employed in a faith-based setting. There is also a logic that says that if we do not give public funding to support minority faiths such as Islam, Sikhism and Judaism to set up their own schools, we will have to withdraw public funding from Christian-based schools. This would have far-reaching effects on the British education system; many schools are Church of England (C of E) schools and withdrawal of state funding could lead to the closure of these schools – in many villages, the C of E school is the only school.

What the law says

The way we interact with one another in society is regulated by the laws of the land in which we live. Laws set a framework of what society as a whole considers to be appropriate or inappropriate behaviour; they set limits to what citizens may do; they describe what must or must not be done. Laws cannot alone change prejudiced attitudes and assumptions or influence the way people think, but they are important in reducing practical aspects of discrimination. In the UK, the state has intervened to pass laws which limit certain types of behaviour in the context of ethnicity.

The Race Relations Act 1976 aimed to protect people from discrimination on grounds of ethnic or national origin or colour (but not religion). This includes:

◆ direct discrimination (such as refusing to admit a child to a setting because he or she is black)

◆ indirect discrimination (such as allocating places in a setting by relying on 'word of mouth' rather than advertising openly in the local community, because this could lead to exclusion of families of specific ethnic groups who do not get to hear of vacancies).

All laws are broad in their intentions and it is only when they are applied to real situations that detailed meanings are worked out and precedents are set by case law. Case law has established that Sikhs and gypsies/Romanies are distinct ethnic groups entitled to the protection of the Race Relations Act.

The 1976 Act set up the Commission for Racial Equality (CRE), giving it statutory authority to enforce the Act, using its legal powers to combat discrimination and promote equality. It has worked to improve relationships between people of different ethnic groups, raise public awareness of discrimination and win support for efforts to create a fairer and more equal society.

More legislation followed in subsequent years:

◆ The Public Order Act of 1986 made incitement to racial hatred an offence.

◆ The Racial and Religious Hatred Act 2006 did the same for incitement to religious hatred.

◆ The Race Relations (Amendment) Act 2000 put a duty on public authorities to promote equality of opportunity and work towards the elimination of discrimination on grounds of ethnicity.

◆ The 2006 Equality Act made it illegal to discriminate in the provision of goods and services on the grounds of religion or belief. It also replaced the CRE with the Commission for Equality and Human Rights (see page 192).

The Children Act 1989 and Care Standards Act 2000 set out the arrangements for the registration and inspection of early years and childcare provision. The Acts actively encouraged anti-discriminatory practice and set requirements for providers to take account of the religious, racial, cultural and linguistic needs of children. People who work with young children were expected to have knowledge and commitment to treat all children as individuals and 'with equal concern'.

The Childcare Act 2006 introduced the statutory framework of the Early Years Foundation Stage (EYFS). This requires registered providers to 'have and implement an effective policy about ensuring equality of opportunities', including 'how the provision will promote and value diversity and differences', 'how the provision will encourage children to value and respect others', and 'how inappropriate attitudes and practices will be challenged'. This legislation sets a strong framework, but its effects can only be as effective as the daily practice of individual practitioners, which in turn relies on your readiness to take on new ideas and turn them into reality.

REFLECTING

You can find out more about these laws from www.equalityhumanrights.com or www.homeoffice.gov.uk . How does your setting comply with these laws in its policy and practice?

Gender

For gender, you can again look to the past to enhance your understanding of stereotypes and discrimination, and of the need for a legislative framework.

Women today have many rights and privileges, and in many areas of life have equality with men. The physical aspects of the work of caring for a home and family were made much less onerous and time-consuming by the development of the technology of vacuum cleaners, fridges and freezers, electric irons and washing machines. Girls and young women growing up in the 21st century have more opportunities and choices than any previous generation.

However, it would be easy to take for this for granted and forget how recent a development it is. We should remember that until well into the 20th century, women (especially married women) in Britain had restricted legal human rights and didn't have access to many of the opportunities in education and employment enjoyed by women today. It took 30 attempts to change the law in Britain before women over the age of 30 years were given the right to vote in 1918 (and it was another 10 years before women got that right on equal terms with men). Until 1886, the law assumed that children were the father's possession and a mother had no right to seek custody of her own children. Until 1923, it was more difficult for a wife to divorce a husband than vice versa. Even after the Second World War (1939–45), women who were teachers and civil servants had to give up their jobs when they got married, and they did not achieve the right by law to equal pay with men until 1970. Maternity leave and pay were only introduced in 1975. It was also as late as the 1970s before financial and other institutions began to recognise women as independent individuals; until then it was common practice to require a woman's husband or father to sign that he would guarantee any loan she obtained.

The battle for gender equality has not been completely won and women and girls still face measurable restrictions on opportunities in their lives compared with their male counterparts. Women's earnings remain significantly lower on average than men's (women's average earnings are 70 per cent of men's). In many occupations, women find their chances of promotion are restricted, especially once they have to juggle their work life with their responsibilities as a mother. Although men, too, find that becoming a parent brings responsibilities and earmarks part of their time, women are the ones whose work prospects are most affected. Care of elderly and disabled family members also continues to be done largely by women.

Most of the more overt barriers to the education and training of girls, like the old eleven-plus exam and university and medical school gendered intake (see pages 37–8), have disappeared. However, girls still tend to get guided into apprenticeships in hairdressing and working with young children, which are much less well paid than plumbing and car maintenance (which are largely the preserve of boys). Even though girls do better than boys in maths and science in school (as in all other subjects), they are still under-represented on science, engineering and technology courses in further and higher education, and so women are still in a small minority in related careers. There may be an element of this which reflects attitudes of previous generations to the appropriateness of women engaging in work involving machinery: before the First World War (1914–18), all typists were men because it was thought that typewriters would take away women's femininity in some way.

The women's movement began to gather momentum in the 19th century and focused primarily on the right to vote – suffrage. During the First and Second World Wars, women took on dangerous and physically hard roles which had previously only been held by men – working in factories and on the land – and nurseries were opened to provide childcare. Women showed that they could be men's equals, but once the wars ended they were expected to go back to their traditional roles and many nurseries were closed. The feminist or women's liberation movement in the later decades of the 20th century asserted robustly the equal (or even superior) value of women and the rights of women and girls in the arenas of education and employment, as well as influencing changes in women's role in the family and home. One of its preoccupations was the key factor of women's control over their own fertility, through contraception and, more controversially, abortion. It was also concerned with male violence towards women and helped to focus attention on domestic violence.

Women working in a munitions factory during the Second World War

Look at the evidence in the written and broadcast media about the balance of men and women holding positions of power in Britain today. Find out about the people who make laws – how many women MPs are there in Westminster compared with men? Are things any better in the Scottish Parliament and Welsh Assembly? Find out, too, about those who implement the laws – how many senior women police officers are there; how many female judges and magistrates? What about the top posts in industry and commerce – how many women break through the 'glass ceiling'? You may find the website of the Fawcett Society (www.fawcettsociety.org.uk) an informative and interesting starting point.

The denial of equality of opportunity to girls and women, both in the past and lingering on, arises from long-held opinions about the respective value of males and females, and the appropriate roles for men and women in society. The value placed on males and females varies from society to society and culture to culture, but there are many examples of women holding subordinate roles to men, and of boys being more highly prized than girls. In certain social classes, there is an emphasis on the need for a son, whether to inherit land and a title or simply to 'carry on the family name'. Many religions debar women from playing an active or full part in rituals and ceremonies or holding ecclesiastical office, and even regard them as 'unclean' after childbirth and when menstruating.

It cannot be denied that in many places at many times there have been and still are widespread attitudes that see females as inferior to males. Sometimes this is expressed in assertions that men have intellectual or creative abilities that are superior to those of women. Individual women in the past have proved this wrong by demonstrating their abilities, talents and creativity in many fields of human activity, but their achievements have often been given less prominence.

FOOD FOR FURTHER THOUGHT

Find out about women artists, writers, scientists and travellers from previous centuries whose abilities and achievements have been given less prominence than those of men. Look for information about Berthe Morisot (one of the 19th century French impressionist artists), Aphra Behn (in the 17th century, the first Englishwoman to earn a living by writing, as well as being a spy!), Mary Somerville (the brilliant 19th century mathematician), Freya Stark (the explorer and writer), and other pioneering women.

Mary Somerville (1780–1872), the mathematician and science writer

A key factor, of course, is the assumption that women's natural biological role of bearing children inevitably excludes them from giving sufficient time to creative activities or taking responsibilities in the world of work or in public roles. This is coupled with the belief (widely held among many women as well as men) that they should devote the majority of their time to domestic and caring responsibilities. The lower status of women is exacerbated by the fact that society tends to attach a lower status to those domestic and caring activities than it does to the activities undertaken by men outside the domestic sphere – even though women's caring work is central to the welfare of communities. It has been argued that men have much to gain from excluding women from power and influence, while depending on them to run the practical details of their lives – cooking, cleaning and childcare.

Sometimes, the arguments about the 'proper' relevant roles for men and women in society crystallise into whether it is right or wrong for women, especially mothers, to work outside the home. At frequent intervals, the media seize on research that 'proves' that children, especially the youngest, suffer when their mother goes out to work, and women are made to feel guilty about the choices they make about earning a living. This research usually turns out to indicate that children who spend too much time in poor-quality childcare services fare less well than their contemporaries, rather than measuring the effect of their separation from their mother for some part of their day and week. Government policy over the last ten years has emphasised the importance of supporting women to work outside the home as a key route to lifting children out of poverty.

Even though many battles for women's equality have been fought and apparently won, we must still endeavour to ensure that girls and young women have opportunities open to them which enable them to make their own choices and decisions, not limited to narrow options. Stereotypical opinions lurk just below the surface of society and emerge at regular intervals. This matters for everyone – men as well as women. If we deny opportunities for personal development of potential to women, we deprive ourselves as a society of the benefits of the abilities and talents of half of the population. We need to remind ourselves that gender equality is not all about the rights of women and girls. It is also about the right of men and boys to have choices and not be restricted to taking on stereotyped roles, including the freedom to enter the female-dominated sectors of working with children.

What the law says

The main piece of legislation is the Sex Discrimination Act and Equal Pay Act 1975, which aimed to ensure that neither men nor women suffer discrimination on the grounds of their gender in the context of employment, education and training, and the supply of goods and services. The Act set up the Equal Opportunities Commission (EOC), with statutory powers to enforce the law. It has worked to promote equality and combat discrimination on the grounds of gender. The EOC focuses on issues such as equalising pay and training opportunities, pensions and childcare, as well as supporting individual women who have been treated unfairly by employers.

The Equality Act 2006 gave public authorities a duty to promote equality between men and women and prevent discrimination in the workplace. It also replaced the EOC with the Commission for Equality and Human Rights (see page 192).

REFLECTING

You can find out more about these laws from www.equalityhumanrights.com or www.womenandequalityunit.gov.uk. How does your setting comply with these laws in its policy and practice?

Disability

The link between attitudes to disabled people in the past and current issues facing disabled people in the UK is strong. Major legislation to tackle disability inequality is much more recent than that related to ethnicity and gender.

Attitudes to disability in the past have mostly been very negative. Having a disabled child might be seen as a curse or punishment for previous wrongdoing. Women who gave birth to a child with impairments were often blamed – it was thought they must have committed a sin for which they were being punished. Children with learning difficulties were often seen as possessed by evil spirits. In some societies, disabled children were deliberately killed, and even in comparatively recent times, midwives and doctors would 'put to one side' a child born with an identifiable impairment, not caring for them in the early minutes and hours of their life, so that they perished. In many cultures, not only in the past but still today, having a disabled child is seen as a source of shame; something to be hidden away.

Until well into the 20th century, many disabled people, especially those with learning difficulties, were shut away from society in asylums or workhouses. When anything is hidden away, the result can be suspicion or even fear because it is unknown. Although disabled people are now far more visible in British society, there remain some people who don't want to have to acknowledge their existence or be expected to respond to them in respectful ways. Suspicion, hostility and negative attitudes surface from time to time when, for example, residents oppose accommodation for people with learning difficulties in their neighbourhood.

When primary (or elementary) education first became available to most children in the UK at the end of the 19th century, no specific provision was made for disabled children. A few 'training establishments' for children with sight or hearing impairment were set up and the children in them had little contact with the outside world. Children with learning difficulties were referred to in official documents as 'mentally defective', 'idiots' and 'imbeciles', and those who had fits were likely to be seen as uneducable.

At the beginning of the 20th century, local education authorities were given legal powers to make provision for the education of 'mentally defective and epileptic' children. The decision about whether a child fitted into that category was made the responsibility of medical officers. Decisions about whether or not a child was educable were made entirely on medical grounds for many years.

The belief developed in some circles that 'mentally defective' people undermined a nation's health. The view was that society should be protected from these 'degenerates' by segregating them, thereby preventing them from contaminating other people and from 'breeding'. These eugenicist beliefs started from some valid liberal intentions about producing a healthier and stronger society, but underpinned the thinking that led to disabled people being sent to concentration camps and killed during the Holocaust – a form of 'cleansing' of society.

For much of the 20th century, the only form of education provided for disabled children was training designed to ensure that they were able to work, so they did not beg, steal or live on the 'poor law' (an early form of social security benefits). From the 1920s, 'handicapped' children were brought into the education system, but only in special schools with restricted contact with the rest of society. Until the 1980s, children with learning difficulties were referred to as 'educationally sub-normal' (ESN). Provision for disabled children was largely made by voluntary organisations and charities, so the resources they required to function effectively in life were made available as a donation or a gift, rather than provided as a right. This resulted in patronising attitudes of pity for disabled people as helpless and dependent, and prevented them from being seen as people with potential and able to contribute to society.

In the 1980s, government policy changed and the large institutions in which so many disabled people had been incarcerated were closed. Disabled people were now moved into smaller supported residential settings or back into their families' homes. This was a well-motivated policy known as 'care in the community', and in many instances gave disabled people their first taste of independence. However, in some areas, insufficient resources to provide the necessary support structures and expertise left some disabled people as badly or even worse off than they had been in the bleak institutions.

Towards the end of the 20th century, disabled people began to become more vocal on their own behalf, seeking their civil rights and rejecting the passive role they had previously been expected to take (grateful for handouts of resources and attention). Disabled people's organisations developed the social model of disability (see pages 66–7) and made non-disabled people think more effectively about how society is responsible for disability.

FOOD FOR FURTHER THOUGHT

Find out about the disabled people's movement in this country. Take a look at www.disabilityinformation.com.

As we saw in Chapter 2 (page 71), the introduction of the Early Support Programme has been a great step forward for young disabled children and their families.

What the law says

Various laws have gradually changed the way in which the education of disabled children and children with special education needs is approached. The Education Act 1981 was a turning point, introducing the concept of special educational needs (SEN). Its main feature was that local education authorities (LEAs) were given the duty of **statementing**.

Since 1981, local authorities have had a duty to provide a statement for a child who is thought to have special educational needs. The authority should:

◆ *assess the child's special educational needs*

◆ *issue a 'statement' which sets out the child's specific learning needs*

◆ *identify the provision required to meet these needs and what the authority will do.*

This is the process of **statementing**.

The Education Acts 1993 and 1996 replaced and improved on this Act, with greater rights for parents and rules about statementing which set time limits for each stage of the process. A very important improvement was the introduction of the SEN Code of Practice (see pages 69–70). The Special Educational Needs and Disability Act 2001 (SENDA) strengthened the rights of children with SEN to be educated in mainstream provision, and brought new duties to LEAs to offer parents advice and information.

The Disability Discrimination Act 1995 (DDA) was a landmark in the way society regards disabled people. It made it unlawful to discriminate against disabled people in the provision of services or to treat a disabled person 'less favourably' than someone else for a reason related to their impairment. This means that a setting providing a service for children must not:

◆ refuse to provide a service to a disabled child in circumstances where they would offer that service to a non-disabled child

◆ offer a lower standard service or a service on worse terms than they would to a non-disabled child.

The setting also has a duty to make 'reasonable adjustments' to:

◆ policies, practices and procedures for disabled children

◆ the environment to overcome barriers to access.

The duty to make reasonable adjustments is 'anticipatory'; a setting must not wait until they are asked to offer a place to a disabled child, but think ahead about the sort of changes they could make to policies, routines and the environment so they would be able and ready to provide a service for a particular disabled child. However, the word 'reasonable' to describe the adjustments indicates that a setting is not expected to make huge financial outlay beyond their budgetary means on equipment or on major alterations to the building.

REFLECTING

You can find out more about the Disability Discrimination Act (DDA) from *Early Years and the Disability Discrimination Act 1995* (National Children's Bureau, 2003) and www.equalityhumanrights.com. How does your setting comply with this law in its policy and practice?

The Disability Rights Commission Act 1999 set up the Disability Rights Commission (DRC) to promote the rights of disabled people and work towards their fuller inclusion in society by fighting discrimination. The Equality Act 2006 replaced the DRC with the Commission for Equality and Human Rights (see page 192).

Integration or special provision?

One key issue in the sphere of disability which continues to be debated is whether *all* disabled children should be integrated into mainstream education and special schools closed down. The main thrust of public policy is currently aimed at achieving integration.

The arguments for integration are particularly strong for children with physical impairments. Some adults with physical impairments tell of their restricted opportunities to learn and progress because they were educated alongside children with learning difficulties, whose needs sometimes took precedence over providing a challenging curriculum. Being educated alongside the main cohort of their contemporaries enables children with physical impairments to share learning opportunities appropriate to their intellectual capacity, and to develop social relationships with non-disabled children. The non-disabled children also benefit from sharing their school with disabled children by learning about disability.

Integration encourages the development of social relationships

For some children, the policies of integration have been a success. As a result of the push for integration, many more disabled children now attend local schools alongside other children, fully integrated into those schools. Statementing has in many instances led to the provision of resources which enable disabled children to participate in mainstream schools, such as aids to hearing and sight. It has also resulted in funding for assistants to work alongside a teacher in a classroom, providing an individual disabled child with one-to-one support, both to help with practical issues of personal care and to help those with learning difficulties to appreciate what is expected of them in the classroom. The DDA has put pressure on local authorities to ensure that schools adapt premises appropriately.

However, there are reservations for some teachers and parents about whether the policy of inclusion and integration can or should be extended to *all* disabled children. The closure of special schools and the movement of children into mainstream schools is opposed by many and has become a party political issue.

The arguments against integration are wide ranging:

◆ Sufficient resources have not been made available to make statementing effective everywhere.

◆ Some parents and teachers feel that the closure of special schools for children with sensory impairments has limited the availability of the specialised teaching these children require.

◆ There are concerns about whether children with complex medical needs can be properly catered for in mainstream schools.

◆ Some parents of disabled children feel that part of the aim of integration is unrealistic for children with significant learning difficulties, since their stage of development diverges so widely from that of other children of their own age that genuine social relationships are not possible. They fear that the gap in development between their children and others of the same age is so pronounced that the disabled child will inevitably experience feelings of low self-esteem if they compare themselves with their contemporaries.

◆ Many of the reservations centre on children whose behaviour is affected by their impairment – primarily children with autism. Some parents fear that their children cannot cope with the atmosphere of mainstream schools, and feel they thrive better in smaller groups. It is difficult, for example, for many children with autism to cope with moving from one part of a school to another for different lessons: they need the security of a consistent environment. Some teachers feel that they cannot cope with children whose needs for support related to their behaviour are very great. They are also concerned that the other children in their classrooms are not able to progress effectively because adult time and attention has to be focused on the autistic child. Others share some of those concerns but point to the solution of more resources for support staff and better professional development opportunities for teachers.

The most helpful way to approach this debate is to emphasise the imperative of assessing the requirements of each child as an individual and aiming to meet these requirements in an appropriate environment with adequate resources. Sometimes, this will be best achieved in a small specialised unit within a mainstream school, but for some children it seems that a special school is still the best option.

REFLECTING

How far has inclusion of disabled children happened in your work setting? What challenges has this brought you as a practitioner? What successes have you achieved?

Sexuality

Attitudes towards **homosexuality** are often polarised – opinions at either end of the spectrum are held passionately and discussed in strong terms, although prejudice against lesbians does not seem to have been as pronounced as that against male homosexuals.

WHAT DOES THIS MEAN?

Homosexuality *refers to being attracted by and having sexual feelings towards people of the same sex as oneself. It is most often used to refer to men, but it can be applied to both men and women – the 'homo' part of the word means 'same'. Homosexual men are usually referred to as gay, and homosexual women are usually referred to as lesbian. People who are attracted to people of the opposite sex are referred to as heterosexual, and those who are attracted to both sexes are referred to as bisexual.*

Various religions debate whether homosexuality (usually referring to men) is explicitly condemned by parts of their religious scripture or not. Arguments continue about whether a person's sexuality is innate or acquired / learned. The legal position of homosexual people has changed radically in the last 50 years, and the pace of change accelerated in the first decade of the 21st century.

In ancient Athens, friendships between older and younger men were highly valued, even including physical relationships. Male beauty was much prized and attraction between men was seen as normal and natural. Indeed, close relationships between men were seen to strengthen comradeship in the army. Ancient Rome had a fairly relaxed, laissez-faire attitude towards such relationships, until Christian influence on the Roman Empire led to the execution of homosexuals. In medieval Britain, homosexuality seems to have been openly practised, not least in monasteries, and poetry celebrating homosexual love has survived from that period. At least three British kings are known to have been homosexual (Edward II, James I and William III), but it was Henry VIII who made sodomy (buggery) illegal and punishable by hanging in 1533. This law remained in force in England until 1861. In 1885, sexual touching between men ('gross indecency') was made illegal; perhaps the highest profile conviction under that law was of the playwright Oscar Wilde in 1895. No such prohibition was placed on intimate contact between women.

In the 19th century, psychiatrists suggested that homosexuality was an illness which could be 'cured': Krafft-Ebbing said it was due to the inheritance of 'degenerated' genes, while Freud thought it was due to mistakes in a child's upbringing. The American Psychiatric Association did not remove homosexuality from its official list of 'disorders' until 1973.

A government committee of enquiry in Britain in the 1950s produced the Wolfenden Report, proposing that private acts between 'consenting adults' should no longer be criminalised. This was eventually transformed into law for England and Wales in the Sexual Offences Act of 1967 (similar legislation did not happen in Scotland and Northern Ireland until the 1980s).

The Gay Liberation Movement took off in the 1970s, and gradually representation of gay relationships appeared more openly in all forms of literature, drama and popular entertainment, such as cinema and television. Increasingly, public figures, including politicians, were prepared to acknowledge their homosexuality, although this was not always voluntary since some parts of the press resorted to vicious 'outings'. Against this tide of change, Section 28 of the Local Government Act 1988 forbade the 'promotion' of homosexuality in schools, and was not repealed until 2003. The HIV/AIDS epidemic which gained momentum in the 1980s resulted in great compassion about the premature death of so many young gay men, but also brought out malevolent expressions of hatred from those who saw the 'gay plague' as divine retribution for the 'sin' of homosexuality.

The 1990s saw progress in the development of gay rights on many fronts, such as reducing the age of consent for sex between two men from 21 to 18 years (1994) and then to 16 years (2000; the same age as for heterosexual couples). In 2002, fostering and adoption by single homosexual people was permitted and, subsequently, by same-sex couples (2005). The British armed forces were forced to cease their practice of dismissing homosexual people following a ruling of the European Court. In 2004, the Civil Partnership Act enabled gay and lesbian people to register legal partnerships offering mutual rights and responsibilities similar to marriage. The 2006 Equality Act made it illegal to discriminate against gay men and lesbians in the provision of goods and services.

Many more homosexual people in all walks of life now feel able to be open about their sexuality. However, harassment, abuse and even physical violence against homosexual people – especially gay men – remains a feature of UK society, so there is still some way to go to creating respectful attitudes. The website of Stonewall, the organisation which campaigns on behalf of gay and lesbian people, is a useful source of information (www.stonewall.org.uk).

Commission for Equality and Human Rights

The approach of this book is largely to look at all aspects of equality together, so you can see the common threads that run across issues related to ethnicity and culture, gender, disability, sexuality and other aspects of diversity. As you have seen in this chapter, different bodies had responsibility in the past for issues relating to ethnicity, gender and disability. This changed with the introduction of the 2006 Equality Act, which set up the Commission for Equality and Human Rights (CEHR) to replace the CRE (Commission for Racial Equality), EOC (Equal Opportunities Commission) and DRC (Disability Rights Commission). The CEHR aims to:

◆ reduce inequality

◆ eliminate discrimination

◆ strengthen good relations between people

◆ promote and protect human rights.

It enforces equality legislation on age, disability, gender, race, religion or belief, sexual orientation or transgender status, and provides individuals and employers with advice.

The laws it has power to enforce are those listed in the previous sections of this chapter, as well as the Employment Equality (Age) Regulations which came into effect in 2006 and made it illegal to discriminate against someone on the grounds of age.

The scale of the task of the CEHR was apparent when it was launched on 1 October 2007, reporting a survey which said that 46 per cent of people in the UK felt they had been discriminated against in some way, mainly in the workplace. The most frequent causes of the discrimination were ethnicity, sexual orientation, age, religion and disability.

FOOD FOR FURTHER THOUGHT

You can keep up to date with the CEHR's work and check archives for the three bodies it replaced on the website www.equalityhumanrights.com.

The UN Convention on the Rights of the Child

Following the Holocaust and other events of the Second World War, there were moves to establish the principle that all human beings have certain rights. Human rights came to be acknowledged as arising from 'the dignity and worth of the human person'. Various international treaties were developed, including the United Nations Convention on the Rights of the Child (UNCRC), which was an international treaty launched in 1989. The UK ratified the Convention in 1991, which means that British governments are committed to making sure that laws, policy and practice in the UK are in keeping with the articles of the Convention. All countries that are members of the United Nations have accepted this Convention, except Somalia and the USA.

The UNCRC recognises that children need particular protection of their rights because they are immature and vulnerable; they often cannot assert their own rights and need the adults around them to protect them and ensure they have the best opportunities in life. However, there is still some resistance to the idea that children have 'rights'. Many people see the proper place for children in society as being passive and under the control of adults, who should make decisions on their behalf and organise their lives for them. They do not see children as autonomous human beings who need opportunities to make choices and decisions, and to build their self-esteem and self-confidence so they are able to take charge of their own life. It is a strength of the Early Years Foundation Stage that it declares, 'All children are citizens and have rights and entitlements.'

The rights set out in the UNCRC are in three main groups. All children and young people aged under 18 years have the right to:

◆ provision (e.g. access to food, clean water, housing, education and healthcare)

◆ protection (e.g. to be protected from abuse and discrimination)

◆ participation (e.g. to have their views heard and participate in making decisions).

PUTTING PRINCIPLES INTO PRACTICE

You can find a summary of the UNCRC at www.unicef.org.uk/youthvoice/crc.asp and a full copy at www2.ohchr.org/english/law/pdf/crc.pdf.

Take a look at the most significant articles of the Convention for your work with children. Consider some of the ways you put them into effect in your work, and think how you could develop your practice further.

Article 2 requires that children are 'protected against all forms of discrimination'. In what ways do you value the individuality of each child and aim to treat each child 'with equal concern' so you meet their individual needs? How do you operate anti-discriminatory practice such as avoiding stereotypes, offering all children equal opportunities to achieve, and celebrating diversity? How effectively do you challenge prejudice and discrimination?

Article 3 declares that the best interests of the child should be paramount. In what ways do you strive to put the interests of the child first, before other people's interests (including their parents, your colleagues and yourself), especially in the context of protecting children from abuse?

Article 12 assures children of the right to express their views and have them taken into account, according to their age and maturity. What methods do you use to listen to what children tell you about their ideas and feelings, and respect their views, so you are more aware of their opinions and take them into account? How do you help children to have a say in decisions which affect them?

Article 16 sets out children's right to privacy. In what ways do you maintain confidentiality regarding information you hold about children?

Article 23 provides that disabled children require special care. In what ways do you use your knowledge of disability issues, such as the social model described in Chapter 2, to include disabled children?

Article 28 describes children's right to education and healthcare.

Article 29 provides that the aim of education is to develop the child's personality, talents and mental and physical abilities to their fullest potential.

Article 31 recognises children's right to play, rest and leisure. In what ways do you promote all aspects of children's learning by assessing their development so far and providing play and other activities and experiences which will help them to progress? How do you promote their health and well-being through their diet, exercise and rest?

Whenever someone acquires rights, they automatically acquire responsibilities to:

◆ ensure that others get their rights

◆ use their own rights in ways which do not harm others or deprive them of their rights.

You have already seen in previous chapters that part of your work is to help children appreciate and respect the rights of others, and we will look at this again in Chapter 6.

The UNCRC helps practitioners to see that children are entitled to be treated as individuals, and have their needs and requirements met. As has been emphasised in this book, children and their families are entitled to respect and to live free from the harmful effects of inequality, prejudice and discrimination. Childhood is brief, so children need to make the best of their chances to learn and develop and to enjoy being a child.

Children's Commissioners

A Children's Commissioner has been appointed in each of the UK nations. Those in Wales, Scotland and Northern Ireland have a specific brief to promote the rights of children and young people, but the brief of the Children's Commissioner in England is less clear, being expected only to promote *awareness* of rights.

You can find out more about the Children's Commissioners from their websites:

◆ England: www.childrenscommissioner.org

◆ Wales: www.childcom.org.uk

◆ Scotland: www.sccyp.org

◆ Northern Ireland: www.niccy.org

Positive discrimination

One approach to counter-balancing the discrimination faced by certain groups of individuals in society is **positive discrimination**.

> ### WHAT DOES THIS MEAN?
>
> **Positive discrimination**, *or affirmative action, aims to take an active role in extending opportunities for people (for example, for employment or education) who are often excluded or discriminated against.*

The argument for positive discrimination is that in the past the odds have been so badly stacked against women, minority ethnic groups, disabled people, working-class children, and so on, that educational establishments and employers must now make conscious efforts to reach out to such groups and ease the path for individuals to be included and succeed. The argument against positive discrimination is that this is itself a form of discrimination, and that opportunities should always be made available on the basis of the abilities and talents of the individual, not because they are seen as belonging to a particular group.

Positive discrimination can take many forms. A fairly crude approach is to set quotas, such as in Finland where a certain proportion of places on some university courses are reserved for Swedish speakers. Quotas of this type are illegal in this country, but the Labour Party has tried to increase the number of women in Parliament by creating women-only shortlists, so a local party has to select a woman as its candidate. A more widely-accepted approach is to target advertising for a job or university places in media which will be more commonly seen by traditionally excluded groups. An employer might advertise a post in a newspaper like *The Voice*, which has a predominantly black readership, or a university might place information in magazines read mainly by young women. Sometimes, you will see an advertisement for a job which says something like, 'Women, ethnic minorities and disabled people are underrepresented in our workforce and we particularly welcome applications from these groups.' Some of the élite universities run projects to visit state schools to try to increase the number of applicants from these schools, especially comprehensives.

These methods can all help to give the message that applications are welcome from all groups, that this post or place is not reserved for men or white people or non-disabled people. Individuals who might have felt 'that isn't for the likes of me' will be more likely to apply, and the employer or educational establishment will benefit from being able to make choices from a wider range of people. If they only ever thought in terms of men or white or non-disabled people for a job, employers would be missing out on able, talented candidates; when some universities reserved places for students from specific public schools, they denied places to more able youngsters from state schools and lower social classes.

However, when it comes to selecting the employee or student, the wisest path is to make a decision based on who is most suited for the job or most able to benefit from a university education. It does not help if interviewing panels are swayed by one part of an individual's identity and make their selection primarily based on gender, ethnicity, disability or social class. If the person does not have the ability, qualifications or experience to succeed in the role, they are not being done a favour but are more likely to be being set up to fail. When it turns out that they are unable to cope, the views of the bigots that women, black people, disabled people or working-class students are not up to the job or course are just reinforced and it becomes more difficult for the next able woman, black person, disabled person or working-class student who comes along.

REFLECTING

Does your setting operate any form of positive discrimination when appointing staff? If it doesn't, how do you think it might benefit from doing so? What advantages might be brought to the children and families?

Knowing about events of the past will help you to understand issues in society today and be in a position to tackle some of the aftermath of history, and also to see why certain laws and formal policies are necessary and helpful.

Chapter 6

When attitudes get in the way

By reading previous chapters in this book, you have had the opportunity to build up your knowledge and understanding of issues related to inclusion, equality and diversity, and to explore the implications for your own work with children. In this chapter we will consider occasions when you will need to draw on all that knowledge and understanding to respond to people and situations where there are barriers to inclusion and equality arising out of the attitudes of other people. We will consider issues relating to 'political correctness' and, in particular, the value of thinking carefully about the language we use. We will also look at how you can challenge expressions of prejudice, from children and from adults. Finally, we will consider how having a policy about inclusion, equality and diversity provides a framework to support your practice and make your intentions and commitment clear to others.

Not a Down's child but a child with Down's syndrome – a child first and foremost

Politically correct or showing respect?

Towards the end of the 20th century (from the 1970s), the idea of **political correctness** emerged.

> ### WHAT DOES THIS MEAN?
>
> **Political correctness** *is about avoiding certain expressions, actions or policies which appear to exclude, belittle or malign groups of people who are often discriminated against, and instead using alternative ways of speaking and writing which show respect for others.*

By the 1990s, it was being suggested by certain political groups and parts of the media that freedom of speech was being limited by those who advocated political correctness, or 'PC'; in fact, you can find several websites devoted to this theme. Those who support this viewpoint claim that liberty is threatened by the 'PC brigade'. They deplore developments in recent years over a wide range of topics, including health and safety regulations and precautions, the right to smack children, the bans on smoking and hunting, speed cameras, and many other issues. They express views about the 'nanny state' interfering in too many aspects of people's lives.

Most of these claims about limiting freedom are exaggerated, and often based on inaccurate or even false claims about what those pursuing equality and anti-discrimination suggest, particularly about the use of language.

Being sure of your PC position

To be strong in your commitment to inclusion and equality in the face of this sort of criticism, when proposing actions and behaviour which are intended to be respectful and inclusive, you should make sure you are on really firm ground about whether your proposals are in fact necessary or likely to achieve your aims. Anyone who is committed to achieving greater inclusion and equality in the UK's diverse society needs to give careful thought to their motivation for apparently being PC in certain situations. You should be able and ready to defend your values if necessary, being sure of your ground and able to explain your actions and behaviour.

Good intentions about respecting all cultures can lead to taking unnecessary steps which get targeted for ridicule. An example of this is moving from understanding that the Qur'an forbids Muslims to eat pork and other pig meat, to deciding that young Muslim children should not be exposed to stories and rhymes which talk about and show pictures of pigs or be taken to visit a farm where there are pigs. Some Islamic leaders in the UK have indicated that whilst they appreciate the attempt at cultural sensitivity of settings which have excluded Wibbly Pig, the Three Little Pigs, Pooh's friend, Piglet, or Wilbur the pig in *Charlotte's Web*, there is no necessity for this. Once again, the key to showing true respect is to consult the people you wish to avoid offending.

Similar principles apply to the debate over whether celebrating Christmas in settings for children risks offending people of other religious groups. The issue seems to have arisen out of well-intentioned attempts by settings to avoid giving Christmas a prime position in the year, which would imply that the Christian religion is seen in the setting as superior to other religions or that Christian festivals should take precedence over the festivals of other religions. Whilst this is commendable, it is not a reason for taking the festival out of a setting's calendar altogether. More important is to give equal recognition and significance to the festivals of all religious groups represented amongst the children and families in the setting, as well as helping children to learn a little about key aspects of other cultures.

Another side of this debate to consider is that Christmas is not just a Christian festival, but a secular celebration of light and warmth in the middle of winter which long pre-dates Christianity, coming at the time of the winter solstice, the shortest day in the year. It is a festival celebrated and enjoyed by people of many cultures, including those with no religious allegiance, all over the world. My Sinhalese friend, who was brought up as a Buddhist, phoned me on Christmas Day with her greetings and told me about her sister serving a turkey dinner under the Christmas tree in the tropical heat of Sri Lanka. These are leftovers from the British Empire, but ones they enjoy and choose to keep. Above all, don't assume that non-Christians will be offended if you celebrate Christmas. Follow the usual rule – ask them what they think and feel.

Christmas is a secular as well as a Christian festival

PUTTING PRINCIPLES INTO PRACTICE

How does your setting celebrate Christmas? Do you help children to learn something of the nativity story, even if they are not members of church-going families?

Do you also emphasise the aspects of the mid-winter festival which are not exclusively Christian – the pleasure of being with our families, visiting friends, exchanging gifts, having special meals, decorating the home and the symbolism of light in the darkest part of the year? How could you extend and develop your celebrations at Christmas time to be inclusive of everyone?

Do you also make sure that children of religions other than Christianity have a chance to share the pleasures of their celebrations for their religious festivals? How could you develop this aspect of your practice?

Use of language

One aspect of the condemnation of political correctness concerns the use of language in the context of inclusion and equality. You may find that if you take care to avoid certain forms of wording because you see this as an important part of best equality and inclusion practice, you may be accused of simply giving into pressures to be politically correct and 'toe the line' in order to meet with approval.

If someone is adapting the way they speak only because they feel under pressure to do so and for no other reason, then that is to be regretted. There is no point in simply complying with explicit or implicit rules about your use of language if you don't really understand the basis for guidelines on what is and is not acceptable. Unthinking following of such guidelines has resulted from time to time in incidents which distort the equality and inclusion message and provide fodder for the ridicule of the 'anti-PC brigade'.

There are some powerful reasons for being thoughtful about the language we use.

◆ *Showing respect*. We have emphasised in several contexts in this book the need to show respect for individuals and be sensitive to difference. Part of this is to be alert to language which perpetuates prejudice and discrimination.

◆ *The effect of the language we use on our ability to think clearly and fairly*. If we have not sorted out our ideas about equality and inclusion, we are unlikely to be able to care for children with due attention to their individual needs or promote their development and learning in ways which open up opportunities for their future. The words we use to express ourselves can affect the concepts, values and attitudes we develop; they mould the way we think and may lead us to distorted or limited opinions. Language both reflects and influences how we think about ourselves and others. It can reinforce the development of stereotyped and prejudiced ideas, or it can help us to think more constructively and treat others respectfully.

REFLECTING

Think about the word 'black' and its many negative uses, such as referring to someone as having a ' blackened character', being on a 'black list', being 'black hearted', or giving someone else a 'black look'. Consider phrases such as 'it was a black day when…', or referring to the financial crisis of 1992 as 'Black Wednesday', talking about the 'black market' for unauthorised goods or labour, or the evil of 'black magic.' These and many other usages of 'black' give the word the meaning of bad, dirty, ugly, evil.

Now think about the cumulative effect on a small child who knows they and their family are black and constantly hears the word 'black' used in these negative ways. It is not surprising that the self-esteem of many black children suffers as they learn to think of themselves as undesirable in some way, and become ashamed of their skin colour, wishing they could be white instead.

Does this make you feel that it might be better to avoid using the word 'black' with such negative meanings whenever you can?

Of course, this doesn't mean that we can't use the word 'black' at all. There are many uses of the word which do not carry negative connotations, but simply refer in a straightforward way to the darkest colour. So, you should not feel inhibited from talking about a black belt in Karate, a blackboard in the classroom, a black box on an aircraft, a black tie dinner, black ice on the road (it's invisible so the black tarmac is not hidden), blackberries, black swans, blackbirds or black fly in the garden. And there is no problem about black coffee; maybe insisting on 'coffee without milk' *is* political correctness gone mad! For a while, people got very hung up about asking for the colour they preferred their coffee, but this was an example of not really thinking through the full reasoning behind the idea of using language carefully: describing a cup of coffee as 'black' is not using the word negatively but descriptively.

As for the furore stirred up in some of the less responsible tabloid newspapers about 'baa, baa, black sheep', there is no evidence that anyone instructed anyone else to sing 'baa, baa green sheep' (or rainbow sheep) – and in any case, there isn't any reason not to sing the traditional rhyme because it's talking about a sheep with a black fleece. However, you might want to think twice about referring to 'the black sheep of the family', because this implies that the family member is a disgrace, so this is a negative usage of the word 'black'.

In the field of disability, too, language plays an important role in shaping how we think about disabled people and how disabled children learn to think about themselves.

Labelling disabled people by using terms like 'a Down's child' or 'a diabetic' can limit our thinking about the person. It can mean that we focus only on their impairment and adopt the medical model of disability, rather than acknowledging the needs and requirements of the whole person. Consider how talking about 'a child with Down's syndrome' or 'a person with diabetes' helps us to put the person first in our thinking, not their impairment. This way of talking about disabled people is more respectful to the individual, seeing their impairment as just one part of them and not the whole of who and what they are. It helps us to work in the social model, seeking ways to adapt our practice and the environment to suit the disabled person.

Think about how using the word 'handicapped' places the problem on the person, as in the medical model of disability, rather than with the society which has not adjusted to meet the disabled person's requirements, as in the social model.

Consider what the phrases 'wheelchair bound' or 'confined to a wheelchair' convey. They carry implications of limitations and dependence on others – that the disabled person is imprisoned or trapped in their wheelchair and unable to make their own decisions or even to speak for themselves. As an occasional 'wheelchair user', I can confirm that a wheelchair is in fact liberating, enabling disabled people to get around, enjoy places they could not walk to, and have more independence and choice.

In each of the above examples, using language differently helps us to develop perceptions and concepts which are more supportive of inclusive practice. Using a term like 'the disabled' lumps all people with impairments together and suggests that they will all have identical needs and requirements. Obviously this is not so: to meet the needs of a wheelchair user will require different resources and strategies from meeting those of someone with sensory impairments or learning difficulties.

Using gender neutral language can help us to move on from some of the assumptions of the past about the limited roles of women, and to widen our expectations for children's futures.

REFLECTING

Consider how using a word which can apply to either a man or a woman helps us to reflect accurately the changing roles of women and the opportunities open to them. If we use a word like 'firefighter' instead of 'fireman', we confirm that women can do dangerous jobs which require physical strength and courage. If we say 'Chair' instead of 'Chairman', we make it clear that women can take positions of authority. A company's 'workforce' clearly includes women, whereas reference to 'manpower' suggests that jobs are not open to women.

Just replacing 'man' with 'woman' (firewoman, chairwoman) does not have the same effect; it simply draws attention to the role being done by a woman and implies that this is unusual. It presents the situation as being extraordinary in that a woman might presume to undertake the role. Gender neutral language does not specify male or female so can be applied to an individual of either gender, and the issue of whether a role is open only to men or only to women becomes irrelevant. (And if someone is concerned that being called a 'Chair' makes them sound like a piece of furniture, you can point out that it is a part of speech known as metonymy, similar to the use of 'the Bench' to apply to magistrates or judges, or 'the Crown' to apply to the monarch.)

The women's movement in the 1970s drew attention to how the usual term of address 'Mr' for all men does not reveal or focus on their marital status, whereas using 'Miss' or 'Mrs' to address women does. Feminists deplored the idea that a woman was thus defined in terms of whether she is married or not, and the growth in couples living together outside of marriage and increased divorce rates have complicated old assumptions. This is what led to the introduction of the usage 'Ms', which can be used to address both unmarried and married women, putting them on a par with men. (The French have always addressed a woman of mature years as 'Madame', reserving 'Mademoiselle' for girls and young women.) As with most attempts to challenge established ways of thinking, the title 'Ms' has had its opponents, many claiming that they don't know how to pronounce it (which is quite simply 'Mizz').

In our quest to promote equality and inclusion in our diverse society, we need to give careful thought to the implications of these and other usages of language. Some words obscure facts and suggest 'foreignness'. As we saw in Chapter 2, talking about someone who was born and brought up in this country as 'an immigrant' is inaccurate. Their parents or grandparents may have been immigrants, but they are British and part of our society. Other usages reinforce prejudiced attitudes.

- Describing African drumming or Maori dancing as 'tribal' or even 'primitive' suggests that they are the product of a less well-developed (or less 'civilised') society. Would you use these words to describe British traditional music of the bagpipes and Morris dancing?
- Talking about 'non-white' people implies that being white is what is desirable and normal.
- We should never talk about people who do not have impairments as being 'normal'; disabled people are not abnormal.
- Referring to someone as 'fussing like an old woman' diminishes respect for women – not only do some old women not fuss, some old men do!

And some usage is just peculiar: a 'disabled toilet' or 'disabled entrance' is surely one which is out of order, so saying 'accessible' makes more sense.

It is also important to be accurate in use of words. For example, the word 'invalid' means someone who is not well, so it is not accurate to apply it to a healthy wheelchair user. Similarly, it is best to avoid referring to someone as 'suffering' from their impairment. The impairment may mean that a person has to adopt different strategies to ensure their mobility, independence and access to opportunities, but they may not be suffering in the sense of being in pain or deprived of life chances. If you call someone a 'victim' of their impairment, you are also implying that they are defeated by their condition and incapable of being active in running their own life. 'Ethnic' is an adjective which can be used to describe a group of people but it cannot correctly be used as a noun: 'an ethnic' has come to carry negative implications, and is used by people who wish to express prejudiced views.

There are some words which the people they are used about find offensive, and it is a matter of respect to avoid using them. It is unclear whether those who oppose PC language think it is acceptable to give such offence. The usage of words that offend and their impact can change over time. We would not dream of using words like 'imbecile' or 'retarded' today, yet this was the official language of the past to describe people with learning difficulties. It is only in recent years that the term 'educationally sub-normal' has dropped out of use, and that charities set up to help disabled people have taken words like 'cripple' and 'spastic' out of their names. The first law identifying certain groups of migrants as 'undesirable' (including 'lunatics' and 'idiots') and trying to keep them out of Britain was the 'Aliens' Act of 1905.

Words like 'wop', 'yid', 'wog' and 'Paki' were always used with racist intentions. Many white British people born in the 1940s and 50s were brought up to think that it was polite to refer to people whose skin is not white as 'coloured', but most black people now find this offensive. This is partly because of associations with apartheid in South Africa, and partly because of the use of the word in previous times in the United States. Similarly, the old term 'half-caste' for a child whose parents are from different ethnic groups is likely to give offence, and 'mixed race' focuses on the dubious concept of race. More up-to-date terms are 'mixed origins' or 'mixed (or multiple) heritage', but as you saw in Chapter 3, even these terms are problematic: we need to remember that we are all of mixed ethnic backgrounds.

One source of offence can be the way some phrases suggest that the users are (or feel themselves to be) superior to the person being spoken to or about. This is still apparent in the language some men use to talk to and about women, such as addressing a woman as 'dear' where a man in a similar situation is called 'sir', or referring to women as 'girls' and their male equivalent as 'men'. A good rule is: if you say 'ladies', say 'gentlemen'; if you say 'girls', say 'boys'; if you say 'women', say 'men'. This shows equal levels of respect to each gender.

REFLECTING

Have you experienced language being used to or about you which you found upsetting, disrespectful or even hurtful?

How did you feel? How did you respond? Did other people offer you support? What did you think the intentions of the person who used the language were?

If you cannot recall such an experience, think about whether you have witnessed or heard about such use of language and what your reaction was.

You may come across disputes over whether certain terminology is acceptable. For example, there still seems to be some lack of clarity over whether it might give offence to refer to someone as blind or deaf – would it be more acceptable to say 'sight (or visually) impaired' / 'partially sighted' or 'hearing impaired' / 'hard of hearing'? Most organisations for those with such impairments seem to use both terms, with 'blind' and 'deaf' applying to those with little or no sight or hearing, while the other terms are used for those with lesser impairments to their senses. There are similar debates about the use of 'learning difficulties' and 'learning disabilities'.

Some people argue that the term 'disabled people' (most often used in the UK) makes the point powerfully that it is the failure of society to get the environment, resources and attitudes right that disables people. Others feel that saying 'people with disabilities' (used in North America) puts the person first and the impairments afterwards. However, using a clumsy term like 'differently abled' is full of pitfalls. It is essentially meaningless, since each one of us has different abilities and capabilities from everyone else, and it underplays the fact that society does disable some people by failing to meet their needs appropriately. The term 'X challenged' (as in 'visually challenged') leaves the problem (in medical-model style) with the disabled person, not with the unadapted environment. It is also open to ridicule when it gets extended to 'vertically challenged' for short people and similar usages.

These debates are useful because they make us explore what we mean when we use certain terminology, and consider how the way we describe people reveals something of how we view and value them. What is essential is to find out how the people concerned prefer to be referred to. Listen to their views and respect what they say they want – don't try to guess or make the decision on their behalf. ('Don't assume. Ask.'). Some people whose ethnic origins lie in the Indian sub-continent object to being referred to as 'black', pointing out that their skin is brown, and prefer to be referred to as 'Asian'. Remember, not everyone with similar impairments or ethnic background will hold the same viewpoint – make sure you respond to the wishes of individuals.

An interesting development in the use of language has been the way some disabled people have started to refer to themselves and other disabled people as 'cripples' and some homosexual people use 'queer' to talk about themselves. This is part of their assertion of their identity and self-confidence, but it is not a licence for someone outside the group of disabled people or homosexual people to revive these otherwise out-dated and offensive words.

And, of course, it is not only white people who use racist language about black people. When a black person calls a white person a 'honkie', they may well intend to be offensive!

Closely linked to the issue of use of language is that of 'jokes' of a racist, sexist or homophobic nature or which ridicule disabled people. There are entire websites devoted to listing such 'jokes', and those who do not find them funny are accused of lacking a sense of humour. Yet jokes which rely on mocking how people look, speak, dress or live their lives, especially when they are based on stereotypes, reinforce prejudiced thinking and contribute to making prejudice respectable and acceptable. If you challenge the telling of such jokes, you may find yourself told to lighten up, it's just a bit of fun, but remember that this sort of thing can be very hurtful. If jokes and teasing become cumulative, this can amount to a form of harassment or bullying.

We can see that thinking seriously about these issues is not just a case of being PC in order to fall into line with some unspoken code for how we speak and act. It is about respecting the dignity and individuality of others, valuing people equally and seeking to include them in our settings and society. It is not helpful to become so nervous about saying the wrong thing that you feel inhibited and powerless, but it is important to become alert to how you talk because of its powerful influence on the way you think. Your patterns of thought affect the way you treat others and the role model you present to children. If they hear the language of stereotypes, prejudice and discrimination, they will learn the concepts of stereotypes, prejudice and discrimination, and inequality will be perpetuated into the future.

Challenging stereotypes, discrimination and prejudice – children

As someone who works with children, you have a major role to play by:

◆ setting an example in the way you talk and behave

◆ guiding children when they speak or behave in ways which cannot be accepted in your setting.

Your approach to issues concerning diversity in all its forms has to find a way of combining:

◆ open discussion with children, building up their knowledge and understanding of people different from themselves

◆ guiding them to appreciate respectful ways of talking about and behaving towards others.

The aim is summed up in the Early Years Foundation Stage (EYFS): 'Children should be helped to learn to respect and value all people and learn to avoid misapprehensions and negative attitudes towards others.'

You may find it useful to approach this through using puppets or dolls (especially Persona dolls), who can take the role of a child who is experiencing prejudice or discrimination. Be wary of being too negative about the views children express for fear of discouraging them from feeling able to express their views to you. Instead, point out that you see things differently because of what you have learned about others through your own observations and experience.

You saw in Chapter 3 that children learn stereotypes and prejudice from an early age. This can lead on to them sometimes expressing stereotypical or prejudiced views, for example through name-calling and behaving in discriminatory ways, such as excluding certain children from play and activities. At its worst, this sort of behaviour becomes **bullying**.

WHAT DOES THIS MEAN?

Bullying *is:*

◆ *deliberate – it sets out to hurt*

◆ *persistent – it is repeated over time*

◆ *exercising power over another person – the bully gains satisfaction from their ability to manipulate and intimidate others.*

It may be:

◆ *physical – punching, slapping, kicking, pushing, poking, damaging belongings*

◆ *verbal – teasing about appearance, ethnicity, disability or sexual orientation; taunting about family or friends; threats; spreading rumours (in person or by text or email)*

◆ *exclusion – from activities, the group; by ridiculing, humiliating*

◆ *extortion – demanding money or possessions with threats of physical attack.*

One-off incidents of name-calling or exclusion don't amount to bullying – it is sustained repetition which amounts to exercise of power.

Challenging bullying and discriminatory behaviour

You cannot ignore bullying or any other form of discriminatory behaviour. If it occurs, your role and responsibility is to intervene promptly and try to create a positive learning situation. As the EYFS says, 'Always intervene in play if it is racist, sexist or in any way offensive.'

PUTTING PRINCIPLES INTO PRACTICE

Good practice in response to a child who makes an abusive remark or bullies another child because of their skin colour, gender, disability, social background or appearance includes the following:

- Never ignore or excuse one child's bullying or discriminatory behaviour towards another child, any more than you would ignore or excuse them if they inflicted physical pain on that child.

- Don't feel that you will make things worse by drawing attention to what has been said and done – if you do not respond, you give the impression that you condone the behaviour.

- Intervene immediately, pointing out to the child who has behaved in a bullying or discriminatory way that what was said or done is hurtful and that the behaviour cannot be accepted (using words like 'unfair' or 'cruel'); but don't suggest that the child will be punished.

- If necessary, point out anything that is untrue and give correct information and new vocabulary.

- Help the child to learn from the situation – to see the consequences of their actions and to understand why their behaviour is regarded as inappropriate (ask 'how would you feel?').

- Don't leave the child with the feeling that you dislike them personally for what they have said or done – make it clear that what you won't tolerate is what they have said or how they have behaved.

- Help the child to find ways of expressing their own strength through the things they are good at and can achieve, and support them in building their self-esteem in positive ways, showing that you value them for who and what they are.

It does not help to overreact to a child's prejudiced comments or discriminatory behaviour and resort to labelling a child as racist, sexist or a bully. The child will be in the process of learning some complex concepts and may not yet have developed empathy (the capacity to feel with or for other people), so won't necessarily realise how much their behaviour hurts other people. As you saw in Chapter 3, children are very influenced by the adult world around them – at home, in their local community and in the media. Younger children may not understand that the language and behaviour they are repeating is wrong, because they may have heard and observed adults and older children speaking and behaving in a similar manner. They may learn to behave in aggressively discriminatory ways because they see members of their family and local community behaving like that, using prejudiced language and showing little respect for others. You may have to acknowledge that other people do speak and

Always intervene to stop bullying or discriminatory behaviour

behave in prejudiced and discriminatory ways, or hold stereotypical views, but emphasise that it is not accepted in your setting because it is rude or unfair.

PUTTING PRINCIPLES INTO PRACTICE

A group of practitioners who met at a workshop exchanged information about their experiences in encountering situations where children made stereotypical or prejudiced comments or behaved in discriminatory ways, and described how they responded.

'I found two of our Muslim boys in Year 2 in floods of tears, looking really frightened. I eventually got it out of them that a group of bigger white boys had been threatening them in the playground and shouting at them 'Terrorists. Go home.' After I'd said how nasty I thought the big boys had been and dried their tears, I took them back to their classroom. I found a colleague to help me track down the boys concerned. We had a very serious talk about their behaviour, getting them to say what they thought terrorists did to hurt people. We asked them what made them think the two younger boys were terrorists since they hadn't hurt anyone. We are trying very hard as a whole school to show that the Muslim families we have at our school are fully accepted and respected, but we know there is so much being said out in the wider community and in the children's homes – it's not easy.'

Razia, classroom assistant

R has Down's syndrome and when he first started coming to the playground with his sister, F, some of the kids were calling him 'dumbo', 'thicky' and 'spazz'. R – and F – were very upset and my colleagues and I had to really take firm action. Tammy took R and F off to another area to play and I gathered the name-callers and a few of the bystanders around for a serious chat. I reminded them about their contribution to our discussions on what rules we would have in the playground and how we had said we couldn't have bullying, which is what it would be if they went on speaking to R like that. We talked about how hurt R and F had been. A few of the bystanders set off to join in playing with R and F. It was a few weeks before the name-callers really spent time with R, but the bullying didn't develop – I think we nipped it in the bud.

Gary, adventure playground worker

The first time H, a three-year-old white girl, walked back from school with the older children, she wouldn't hold hands with K. She said his hands were dirty and he should wash them properly. I explained that K wasn't dirty, his skin was a different colour from hers – a lovely dark brown. I said she could hurt K's feelings by not walking with him and asked him to come and hold my hand.

Sally, childminder

One little girl who comes into the crèche while her mum has a swim loves playing with the dolls, cuddling them and putting them to bed. But she won't let the boys anywhere near 'because boys don't play with dolls'. I have to help the boys get a look-in and keep reminding her that boys can help put the dollies to bed and give them a cuddle. I keep saying that daddies and uncles and grandpas help to look after babies too, and she shouldn't be so unfair to the boys who want to play with the dolls.

Dawn, crèche worker

Some of the older children had seized J's patka and were throwing it around the room, chanting 'J wears a hankie on his head'. I retrieved the patka, returned it to J and really gave the other children a piece of my mind about their horrible behaviour. I made them see how upset J was and how cruel they had been, so many setting on one person. When we'd all calmed down, I talked with the whole group about Sikh boys and men wearing patkas and turbans to cover their hair, and how important it was to them. I got some help from J's family to find out about the five Ks of Sikhism.

Kirstie, pre-school worker

We have a lad, T, whose two mothers live together in a lesbian relationship. Last month, the mothers registered their relationship in a civil partnership ceremony, and this has become known in the area. Since then, T has been subjected to bullying comments at school and in the club. I overheard two children, L and D, saying to T, 'My Mum says you'll grow up all wrong because your mum is disgusting.' 'My Dad says that she'd be more normal if a bloke like him gave her a good seeing to.' I spent a bit of time with T, saying how lucky he was to have two mums who loved him, and that it was none of the other children's business. Then I went off to have a word with L and D, and told them in no uncertain terms that we didn't have bullying like that in our club, and they had really hurt T's feelings. They haven't a clue about lesbians really, but of course they hear all this stuff at home.

Chris, after-school club worker

We had some problems with some of the lads who didn't want S on their team. They claimed they couldn't understand a word he said and he and his dad couldn't speak properly. I said 'That's not true, is it? S and his dad speak two languages – English to us and Polish at home. I've been trying to learn a bit of Polish and it isn't easy – maybe we should all have a go.' I asked S to be my partner for some practice exercises, and made it very clear that he was in the team to stay because he's a good player and I expected them to treat him better.

Pete, from the under-12s football club

Note that these practitioners used children's initials when talking about them in order to maintain professional confidentiality.

It is vital that practitioners do not think of name calling, such as 'fatty' or 'four eyes', as a minor or unimportant matter and dismiss it as merely teasing. When it is repeated and done with intent to hurt, it becomes bullying or harassment. Some adults play down what they see as 'just toughening children up for the real world' and don't intervene. But you should question why a child should be expected to endure comments that undermine their self-image and self-esteem, and be ready to support them in facing such torment.

The word 'gay' has come to be a general term of abuse and contempt, rather than referring to someone being homosexual, and 'spastic' or 'spazz' are often used to refer to anyone who is clumsy or awkward, not just to a disabled child. You may need to tackle this, unpicking what the words mean and how they are used, and the disrespectful attitudes they may show. Terms like 'coon' and 'nigger' are absolutely unacceptable and that should be made clear.

Children reach a stage in their development in primary school where they begin to regard the opposite sex as 'useless' and may have very stereotypical and limited views of what each gender can or should do. As they reach secondary school age, they may start to use abusive language about one another, such as 'slags', 'bitches' or 'morons'. Your role is to make clear that such disrespectful ways of talking about one another is not acceptable in your setting.

Don't assume too quickly that because there is an incident between children of different genders or ethnic groups that there is necessarily a sexist or racist element involved. Be sure to check out the details of what has happened, listen to the children's versions of events and don't jump to conclusions.

Supporting children who experience bullying and discrimination

All the practitioners in the examples on pages 209–11 told of how they focused on the child who had been the target of the bullying or discriminatory behaviour. A child may be bullied or experience discrimination because something about them or their family – their skin colour, their impairment, or the way they look, speak or dress – marks them out as 'different'. Never blame a child who is bullied or see them and their differences as the problem. They have a right to their difference and to have it respected. Some children seem to be frequent targets of bullying and this is often because their self-esteem is low: because they don't have the feeling that they deserve better, they don't resist the bullying so it happens again and again.

PUTTING PRINCIPLES INTO PRACTICE

Support a child who has experienced bullying or discriminatory behaviour by:

- comforting the child who is the target of the bullying or discrimination
- making it clear to them that you do not share the views expressed
- telling them that they do not have to put up with such comments and behaviour
- building their self-esteem through showing how much you value them for who and what they are
- helping them to respond to the other child(ren) so you build their resilience and give them strategies to deal with any future incidents of a similar nature.

A bully won't waste their time on someone with high self-esteem – such a person won't accept the bullying because they know they are worthy of being treated well. Someone who is certain enough of their own value to think 'How dare you do that to *me*' denies the bully the power they want. So, to help children resist bullying and discrimination and build their emotional strength, you can introduce them to some of the techniques of 'empowerment'. These include:

- walking away when the bully appears – this is sensible, not cowardly
- not fighting back, because that could lead to you being hurt more
- using phrases like 'I don't like this' and 'that's not fair', or just saying 'no'
- reacting as little as possible – don't reward the bully with responding (this is known as 'fogging' and though it is not easy for a child, you can practise the method with stories, using puppets or dolls)

- being with other children in a group as much as possible, not on their own
- 'walking tall' – standing up straight with shoulders back, walking confidently, making eye contact (this also benefits from practice, perhaps with mirror).

For more information about tactics for resisting bullying, see the website of Kidscape at www.kidscape.org.uk.

'Walking tall' is a way of defeating bullies

Building self-esteem

Both children who discriminate or bully and those who are the targets of such behaviour may need help in building their **self-image**, **self-esteem** and **self-confidence**.

> ### WHAT DOES THIS MEAN?
>
> **Self-image** *is the picture we have of ourselves – who we are and what we are like – and how we fit into the world.*
> **Self-esteem** *is valuing ourselves, and seeing ourselves as having value in other people's eyes.*
> **Self-confidence** *is feeling able to do things and capable of achieving.*
> *People with a clear self-image and high self-esteem are confident enough to tackle new activities and experiences, to take responsibility for themselves, to care for others, and to make choices and decisions for themselves.*

Practitioners who work with children of all ages have a significant part to play in helping those children to grow up with the sort of strong self-image that engenders self-esteem and self-confidence.

PUTTING PRINCIPLES INTO PRACTICE

There are many ways of boosting children's self-image, self-esteem and self-confidence.

- Show children that you respect and value the way of life and traditions of their family, as discussed in Chapter 3 (this gives them a feeling of 'my family and me are good; other people like us').
- Make children feel welcome in your setting through the use of visual images that reflect the child and their family, as described in Chapter 4 (this gives a feeling of 'they want me here').
- Pay children compliments – admire aspects of their appearance such as their hair colour and texture, their features, their skin tone (this gives a feeling of 'it's good to be like me; I look good').
- Include positive images in your setting, as described in Chapter 3, to help children develop an image of people like themselves in various possible roles (this gives a feeling of 'I'm good enough to be like that').
- Provide activities which enable children to experience success (this gives a feeling of 'I did it! I can do other things, too').
- Encourage them to try new things (this gives a feeling of 'Maybe I could do this as well – bet I can').
- Help them to discover how to solve problems (this gives a feeling of 'I can work things out for myself – I can overcome!').
- Offer them choices and chances to make decisions (this gives a feeling of 'I can manage this for myself').
- Give them opportunities to take responsibility (this gives a feeling of 'I can help other people and they like me for doing it').
- Give praise for achievements (this gives a feeling of 'Well done, me. I'm great!').

Strategies like these can contribute to empowering children to be strong enough and resilient enough to deal with their experiences of discriminatory behaviour and bullying. They will feel strong enough to deal with situations for themselves, and will not be interesting to bullies because they are not easily intimidated or cowed. Such strategies can also contribute to reducing the likelihood of children discriminating against or bullying others, because they won't need to feel the power of the bully to feel good about themselves.

Being given responsibilities helps build self-esteem

Challenging discrimination by adults

Responding to children's expressions of prejudice or discriminatory behaviour takes patience and a consistent approach, but responding to the comments and behaviour of adults can be very daunting. This requires strength and, at times, courage.

FOOD FOR FURTHER THOUGHT

If it becomes necessary to challenge adults, use a similar approach as with children.

◆ Challenge the remark, politely but firmly.

◆ Choose your time and place – you may not want to speak strongly in front of children, but you should act as soon as you can.

◆ Remain as calm as possible but make clear that you find the remark or behaviour offensive or inappropriate.

◆ Remember that if you let the incident pass, you are contributing to the person feeling that it is acceptable to speak or behave in that way.

◆ Offer support to the person who has been the object of the remark or excluding behaviour.

◆ Offer accurate information if the person's comments or actions seem to arise from ignorance of the implications of what they are saying or doing.

It takes determination and energy to challenge the prejudice of adults, and sometimes you may not feel up to it. But you must be ready to protect the children you care for if they are discriminated against.

Practitioners share their experiences of challenging discrimination

PUTTING PRINCIPLES INTO PRACTICE

The group of practitioners in the workshop discussed how they would try to respond to various possible incidents in which adults expressed prejudiced views or behaved in discriminatory ways. They did this by considering a series of scenarios.

They began by talking about how difficult they found challenging adults. Razia described how she had recently challenged a parent she had overheard referring to the disabled children in her class as the 'spazzes' and the 'crips'. She said, 'I found it really difficult and I was shaking when I spoke to him, but I'm so glad I did it. I think he actually didn't realise how offensive he was being and how he had hurt the feelings of the parents of those children.'

Scenario 1:

> Imagine that you are feeding the ducks in the park with a couple of the children from your setting. One of them is an African Caribbean boy, Leroy. An elderly man walks past when you are on the way to the swings and he glares at Leroy and says, 'There's too many of these coloureds over here, destroying our way of life. England for the English, I say.'

Shahida said, 'I'd be so angry, I'd find it difficult to say anything.'

Kirstie said, 'So would I, but you really can't ignore something so blatant as that. You've got to say something.'

Gary said, 'I would certainly point out that you don't have to be white to be British and Leroy is as British as any of us. I'm not sure if I could go into why it's so unpleasant to use the word 'coloureds' – probably not the time and place.'

Sally said, 'I would say that Leroy is very welcome in my setting and I'd be careful to tell Leroy that I loved him and I thought he was great. Isn't it dreadful to think that even little children have to hear such horrible stuff?'

Scenario 2:

> You often take a small group of children from your setting down to the local park. Ten-year-old Laura loves being taken in her wheelchair. She finds it difficult to control her head movements, and her speech isn't very clear. On your way back to the setting, you sometimes pop into a shop to buy fruit. The shop has plenty of room for Laura's wheelchair. The children are all learning to work out how much things cost and buy them with the right money.
>
> One day, the shopkeeper asks you not to come into the shop again because he's had complaints about the wheelchair getting in the way of elderly people and babies in buggies, and it knocks stuff off the shelves.

Pete said, 'He's another one with a problem that he's trying to put onto other people. It's not the chair that's the issue – he's got a thing about disabled kids being out in public.'

Chimelu said, 'Laura shouldn't have to give up her outings, and she and the other children shouldn't have to give up their chance to learn about shops and money just because he's such a bigot. If you don't let children into places like shops, how are they going to learn how to behave properly in such places?'

Razia said, 'I think I'd be able to deal with this one because I would remind him about the Disability Discrimination Act and how he is not allowed to treat disabled customers less well than his other customers. He's just got to learn to live with it!'

Gary said, 'That's a really good example of where having a law is such a support, isn't it? It probably won't do a lot to change his way of thinking about disabled people, but he can't discriminate against them.'

Kirstie said, 'I'd talk to the children on the way back about what had happened, to reassure them, especially Laura. I expect they'd be quite upset, especially if I'd had to get a little bit stroppy with him.'

Responding to colleagues

If the adult who is talking or behaving in a prejudiced or discriminatory way is a colleague, this brings another set of considerations into the matter. You may encounter colleagues who use language carelessly without thinking of the implications of what they are saying and how it may show lack of respect or even be offensive. Or they may express stereotypical views that show that they have not thought about equality and inclusion issues. At best this may make you wince; at worst it might make you furious.

As you saw in the introduction to this book (pages 6–10), prejudice and discrimination should always be challenged, especially amongst those who are responsible for the welfare of children and have a particular duty to be committed to inclusive and anti-discriminatory practice. You should not let an incident pass without taking action, but, as a member of a staff team, you have to go about it in a way which does not undermine professional working relationships.

Be prepared to challenge colleagues' prejudice

Confrontation is not going to be an effective strategy, and neither is ostracising a colleague. It is unlikely to be appropriate to challenge a colleague in the presence of children or members of their families, and you are likely to achieve more by a quiet conversation in private than by, for example, making accusations in a team meeting. The situation may have arisen simply from lack of information or understanding, and you may be able to help by offering explanations. However, if the colleague is unwilling to address the issues involved, you may have to share your concerns with their manager and leave them to pursue the matter. Strategies involving training are more likely to be successful than disciplinary actions.

PUTTING PRINCIPLES INTO PRACTICE

The group of practitioners in the workshop also exchanged information about their experiences of colleagues who had expressed stereotypical, prejudiced or discriminatory views, and described what had happened as a consequence.

We had a young woman, T, who had just started working with us when we were joined by R, a little boy who had lost a leg. T didn't say anything at first but rarely played with R and always managed to avoid changing his nappy. I wanted her to support R's key worker so I insisted that she change his nappy and she just refused. She said it made her feel creepy to touch him. I was quite shocked that she could say such a thing, but didn't want to make a fuss during the crèche session. But at the end of the day, I took T aside and told her that I thought her attitude was worrying. I explained quietly that she had come into a profession which had principles of including all children. I asked her to go away and think about what she had said and consider how she could develop her commitment to practice which treated all children with equal concern. I said I wouldn't insist on her changing R's nappy for the next couple of weeks, but I wanted her to spend time with him, getting to know him as an individual, so she could learn to see disabled children as children first and foremost, not just in terms of their impairment. It took her a long time to be comfortable with the situation, but I think things improved after she went on a disability equality course.

Shahida, crèche worker

We had one coach who was always saying things to the lads like 'Get on with it, stop prancing about like a lot of girls' or 'You were useless today, playing like a spastic'. A couple of us had a go at him, telling him that he shouldn't refer to girls in such a derogatory way and explaining that it wasn't acceptable to use the word 'spastic' like that. At first, he told us not to be such a lot of 'PC pansies', so we got hold of some copies of 'Equality in Your Coaching' and used them as the basis of a few discussion meetings. I'm not sure he really saw the point or accepted all the ideas, but at least he stopped talking like that so the kids weren't exposed to it. He realised we weren't going to put up with it and he had to change if he was going to continue to work with us.

Pete from the under-12s football club

When it became known amongst the staff that one of our new children was being fostered by a gay couple who hoped to adopt her, one of my colleagues was very vociferous in the staff room about how disgraceful that was. He used some very aggressive and quite unpleasant language, talking about gay men as if they were all promiscuous and paedophiles. He said it would ruin the child's future and it was irresponsible of social services to place her with them. Several of us were flabbergasted by the way he spoke – so extreme and vitriolic. Fortunately, one of the other teachers told him he was completely out of order to churn out such stereotypical and inaccurate opinions. She said that it wasn't any of his business but in fact she happened to know that the two men had recently had a civil partnership ceremony after being together for over ten years. She said that the child was flourishing in her new home with two parents who were committed to her and to one another, and reminded him that the little girl was disabled and it had not been easy to find a prospective adoptive family for her. I thought she was terrific and added my view that to have two loving parents was what gave children a good start in life. The Head had him into her office the next day and he looked a bit subdued when he came out.

Kirstie, classroom assistant

I worked with an older woman who was very unsettled when a black family moved into the village and their two boys joined the club. She was sure they would be a lot of trouble and disruptive. She had formed the idea that all African Caribbean parents were harsh disciplinarians and she kept on about how we'd 'have to keep on top of them like they're used to at home'. It took us some time to convince her that we shouldn't make pre-judgments about a family, and certainly not make assumptions about children on stereotypical grounds before we'd even met them. In fact, the boys were quite studious types and very well-mannered. Once she got to know them, she did have the good grace to admit that they weren't at all what she'd expected.

Chimelu, after-school club worker

When one member of staff joined the team, she claimed she couldn't get her tongue round the names of some of the children, so gave them Anglicised names instead. She claimed they liked their new names, but we had to be very firm with her that she had to learn and use their proper names. We spent a little while in a staff meeting talking about how important our own names are to us. Each of us said what our names meant and who had chosen them for us, if we were named after someone in the family, whether we preferred not to have our names abbreviated and so on. It helped her to see that names are an important part of a person's individuality and that we must take care to use other people's names accurately.

Razia, pre-school worker

Teams are most effective when each member of the team has a clear understanding of the overall aims and policies of the setting and feels a sense of commitment to those aims and policies. This means that it is worth giving time in staff meetings to highlighting inclusion and equality issues and practice. It is also worth talking through how you can best implement your intentions about including all children in your setting and promoting their equal chances in life.

To be able to work with colleagues effectively, you need to respect and support each other, maintaining a professional working relationship and not letting personal feelings get in the way. If you encounter incidents like those explored in this chapter, you need to approach the situation in a calm way, even if you find a colleague's behaviour offensive. Express your views in constructive ways which will help the colleague to develop their understanding and change their practice.

Remember, colleagues may also pick you up on your behaviour or use of language. You could slip up if you are under pressure of some sort or just not being as thoughtful as usual. You might feel very upset if this happens. Your colleague should raise the matter with courtesy and sensitivity, not attacking you. Don't feel guilty – we all make mistakes and are learning all the time; try to use such an experience as a positive learning point.

Responding to families

Sometimes, the adults who express stereotyped or prejudiced views are the parents of the children you work with. This may put a strain on that all-important parent–practitioner relationship. You may find yourself working with families whose values are different from your setting's values. This may centre, for example, on a conflict between the cultural values of the family and the gender equality values of the setting. Some cultural and social groups have very deeply held perspectives on what is appropriate for girls and boys, and will not be readily open to ideas of equality of treatment and opportunity. Some parents will be wary of suggestions that inter-racial relationships are acceptable or be unsettled by anything which suggests that same-sex relationships are normal.

It is important to maintain the parent–practitioner relationship by being open and courteous

This can be very difficult to deal with. On the one hand, you want to maintain good relationships with parents and be respectful of their culture and traditions. On the other hand, you are committed to ensuring equality of opportunity for the children, but without presuming that you know better than their parents what is right for them. It is important to be open, honest and courteous in how you respond to parents but still retain your commitment to inclusive and egalitarian principles and practice.

PUTTING PRINCIPLES INTO PRACTICE

The group of practitioners in the workshop also used scenarios to help them think through how they might respond to parents' stereotypical or prejudiced opinions.

Scenario 1:

> Imagine that the parents of two children, Daniel and Ahmet, arrive at your setting to collect their children at the same time. Ahmet's mother talks to him in Turkish as they gather up his belongings. When they have left, Daniel's father says 'Did you hear them gabbling away? I think if they come here, they should speak our language and live like us.'

Shahida said, 'If I took my family to live in another country, I'd go on speaking English to my children. In fact, I'd teach them Humpty Dumpty and all the other English nursery rhymes, and we'd go on eating British food.'

Pete said, 'Of course it's important to learn the language of the country you move to so you can get on, but I know I'd want to hold on to my own language and customs as well. I'd want my children to know where they came from.'

Razia said, 'I think I'd be able to point all that out to Daniel's dad. I don't think he's looked at it from the point of view of what he'd do in the same circumstances. He's just feeling put off by their foreignness and thinks they should fit in. I think a Turkish family can do that without giving up their Turkish heritage, and I'd want to make that point to him.'

Kirstie said, 'How rude, to refer to them as "gabbling". How does he think English sounds to Turkish people? Does he think English-speakers "gabble"?

Scenario 2:

> Imagine the parents of a child in your setting has invited each of the other children round to their house (to play or for a party), all, that is, except the two black children in the child's group.

Gary said, 'I would have to take the parents aside at an opportune moment, I think, and say that I was concerned that they had left out the two children in question. I'd have to point out the hurt felt by the black children, and say something about our approach to including all children and making them all feel equally welcome. I think I would be pretty assertive about it all, and say we didn't want any children who came to our playground to feel that they were worth either more or less than any other child. It would depend how the parents responded to this, but if the worst came to the worst, I guess I'd go so far as to say that maybe our playground wasn't the place for their child. But I'd be very reluctant to do that, because we might be one of the few places where their child could have contact with children of other ethnic groups and find out that they could like them and get on with them.'

Scenario 3:

> Imagine that Alice's mother, Gill, comes into your setting one day and says 'I thought I'd let you know we're looking for somewhere else for Alice.' When you ask why, she rather reluctantly says, 'Well, it's that Lucy. She upsets Alice so much – she looks so peculiar, dribbling all the time. Alice says her arms and legs fly about all over the place and she's always knocking her.' Lucy has cerebral palsy. You know that the two children get on well, but Gill never talks to Lucy and avoids looking at her if she can.

Chimelu said, 'It doesn't sound to me that Alice really has a problem. She gets on with Lucy. I think it's the mother's problem and she's putting it on to Alice.'

Sally said, 'I think I'd want to say that I see Lucy as a lovely child, and her impairments are only part of who she is. I wouldn't lose my cool, but I wouldn't let Gill get away with what she said about Lucy.'

Razia said, 'Do you think it would help to ask the mother to come to spend some time with the two girls together? She might get to know Lucy a bit and see how the two of them get on well. That might help her overcome her hang ups about the impairments.'

Scenario 4:

> Imagine you have shown some parents your environment and resources, and explained how you offer all children equal chances to participate, learn and develop their skills.

> One mother says, 'But we want our daughter to grow up in the culture of our religion to become a mother and homemaker like I have, not to get ideas of a career.'

> A father says, 'Well, I don't want my son to play with dolls or play at cooking and ironing. That's women's work. He should be in amongst the cars, like a proper boy.'

> Another set of parents are horrified to hear that sometimes the boys dress up in 'female' clothing from the dressing-up box when they act out 'female' roles. They say 'We don't want our boy growing up to be queer.'

Sally said, 'Each of these is a bit different, isn't it? But they all raise the issue of how far we ought to just 'go along' with what parents say they want for their children. I think I could talk to the father about taking a wider view of gender roles in society today and how they may change even further by the time the child had grown up. (It would be interesting to see how that child's mother saw 'women's work'!) I could also explain to the last parents about how children explore all sorts of roles in their play, and perhaps get them to think about how girls dress up in 'male' stuff too. I'd say that this is just part of them imitating different people they know in their life before they really develop a clear understanding of their own gender.

But I'd find the issue of cultural values very difficult. I want to respect other people's religions but I worry when I see that children's opportunities are being limited – especially for girls. I would explain my position about giving children choices in life, but I'd choose my words very carefully and try to show that I was respectful of the family's traditional views, even if I saw life differently.

In our childminding network, we have been developing our policies, and I think having a policy about inclusion, equality and diversity would help me a lot. I could show the policy to the parents before their children come to me and discuss with them what I'm trying to achieve.'

Your policy for inclusion, equality and diversity

Having a written **policy** can be a great support to your good practice.

> ### WHAT DOES THIS MEAN?
>
> A **policy** *is a written statement about how you work in one area of your practice. It should:*
> - *explain clearly how you go about that aspect of your work*
> - *describe the standards you aim to meet*
> - *explain the principles and methods you base your practice on, and perhaps refer to any legal requirements.*
>
> *A policy does not have to be a complex document; the most useful policies are short, straightforward and communicate clearly in direct language.*

There is little value in just taking over a policy drawn up by and for another setting – you need to develop your own. If you work in a team, everyone needs to be involved in discussing and agreeing the initial policy and in reviewing it regularly to make sure it is still appropriate and useful for the setting, as well as amending it if necessary in the light of new understanding. Each new member of a team needs to be helped, as part of their induction, to understand the meaning behind the policy and think about how their practice can play a part in implementing it.

The whole staff team should contribute to policy

PUTTING PRINCIPLES INTO PRACTICE

Whether you are taking part in drawing up a new policy for inclusion, equality and diversity from scratch or in reviewing an existing policy, check that it includes statements about your intentions to:

◆ welcome all children and families

◆ remove barriers to participation for all children and families

◆ treat all children fairly and equally

◆ meet the needs of each individual child whatever their ethnicity, cultural or social and family background, gender or disability

◆ recognise children's entitlement to a range of activities and learning experiences which offer each child an equal chance to develop and learn

◆ create an environment and use resources which respect the diversity of the children and families and support children's aspirations and learning

◆ help children to learn about people who are different from themselves, and to respect and enjoy the differences between people

◆ guide children away from prejudice and discriminatory behaviour

◆ respond actively and constructively to unacceptable discriminatory language or behaviour of anyone in the setting, including adults.

It is helpful to begin the policy with a general statement of commitment to overarching principles about offering inclusion, promoting equality and celebrating diversity.

Finally, check that your policy:

◆ demonstrates your commitment to principles

◆ provides guidelines for how people should work and behave in the setting

◆ acts as the basis of everyday practice.

Policies are valuable in guiding practice in a setting, but they are of no use unless everyone involved is committed to implementing them and incorporating the principles into their daily practice. Policies should be referred to regularly, both by individual practitioners and by the whole team. This will help you reflect on how far your practice is effective in implementing the policy and how you need to develop the ways you work.

It is important to share policies with parents from the time their child joins your setting, so they are aware how you will work with the child. Discussing a policy with a small group of parents is an effective way of communicating what it says, and gives parents a chance to get to understand what your intentions and aims are. Policies should be reviewed at regular intervals to ensure they are still 'fit for purpose'.

And finally ...

We hope that this book has helped you to be in a position where you can contribute actively and effectively to the development of both policy and practice in your setting, and to communicating the significance of such policy and practice to others, using your knowledge and understanding of the issues involved in inclusion, equality and diversity.

All work with children and families should be underpinned by the principles and practice of:

◆ seeing each child as a unique individual

◆ including all children

◆ promoting equality of opportunity

◆ opposing discrimination and prejudice

◆ valuing diversity.

Children and young people are entitled to high quality in provision and services. This high quality can only be delivered within a framework which focuses on each child as an individual, is inclusive, values differences, promotes equality of opportunity and is anti-discriminatory. This is every child's entitlement and right.

Chapter 1

Department for Children, Schools and Families, 'The Early Years Foundation Stage: Setting the Standards for Learning, Development and Care for children from birth to five', London: DCSF, 2007 (see also www.standards.dcsf.gov.uk/eyfs)

Every Child Matters – everychildmatters.gov.uk

Chapter 2

Sutton Trust – www.suttontrust.com

Early Support – www.earlysupport.org.uk

H. Frisch, 'Sex Stereotypes in Adult-Infant play', *Child Development*, Vol. 48, No. 4, Dec., 1977

C. Smith and B. Lloyd, 'Maternal behaviour and perceived sex of infants revisited', *Child Development*, Vol. 49, No. 4, Dec., 1978

Office National Statistics, Census, 2001 – www.statistics.gov.uk/census

Chapter 3

David Milner, *Children and Race: Ten Years On*, London: Ward Lock Educational, 1983

Paul Connolly and Julie Healy, *Children and the Conflict in Northern Ireland: the experiences and perspectives of 3 to 11 year olds*, Office of the First Minister and Deputy First Minister, 2004

Pre-school Learning Alliance, *Equal Chances*, 1991

Child of Our Time (TV series)

Chapter 4

National Portage Association – www.portage.org.uk

Letterbox Library – www.letterboxlibrary.com

Plain English Campaign – www.plainenglish.co.uk

Contact a Family – www.cafamily.org.uk

Council for Disabled Children – www.ncb.org.uk/Page.asp?sve=785

Asthma UK – www.asthma.org.uk

Children with Diabetes UK – www.childrenwithdiabetes.co.uk

Cystic Fibrosis Trust – www.cftrust.org.uk

Down's Syndrome Association – www.downs-syndrome.org.uk

Epilepsy Action – www.epilepsy.org.uk

Haemophilia Society – www.haemophilia.org.uk

Mencap – www.mencap.org.uk

Muscular Dystrophy Campaign – www.muscular-dystrophy.org

National Autistic Society – www.nas.org.uk

National Blind Children's Society – www.nbcs.org.uk

National Deaf Children's Society – www.ndcs.org.uk

Scope – www.scope.org.uk

Sickle Cell Society – www.sicklecellsociety.org

Chapter 5

The National Archives website has an informative section on the British Empire – www.learningcurve.gov.uk/empire

The website of the National Maritime Museum includes a history resource on the transatlantic slave trade – www.nmm.ac.uk/freedom

Commission for Equality and Human Rights – www.equalityhumanrights.com

Government Equalities Office – www.womenandequalityunit.gov.uk

Home Office – www.homeoffice.gov.uk

Fawcett Society – www.fawcettsociety.org.uk

Website dedicated to the Disabled People's Movement in the UK – www.disabilityinformation.com

Stonewall; Equality and Justice for Lesbians, Gay Men and Bisexuals – www.stonewall.org.uk

Summary of the United Nations Convention on the Rights of the Child – www.unicef.org.uk/youthvoice/crc.asp

Full text of the United Nations Convention on the Rights of the Child – www2.ohchr.org/english/law/pdf/crc.pdf

Children's Commissioner for England – www.childrenscommissioner.org

Children's Commissioner for Wales – www.childcom.org.uk

Scotland's Commissioner for Children and Young People (SCCYP) – www.sccyp.org

Northern Ireland Commissioner for Children and Young People (NICCY) – www.niccy.org

E.M. Forster, *A Passage to India*, London: Penguin, 2000

Paul Scott, *The Jewel in the Crown*, London: Mandarin, 1996

Philippa Gregory, *A Respectable Trade*, London: HarperCollins, 1997

Barry Unsworth, *Sacred Hunger*, London: Penguin, 1992

National Children's Bureau, *Early years and the Disability Discrimination Act 1995: What service providers need to know*, London: NCB Enterprise Ltd. on behalf of the Department for Education and Skills, 2003

Chapter 6

Kidscape – www.kidscape.org.uk

Index

Professional Development Series

Books to last you a lifetime!

From your first year of studying, through placements and right on into the workplace, this series of handbooks provides you with in-depth information on key areas of childcare and education that will get you through your assignments and support you in your career.

How to Observe Children, 2nd edition

- Gives practical guidance on the different techniques for effective child observation and helps you evaluate your observations – fully updated to support the Early Years Foundation Stage.

978 0 435987 66 4

Understanding Early Years Theory in Practice

- Features all the major theorists and theories covered in early years courses, with tips on where to find out more.

978 0 435402 13 6

Working with Babies & Children under Three

- Links the theory and practice of working with children under three years to help you be more professional.

978 0 435987 31 2

Planning Play and the Early Years, 2nd edition

- This popular best-seller is ideal for gaining deeper understanding of children's play and helps you plan successful, curriculum-based activities.

978 0 435401 19 1

Baby and Child Health

- Practical advice on promoting and maintaining health in babies and young children.

978 0 435401 51 1

Inclusion, Equality and Diversity in working with children

- Explains, in a sensitive and easy-to-follow way, how to turn good intentions into effective anti-discriminatory practice when working with children of all ages.

978 0 435402 40 2

Protecting Children

- Informs on the legislation and guidelines in child protection and explains the Assessment Framework and child protection procedures.

978 0 435456 79 5

Managing Children's Behaviour

- Covers the theory and practice of behaviour support from birth to adolescence and provides strategies for empowering children using Individual Educational Plans.

978 0 435455 32 3

Supporting Special Needs

- A comprehensive guide to policies and best practice in the area of special needs.

978 0 435401 62 7

Research Methods in Health, Care and Early Years

- Presents in-depth information on research methods for all early years and care courses.

978 0 435401 68 9

Visit **www.heinemann.co.uk/ProfDev** to find out more about the whole series.

The essential guide to successful planning in the Early Years Foundation Stage

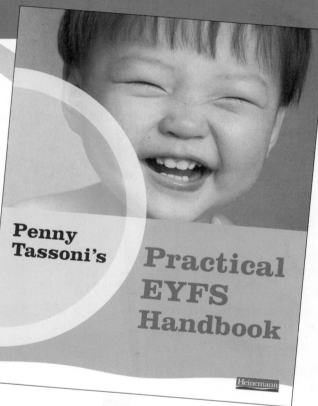

- Written by Penny Tassoni – trained Primary teacher and early years expert – and packed with **the best advice** on applying this key new framework.

- Penny's practical style brings you successful, **ready-made ideas** to use in your own setting or assignments.

- **Full-colour design and photographs** throughout bring the examples and activities to life.

- **Ideal support** for all childcare students, tutors and practitioners, guiding you step-by-step through best practice in the EYFS.

Find out more at
www.heinemann.co.uk/childcare.

N941